Political Grammars

SQUARE ONE
First Order Questions in the Humanities

Series Editor: **PAUL A. KOTTMAN**

POLITICAL

GRAMMARS

The Unconscious Foundations of Modern Democracy

Davide Tarizzo

STANFORD UNIVERSITY PRESS
Stanford, California

STANFORD UNIVERSITY PRESS
Stanford, California

Printed in the United States of America on acid-free, archival-quality paper

Library of Congress Cataloging-in-Publication Data
Names: Tarizzo, Davide, author.
Title: Political grammars : the unconscious foundations of modern democracy / Davide Tarizzo.
Other titles: Square one (Series)
Description: Stanford, California : Stanford University Press, 2021. | Series: Square one: first-order questions in the humanities | Includes bibliographical references and index.
Identifiers: LCCN 2020042646 (print) | LCCN 2020042647 (ebook) | ISBN 9781503614680 (cloth) | ISBN 9781503615311 (paperback) | ISBN 9781503615328 (ebook)
Subjects: LCSH: Political science—Philosophy. | Democracy—Philosophy. | Fascism—Philosophy. | Subjectivity.
Classification: LCC JA71 .T368 2021 (print) | LCC JA71 (ebook) | DDC 321.8—dc23
LC record available at https://lccn.loc.gov/2020042646
LC ebook record available at https://lccn.loc.gov/2020042647

Cover design: Rob Ehle

Typeset by Kevin Barrett Kane in 10/14 Minion Pro

Contents

Foreword by PAUL A. KOTTMAN

Fascism, Tarizzo points out, is "a political disease that infects only modern democracies." For many proponents of modern democratic culture, it will come as a surprise to learn, or to remember, that fascism is not an "other" of democracy but a fate that is possible only within modern democracies. Tarizzo's elaboration of the slippery slope connecting democratic promise and the nightmare of fascism is one of the most compelling and relevant illustrations of what he calls political grammar. He is able to show how smoothly modern democracies can be transformed into pseudo-democratic fascist societies.

At the heart of Tarizzo's argument is a first-order question that has animated political philosophers of all stripes since at least Thomas Hobbes: how does a political "we" get formed out of individuals living together? Or, in other words, how is collective political will formed out of competing individual desires?

Behind this quandary lies the question of the possibility of the political itself: whether there can be—especially in modern democratic societies—a social bond that links individuals, often strangers or people with no ethnic or religious commonality, in a distinctive ethical relationship of citizenship. How, Tarizzo asks, can democratic politics sustain what Hegel called "an *I* that is *We* and *We* that is *I*"? This worry was raised by Jean-Jacques Rousseau in 1750 in his *First Discourse*: "We have Physicists, Geometricians, Chemists, Astronomers, Poets, Musicians,

Painters; we no longer have citizens."[1] In contemporary Europe or North America, the tenor of Rousseau's worry has become deafening. The growing clash between "populists" and "neoliberals" has reopened the debate on the very essence of democratic societies: do we need to be one people in order to keep democracy alive? And, how do we define the concept of a democratic people, anyway?

To explain how citizenship of a modern democratic sort is possible, Tarizzo draws on Jacques Lacan's view that subjectivity should be seen as a process, a grammatical formation, rather than a substance. In practical-political terms, this means that subject-formation is a process, Tarizzo says, "whereby the invariance of the first-person perspective is secured, but the subject's identity cannot be found." Lacan himself did not elaborate a distinct theory of political subject formation; Tarizzo's contribution is to show the usefulness of Lacan's distinction between "subject" and "identity" for an understanding of the workings of modern democratic politics.

Democracy, Tarizzo argues, flourishes when the opening between subjectivity and identity is maintained. Indeed, in Tarizzo's view, democracy turns out to be a process of never-ending recovery from the lack of certain identity, a process that can take different propitious directions depending on the political grammar at work.

Preface

In filmmaking, there is a technique known as subjective camera, or first-person perspective, which consists in filming from the point of view of one of the characters. As a result, we see things as the character in question does. In my view, we should do the same when we study modern democratic societies. Indeed, these are *first-person societies*, whose life and behavior cannot be fully understood unless we adopt, and somehow empathize with, their first-person perspective. *Who are we?* First-person societies raise this question without hesitation and without pause, as they can no longer find peace in mythology, religion, or time-honored beliefs and traditions. Such societies wonder about their own nature and fate relentlessly, and for this reason they release democratic or democratizing effects sooner or later: the reason is because "we the people" start asking each other about our past, present, and future, thereby seeking to grasp what keeps us together, what we aim for, and how to achieve our goals. It follows that a first-person society cannot be compared with a mechanical or quasi-mechanical body politic like the artificial "automaton" Thomas Hobbes had in mind.[1] Rather, it resembles an organism endowed with a spiritual quality, with a genuine soul, and that soul is the *nos*, the first-person plural, that animates the whole of society, just as the *ego*, the first-person singular, animates each one of us. In the modern era, this soul has often been called a nation. As Ernest Renan famously put it, "a nation is a soul, a spiritual principle."[2] This book elaborates on that principle, arguing that first-person—namely, secular and self-questioning—societies are democratic in the first instance and that it is only thanks to the existence of first-person societies that democratic systems and institutions could take root in the Western world.

To prove this, I do not analyze what philosophers such as John Locke, Jean-Jacques Rousseau, and others theorized about democracy or politics in general, nor do I consider how their philosophical views might have influenced the course of history. Rather, I rewind the film of modern history and replay some scenes in the subjective camera mode, taking the first-person perspective of peoples, of nations, of the collective characters that really *made* modern history. Of course, it might be objected that it is impossible to see things through the eyes of someone else, not to speak of someone who lived a long time ago. Moreover, do peoples or nations truly exist? There are many ways to deal with these problems. One way is to immediately strike back with another, more troubling, query: do you truly exist, dear reader? And if that is the case, in what sense of the word *existence* can you claim that you do so? Who are you? What are you? We will need to tackle these issues before asking ourselves whether collective subjects may exist and whether we can learn to see things from their perspective.

If you are a philosopher, you know that the question as to whether it makes sense to say "I am," *ego sum*, in the first person has yet to be answered. Philosophers still quarrel over the mystery of the self. If you are a psychoanalyst, you will know that this problem can be turned upside down by asking not what the self *is* or *is not* but rather how I come to see myself as being an *ego*, a self. Jacques Lacan, in particular, found a way around all philosophical perplexities about the self and developed a theory of subjectivity that accounts for our inescapable, albeit doubtful, *being* in the first person. I will say just enough to make this theory comprehensible for readers who may not be well versed in psychoanalysis. I will then apply some conceptual tools forged by Lacan to collective subjectivities such as peoples or nations. The upside of this approach is that it allows us to take the first-person perspective of someone else by exploring the unconscious grammar, as Lacan would have it, that shapes subjectivity and that allows people to speak and act in the first person, whether singular or plural.

The concept of grammar is key to my entire argument, but it will take some time to elucidate its meaning.[3] As a first approximation, we may say that in order to realize what a certain person is telling us and how she sees things, we must know the language she is speaking and the grammar she is following. Yet there exist many types of grammatical restrictions that condition the way we see things and communicate with each other. In writing these lines, for instance, I am following not only the grammar of the English language but also the grammar, as it were, of the theory that I present in the book as a whole. This grammar dictates that my thoughts be expressed in a particular manner and not others. Grammars, in Lacan's sense of the word, dictate yet another type of syntactic restrictions that lay the groundwork for some "grammatical fictions," as Ludwig Wittgenstein would call them.[4] These are the fictions that make us *be* in the first person. Who am I? Who are we? Briefly put, Lacan's answer is: I am, *ego sum*, what I am not allowed to say. We are, *nos sumus*, what we cannot be.

I began work on this project in 2010, in the wake of the European debt crisis. At that moment, the problem of nationalities reappeared on the Continent, and since then, the problem has worsened. In a matter of years, the British voted for Brexit, Euroskeptic parties became stronger and stronger, and now that the migrant crisis has spiraled out of control, the emblems of national sovereignty are brandished almost everywhere in Europe. Legal and political theorists had not foreseen this situation. A specter is haunting Europe—the specter of nationalism. But what are nations? To begin with, nations can be thought of as *historical constraints*. Let me explain this with an example. Would you lend money to your brother or sister? Most people would answer yes. Would you lend to one of your friends? Maybe. Would you lend to a stranger? Most people would answer no.[5] Likewise, at the outbreak of the financial crisis, German taxpayers did not agree to lend to foreigners, to Greeks, to people whom they did not regard as fellow citizens. Long story short: nations resemble families. A nation, just like a family, is based on mutual trust, a perceived similarity or proximity, and a common sense of belonging that elicits feelings of unity and solidarity among people.[6] As Johann G. Fichte stated in the early nineteenth century, "inner frontiers" (*innere Grenzen*)[7] divide Germans from Greeks, Italians from French, British from Spaniards. The boundaries of nations, like those of families, can be demarcated with little difficulty. But there the similarity ends. Indeed, the nature of nations is extremely difficult to understand. The mystery is so impenetrable that some even doubt the existence of nations. Given that nobody can say with precision what nations are, so the argument goes, there seems to be no valid reason to think that nations are really out there. Yet the fact remains that ordinary people *believe*, more often than not, that they form one people, one nation, together with their fellow citizens. Thus, the question arises as to why people hold this belief and whether or not national feelings, however ill-founded they may be, are the *sine qua non* of modern societies.

Some years ago, two German theorists discussed the matter extensively, with a special focus on Europe. Dieter Grimm argued that in the absence of a European *demos*—that is, in the absence of a common language, a common political culture and history, and a "Europeanised media system"[8]—it was extremely risky to constitutionalize the European Union and deprive European nations of their sovereignty. The consequence of this might have been disintegration rather than integration. Jürgen Habermas replied that a modern *demos* is not the source but the product of constitutionalization. For him, it is the constitution that gives birth to the *demos*, not vice versa. Hence his praise of a European "constitutional patriotism" and his cautious optimism about the rise and consolidation of a European *demos*.[9] In the end, history proved that Grimm's view was closer to reality. Despite the rejection of the European Constitution in 2005, the European Union underwent an invisible yet powerful process of constitutionalization. The Maastricht and Lisbon Treaties, as well as a number of critical rulings of the European Court of Justice, fostered that process, so much so that we may speak of an "overconstitutionalization" of Europe today.[10] Yet nonintegration—not to say disintegration—ensued because no feelings of solidarity and unity among Europeans had arisen in the meantime. As Grimm has recently remarked, "When the Monetary Union was founded in 1992, it was a common understanding among economists that a monetary union of states of very different economic strength could function only if either economic policy was communalized as well or the strong states were willing to pay for the debts of the weaker states. Politicians ignored this warning. The financial crisis showed that the economic experts were right."[11] Today, Habermas himself concedes that something went wrong with European integration, that several countries—including Germany—witnessed the resurgence of nationalism, and that the problem of nationalities therefore remains on the front page: "The problem has surely been that the Federal Government of Germany has had neither the talent nor the experience of a hegemonic power. If it had, it would have known that it is not possible to keep Europe together without taking into account the interests of the other states. In the last two decades, the Federal Republic has acted increasingly as a nationalist power when it comes to economics."[12] Will Europe collapse under the burden of nationalism? Can we continue to dream of a European *demos*? In the following, I will take up these problems from a wider theoretical and historical standpoint, for Europe is not the only issue at stake.

Actually, the question of nations, peoples, and the like can be considered a blind spot in legal and political theory at large. Take, for example, the notion of popular sovereignty or the principle of self-determination of peoples that stands at the center of today's international law. In both cases, what remains rather mysterious is the *subject* that is deemed to have the power to govern itself. As a rule, that power is ratified by democratic constitutions that are authored by people themselves through their representatives. But the people who authored the US Constitution, for instance, the people who solemnly proclaimed "we the people of the United States" in 1787, are no longer there. In light of this, can we really say that the people who nowadays accept the US Constitution and recognize themselves as Americans constitute a self-governing or self-determining people? According to some scholars, there appears to be a fundamental asymmetry between the chartering people and the chartered people of America, or between the "constituent power" and the "constituted power," and such an asymmetry seems to undermine the very idea of democracy, of popular sovereignty, of a self-governing and self-determining people, unless we prove that—and explain why—the people of the past and the people of the present basically amount to one and the same people:

> Apparently, then, there is a dimension of political freedom that we both attribute to the chartering People and deny to the People as thus chartered—that is, the freedom to decide upon procedures of higher lawmaking. The charterers ("We the People of the United States") seem to stand, then, on a different plane of authority from the chartered ("our posterity"), as creators to creatures. How is it possible to construe such an event as one of self-government? . . .
>
> We need to say, then, what it is we think confers political identities on empirical human aggregates, identities of a sort that allows us to check for the sameness of the identities of the People who lay down constitutional law and the People to whom it is laid down. What do we think this people-constituting, identity-fixing factor could possibly be?[13]

Most of the time, legal scholars tackle the problem of the "intertemporal"[14] unity of the people from the perspective of normative theory. In this book, I take another perspective, which I call *clinical*. When one adopts the latter perspective, the normative point of view is not totally discarded. If anything, it is relativized. In other words, there is no normative "view from nowhere" that allows *everybody* to judge what is right and what is wrong, what is good and what is bad, always and everywhere; rather, the normative point of view varies according to contexts and circumstances. Here, normative is not what we the scientific observers consider to be normative but what "we the people" consider to be normative.

To clarify the matter, let us move from legal to political theory. Jacques Rancière and Axel Honneth discussed each other's theories at the Institute for Social Research in Frankfurt a few years ago. On that occasion, both attested that they endorsed a normative point of view on politics based on the abstract ideas of either "equality" or "freedom." According to Rancière, if political emancipation is possible, this is because human beings regard each other as being equal even when they explicitly deny such equality on account of their *identities*. As soon as they talk with each other, Rancière avers, people *have to* acknowledge that they are equally endowed with language and equally intelligent. Equality thus appears as a universal and a priori category of human history. According to Honneth, if political emancipation is possible, this is because modern people cannot be at peace with themselves unless they attain freedom. This entails that people, in particular modern people, *suffer* from not being free and *have to* achieve freedom in one way or another. Freedom thus appears as a universal and a priori category of modern history. I do not share these views, both of which can be labeled normative in the traditional sense of the word. I do not think that equality and freedom are quasi-transcendental categories that mean more or less the same thing for all human beings (Rancière) or for all modern peoples (Honneth). Instead, I would say that these categories gain normative value only within specific historical contexts that determine this normative value in various ways depending on how, each time, equality and freedom are *subjectified* at both the individual and the collective level. Hence, it is from within those contexts, which I call political grammars, that the normative impact of those categories should be evaluated and studied.

Having said this, it seems to me that Rancière and Honneth highlight two key elements of modern political history—subjectivity and suffering—that help us to understand how a sense of collective selfhood is brought to life and the intertemporal unity of the people is obtained. As regards subjectivity, Rancière is certainly right in saying that this notion should not be conflated with that of identity. When we say "I" or "we," *ego* or *nos*, we do not always know what these words mean exactly. It is all too obvious, moreover, that speech acts do not necessarily presuppose that speakers go through a process of identity verification. Yet it is equally obvious that a subject appears every time that "I" or "we" take the floor and speak in the first person. As Rancière makes plain, this discrepancy between subjectivity and identity is of the utmost importance when it comes to political subjects:

> I propose the model of the subject as self-constructed in a process of "subjectivization," and think of subjectivization first as "disidentification." What disidentification means is first of all a certain kind of enunciation. In a political declaration, in political action,

when a collective subject says, "We, the workers, are (or want, or say, and so on)," none of the terms defines an identity. The "we" is not the expression of an identity; it is an act of enunciation which creates the subject that it names. In particular, "workers" does not designate an already existing collective identity. It is an operator performing an opening.[15]

From Rancière's point of view, the question remains as to what makes this "opening" effective—that is, invariant over time. Indeed, from one act of enunciation to another, there must be some continuity such that "we" recognize ourselves as the same subject with the passing of time, else no collective struggle could ever take place, as no political battle could be fought for more than one day. Rancière's theory of disidentification does not consider this problem. With Honneth, emphasis shifts from subjectivity to another ingredient of political history that should not be neglected: suffering. For him, it is always suffering that unleashes the motivational force for the political mobilization of those who, in Rancière's own words, are not counted as equals. And suffering explains in part what first unites people and then ensures the invariance of a political subject, of *one* people:

It's not sufficient to say that there is a miscount, that some are not counted. One has to add that the miscounted also suffer from it; otherwise, it becomes unclear why they act as they do, why they perform "de-identification" and undergo the "subjectivization" process. Becoming a political subject means overcoming the status of an uncountable excluded subject; but as I like to put it, the motivational force for wanting to overcome this status has to stem from some form of suffering, which is therefore part of the political order Rancière and I are describing. It seems to me an added explanatory element is required at this place.[16]

At this point, I am in a position to present the basic idea of this book. As Honneth remarks, once we acknowledge that suffering plays a key role in modern politics, we are in need of something like a "political psychology, in order to be able to explain why certain groups do rebel under certain circumstances"[17] and how they enact their rebellion on the basis of a shared suffering. In some respects, this book attempts to meet the need for a political psychology that Honneth expresses. But there is more to it than that, because modern politics is not only a question of rebellion. It also requires stabilization.

Rebellion and revolutions are surely essential for the process of modern emancipation but stabilization and constitutionalization, too, must be taken into account. In the modern period, if rebellion succeeds, then constitutionalization follows, and the two moments—the insurrectional and the constitutional—are both foundational to the life of *one* people. Take the example of America. The people who declared independence in 1776 and the people who ratified the Constitution in 1787 cannot be seen as two separate peoples; they are one *populus*, the American people, the same political entity to whom citizens of the United States continue to pledge loyalty today. But this entails that there is continuity between rebellion and stabilization and that some sort of suffering, viewed as the motor of insurrectional subjectification, permeates the process of constitutional subjectification as well.

In legal and political theory, the two moments are usually perceived as distinct from each other. Theorists privilege one or the other, dividing themselves into two families: mainstream theorists and critical theorists. What do Frank Michelman and Antonio Negri have in common? If the answer is nothing, this is because they focus on just one of the two moments of political subjectification rather than seeing them as two aspects of the same process. But can we solve Michelman's problem—the problem of the intertemporal continuity between the chartering people and the chartered people—without paying attention to what Rancière and Honneth say about the role that subjectivity and suffering play in modern politics? I do not think so, and what I present here is a theory that endeavors to tie together the insurrectional and constitutional moments of modern political subjectification.

As I have said, the notion of grammar is central to my whole argument, not least because a grammar is that which allows us to distinguish between identity and subjectivity. In my view, however, identity and subjectivity are not diametrically opposed, as Rancière believes. In reality, subjectification amounts to a process of *failed identification* rather than sheer disidentification, and for this reason subjectivity and suffering are closely intertwined from beginning to end of modern political mobilizations. Initially, people do not manage to identify with the community in which they find themselves living. At a later stage, this failure of the people's identification becomes the driving force of a process of subjectification that pushes the people to search for their true identity. A political grammar, as I understand it, is nothing but the *path* that this search follows and that gives shape to a certain form of permanent disease. In the modern era, people definitely suffer from not being able to grasp their true collective identity, even after they have found a way to stabilize and constitutionalize their new political *nos*— which is why self-questioning societies like ours arise and a process of stormy democratization can proceed. It follows that failed identification (not mere disidentification) ensures the continuity between the first and second stages of political subjectification. It is the suffering caused by failed identification that connects the insurrectional and constitutional moments of modern political life.

But what does failed identification mean? To answer this question, we need to bring another notion into the picture, the notion of natural rights. In the modern age, people rebel against the established powers in the name of their alleged natural, or "unalienable," rights. Then, it is in the name of those same rights that people constitutionalize a new political *nos*. Natural rights are therefore crucial from beginning to end, and they are so important because they prevent the modern political *nos* from identifying with itself once and for all. Natural rights are there to point to a kind of remainder, to some secret, inscrutable nature of human beings that becomes the normative end of modern democratic societies as viewed from the perspective of the peoples themselves. These rights are the sign that people continue to suffer from a gap between what can be deemed truly human and what is recognized as human in a certain society. Modern societies are indeed those in which there is a constant interplay between the natural "rights of man" and the "rights of the citizen," yet the gap between them cannot be bridged in any satisfactory way. Every modern *populus* owes its existence to this internal distance from its true nature, from the alleged integrity of all human beings who are part of it and who strive to recover their own being and fulfill their genuine destiny through political mobilization.

A political grammar, very briefly, is the way in which such a pursuit of human integrity and happiness is framed by a single people.

One more remark about the Grimm-Habermas debate might be helpful before moving forward. As I have already stressed, recent developments in Europe proved that the *demos*, not the constitution, comes first. A process of political subjectification *ends in* constitutionalization; it does not *start from* constitutionalization, as Habermas maintains. History is undoubtedly on Grimm's side. Unfortunately, the latter cannot seem to explain why this is the case, and most of his arguments against Habermas—similar to Carl Schmitt's arguments against Hans Kelsen—are far from convincing. Actually, Grimm's conception of the *demos* dates from the nineteenth century. For him—as well as for Fichte, Schmitt, and several others—the key to everything is the notion of social homogeneity. For a *demos* to be possible, people must share the same language and a common cultural background. Apparently, this conjecture makes sense: a common sense of belonging does require a certain degree of homogeneity among people, especially in Europe. A modern *demos*, however, is the expression of a political subjectivity, of a "general will" that struggles for recognition, of a collective quest for happiness and truth, and it is clear to everyone that a strong linguistic and cultural homogeneity does not lead automatically to the political self-affirmation of *one* people. To give just one example: no political subjectivity is detectable in regions such a Sicily or Apulia, in Italy, where local communities are nonetheless characterized by a remarkable level of linguistic and cultural homogeneity. In sum, history is on Grimm's side, but Grimm himself has great difficulty in understanding why. And until we understand why, we run the risk of believing that history is on Habermas's side. As should be evident by now, this theoretical problem has some practical implications that cannot be overstated.

The concept of political grammar serves to address this problem. In a nutshell, the idea is that *objective* elements of social homogeneity are not enough to explain the birth and life of a political *nos*. Those elements become relevant only when they are *subjectively* activated. Political mobilization requires political subjectification, and subjectification entails that people feel the need—at some point in their history and for reasons that need to be clarified—to speak and act chorally, to express their "general will" in the first-person plural, and that they acquire the capacity to do so for a certain period of time. As I will argue at length, political grammars make this kind of collective subjectification possible by imposing restrictions over the acts of enunciation of the people, who thus turn into *one* people and continue to see themselves as *one* people day after day because they all comply with the same grammatical limitations whenever they open their mouths. Most of the time, such restrictions operate on some preexistent resources: language, religion, traditions, and others. But the point is that grammars never amount to the algebraic sum of those symbolic and cultural resources, of those preexistent elements. Rather, a grammar is that which selects from among those elements, organizes them in a peculiar manner, and activates them, animates them, from the point of view of a political subject. Importantly, not even that point of view preexists a political grammar, for a grammar is that which establishes that point of view, thereby giving rise to a political subjectivity.

To recapitulate: I will not develop a normative theory of democracy or of politics—at least, not in the commonly accepted sense of *normative*. I do not intend to explain, for example, why and when violence ought to be condemned. I am more interested in the reasons why conflicts broke out and violence flared up, sometimes with abominable cruelty, in Europe and in other parts of the world. As Judith Butler has remarked, the most pressing problem in political theory is quite simple: "Whose lives are already considered not lives, or only partially living, or already dead and gone, prior to any explicit destruction or abandonment?"[18] Unlike Butler and others, however, I will adopt the view from within, not the view from nowhere.[19] I will not ask myself what the general and abstract criteria for a "good life" are.[20] My problem is what has been done in the past, why, and what lesson for the future can be drawn from this.

Political Grammars

Introduction

The Cartesian Connection

Please close your eyes and repeat: *ego cogito, ergo sum,* "I think, there-fore I am." Thus spoke René Descartes. Readers familiar with the work of Immanuel Kant or Friedrich Nietzsche will know that by drawing the conclusion "I am" from the premise "I think," one falls into a trap, which might be termed a paralogism of pure reason or a grammatical illusion. But let us forget about that. So long as you say "I think," you cannot escape the conclusion "I am," can you? As soon as you appear as a grammatical *subject* speaking in the first person, you cannot help *being*. Stronger than anything, the subject I-think-I-am imposes itself. Today, we all agree that the *cogito* cannot be given any cognitive mean-ing or truth-value. We know that we know nothing when we articulate it. Nevertheless, such a refrain, *ego cogito, ergo sum,* is like a continuo that resounds throughout our existence. Even though the Cartesian *ego* does not pave the way for any true knowledge, even though the subject I-think-I-am is nothing more than a fiction, we must concede that this is a *true fiction*, in that the *ego* I-think-I-am claims to be truly someone or something. Inevitably, we all suffer from such a pretension to truth that leads nowhere. Thus, we end up bewildered by our own *ego,* as we totally ignore how to deal with the true fiction we are. I-think-I-am: *ego cogito, ergo sum.* But then, who am I? What am I?

Modern philosophers tried their best to answer these questions. Since they could not get rid of the *cogito*, the problem became how to make sense of it. Should we see it as being the cipher of a hidden, metaphysical truth? Or should we think of it as a sheer illusion, stemming from more prosaic causes? Whatever the answer, modern philosophy has been constantly puzzled by the *cogito.* As G. W. F. Hegel points out, the *cogito* is "the principle [*Satz*] about which revolves the whole interest of modern philosophy."[1] One can hardly disagree with him. The *cogito* and its product, namely the modern *ego*, the *self*, or our own *being* in the first person, have not been one among many questions for modern philosophy. They have been, and continue to be, *the* question. Despite the fact that nobody can tell what we are saying when we utter the words *ego cogito, ergo sum*, we cannot help but be mesmerized by them.

To take but two examples: when John Locke refutes Descartes's definition of the *res cogitans* as an "immaterial substance," he does not deny the fact that there exists a "thinking thing." If anything, he speaks of "this ignorance we are in of the nature of that thinking thing, that is in us, and which we look on as our *selves*."[2] And when, three centuries later, Martin Heidegger theorizes that "*Dasein* is that entity which in its Being has this very Being as an issue,"[3] it is the same question that comes up again—that is, the question about something or someone, the first-person "I," who claims the truth of her being and yet cannot fill this empty truth with any truthful meaning. "I" eludes true knowledge and fades into a true fiction.[4]

Outside the field of philosophy, there is another branch of research that encounters these problems on a daily basis: psychoanalysis. Lacan, in particular, conceived of psychoanalysis as the clinical science of the Cartesian subject I-think-I-am. In his view, psychoanalysts deal with the true fiction we are and with the various ways in which we try to cope with the empty, meaningless truth we embody.[5] *Ça parle,* "it speaks," as Lacan used to say, and what thus speaks is always the same thing, the Freudian Thing, which is the reverse side of the Cartesian subject: *Moi, la vérité, je parle.* "I, truth, speak."[6] What does it all mean? What is the structure of our subjectivity? What is the real stuff of which our being is composed?

In the following, I will widen the range of problems that psychoanalysis allows us to think through, as I will focus not only on individual subjectivity but also on collective subjectivity. As Sigmund Freud noted, the two issues are strictly interrelated, for psychoanalysis posits that our subjectivity is of a social nature. "Individual psychology . . . is at the same time social psychology as well."[7] In brief, according to Freud, our individual subjectivity is heavily conditioned by the type of relationship that we establish with all the people who live around us from the time of our childhood, and with whom the *ego* shares the capacity to say *nos*—whether these people are parents, families, or communities at large. Unfortunately, however, much about the connection between the *ego* and the *nos* goes unexplained from a Freudian perspective (I will say more about Freud's theory of groups later on). What are collective subjects? How do they differ? How do they emerge and stabilize over time? And how do they relate to individual subjects? Psychoanalysis as it stands today certainly provides a theory—in fact, many theories—of intersubjectivity that accounts for certain aspects of the relationship between one *ego* and another, but it still needs a compelling theory of collective subjectivities. Freud's Oedipus complex, for example, can be considered a theory of intersubjectivity that explains the relationship between children and parents. Lacan's version of the Oedipus complex represents another attempt to explain this relationship with the help of updated theoretical tools. And John Bowlby's attachment theory represents yet another effort to explain how children relate to their mothers and to their environment. But none of these theories explains how many *egos* merge into a *nos*. None of them examines in depth the nature of collective subjects.

Things are no better when we enter the field of political theory. Think about the late John Rawls. On the one hand, he writes an essay on *The Law of Peoples* in which the concept of peoples (in the plural) occupies center stage. On the other hand, when he is confronted with the necessity of defining this concept, he encounters so many problems that he feels forced to take refuge in the venerable John Stuart Mill:

"This account of the Law of Peoples conceives of liberal democratic peoples (and decent peoples) as the actors in the Society of Peoples, just as citizens are the actors in domestic society. . . . Liberal peoples have three basic features: a reasonably just constitutional democratic government that serves their fundamental interests; citizens united by what Mill called "common sympathies"; and finally, a moral nature."[8] Without going into too much detail, Rawls himself concedes that concepts such as "fundamental interests," "common sympathies," and "moral nature" do not clarify the meaning of the word *peoples* but rather require clarification; and this already shows how difficult it is to grasp the essence of the political *nos*—the *demos*, the *populus*. The mystery is so impenetrable that many prefer to regard peoples as optical illusions. According to Hans Kelsen, for instance, there are no such things as "liberal democratic peoples":

> From a concrete point of view, there is nothing more problematic than this unity which goes by the name, the People. . . . Only a juristic fact is capable of circumscribing the unity of the People with some accuracy, namely: the unity of the state's legal order whose norms govern the behavior of its subjects. . . .
>
> . . . Therefore, it is a fiction when the unity, which the state's legal order fashions out of the multiplicity of human actions, poses as a "popular body" by calling itself the "People."[9]

Kelsen's thesis could not be clearer. Liberal democratic peoples have no distinct and prior political existence, because "the unity of the People" does nothing but reflect "the unity of the State's legal order."[10] But then, what about those "peoples" that rebel against the state in which they live, reclaiming their independence? Or what about those "peoples" that ask to join *another* state? In modern history, there are plenty of examples that contradict Kelsen's conclusion—to name but a few: the Jacobites, the Hungarian *honvéd*, the Sudeten Germans, the people of Saint-Domingue, and all other "peoples" that underwent a process of decolonization. In all of these cases, "the unity of the People" cannot be traced back to "the unity of the State's legal order," for the simple reason that those "peoples" did not identify with the state in which they found themselves living. Nor does it make much sense to say that the "popular body" was ultimately the product of political propaganda, because the problem here is not the top-down imposition of an article of faith but rather the rise of a bottom-up sense of belonging that can prompt human beings to die for the sake of their own nation. In short, Kelsen's arguments are far too simplistic. In the modern period, "the unity of the People" and "the State's legal order" enter, more often than not, into a problematic relationship. Modern peoples, whatever their essence and definition may be, surely relate to modern states and cannot be thought of in the absence of states, as Kelsen says, but they are not merely "an element of a particular social order, the state."[11] Modern peoples have an order of their own, however invisible that order may be, and such an order can lay the foundations for the state or else challenge the established powers. Hence the idea of the people's "constituent power," an idea that lies at the core not only of modern democratic constitutions but also of international law, where it takes the name "self-determination of peoples."

In light of the above, the problem arises as to what happens when people start yelling at the rest of the world *nos sumus, nos existimus* and continue to do so for some period of time. What are peoples? How do they materialize? Despite the quite obvious untenability of Kelsen's thesis, only a handful of political theorists and social scientists have tackled this issue in recent decades.[12] Apart from a few exceptions, most of them work in the field of Nationalism Studies.[13]

Here, I will address the same problem from a psychoanalytic point of view and examine the similarities between the two claims *ego sum* and *nos sumus*. My point is that there can be no substantial difference between the ways in which the first-person singular and the first-person plural come into being. Our sense of selfhood, whether individual or collective, always revolves around a true fiction—the subject—which originates in a certain arrangement of the symbolic space.

One of the chief tenets of Lacan's theory of subjectivity reads as follows: subjects stubbornly claim to be someone or something, yet they cannot understand the truth of their own claims. The truth speaks in the first person, "I, truth, speak," but I am deaf to her call. Thus, the truth slips away, hiding behind all I can say about myself. This is how the "unconscious" knocks on the subject's door: *abscondita subiacet veritas.*

Let us return to the *cogito*. I think, therefore I am, but who am I? This question always takes an idiomatic form for each one of us. Why am I stammering, or washing my hands every ten minutes, or falling in love with the wrong person for the nth time in my life? The subject of the unconscious does not know. Yet the subject I-think-I-am is not annihilated for this reason, since it continues to articulate words, doubts, and questions that are organized and distributed around a hole, the *ego*, that cannot be filled up with any truthful meaning. Psychoanalysis investigates this organization and distribution, which Lacan defines as the "grammar" of our unconscious. To a first approximation, Lacan's grammars may be thought of as spectacles (or quasi-transcendental constraints). Through the lens of grammars, we see everything around us. The only thing we cannot bring into focus is the visual field itself—that is, ourselves, our subjective point of view. As a result, all elements inside the field end up revolving around a macula, a blotch, our own *ego*, which appears as a semantic blind spot—as we cannot find any truthful meaning in it—but which attests to a syntactical continuity—as grammars, and nothing else, make the *ego* (the first-person perspective) invariant over time. In sum, I have the feeling that I am always the same because I keep on following the same particular syntax, a kind of private grammar, whenever I open my mouth.

I will argue that the same sort of approach is of some use when it comes to collective subjects such as peoples or nations. According to Lacan, the *ego* is merely a hole circumscribed by words and representations that are syntactically organized and distributed around it. There is nothing that prevents us from interpreting the political *nos* along the same lines. Take, for example, Mill's considerations on nationality:

> A portion of mankind may be said to constitute a Nationality, if they are united among themselves by common sympathies, which do not exist between them and any others—which make them cooperate with each other more willingly than with other people, desire to be under the same government, and desire that it should be government by themselves, or a portion of themselves, exclusively. This feeling of nationality may have been generated by various causes. Sometimes it

is the effect of identity of race and descent. Community of language, community of religion, greatly contribute to it. Geographical limits are one of its causes. But the strongest of all is identity of political antecedents; the possession of national history, and consequent community of recollections; collective pride and humiliation, pleasure and regret, connected with the same incidents in the past. None of these circumstances, however, are necessarily sufficient by themselves.[14]

As the last sentence of this passage makes plain, the problem of nationality cannot be solved by simply enumerating the various components of our feelings of nationality: none of these elements can by itself explain that feeling. Nor does our sense of national belonging arise from the sheer accumulation of a number of national traits such as language, religion, race, history, or culture. In reality, as Mill himself seems to realize, in order to understand why people "are united among themselves by common sympathies," we need to understand how those traits or features *coalesce*, how they become *organized* around a first-person plural, and how they *combine* into a whole that can be passed down from one generation to another. The concept of grammar (in the Lacanian sense) helps us to address these issues.

As I have already said, psychoanalysis offers an intriguing solution to the problem of our being in the first-person singular. Granting that the whole of one's representations of oneself and of the world compose a multifaceted discourse, we cannot identify the *ego* with any of those representations, because the latter change and alternate without a pause, as David Hume explains. Nevertheless, psychoanalysis draws our attention to the fact that our representations always follow an invisible, invariant grammar, which bundles all of them and differentiates one discourse from the other, thus eliciting the feeling that the same *ego* hides behind the same discourse. Importantly, no *ego* can be aware of such a grammar, for the *ego* is shaped by it. Therefore, every time we look into these unnoticed grammars, we are scrutinizing the subject's unconscious.

Nothing keeps us from extending this reasoning to collective subjectivities. Many scholars have emphasized, for instance, how crucial "social imaginaries" are for the understanding of the modern world.[15] In a Lacanian perspective, the problem is how these imaginaries arise out of a process of collective subjectification that is framed by an underlying grammar that provides a certain first-person society with a sufficient degree of invariance. To tackle this particular problem, unusual for psychoanalytic research, we clearly need to take a step beyond Lacan's own conceptualization. Indeed, the private grammars of the *ego*—those that are of interest to psychoanalysts—and the public grammars of the *nos* cannot be the same thing. Yet the very notion of grammar can be preserved when shifting from the first-person singular to the first-person plural and, with it, the idea that the *nos*, like the *ego*, is grounded in a structure of which it is totally unaware.

This step beyond Lacan may seem risky at first. On closer inspection, however, it turns out to be necessary. If we agree with Lacan that one's ontological self-assurance is based on one's private grammar, then it remains to be seen why the *ego* does not think of itself as an island in the middle of nowhere. As soon as we raise this question, the notion of a public, collective grammar imposes itself. If we are not completely isolated from one another, this is because each one of us connects with other people at the level of the first-person plural. But this entails that a kind of collective grammar is always already in force and that this grammar complements our private grammars and integrates each and every *ego sum* into a broader *nos sumus*.

From a philosophical angle, this line of reasoning deserves some attention. According to Ludwig Wittgenstein, the very idea of private language is untenable. For psychoanalysis, by contrast, the unconscious seems to be such a language; remember Lacan's definition, "the unconscious is structured like a language."[16] In spite of appearances, however, there is no contradiction between Wittgenstein and Lacan, for the latter contends that the unconscious is made of private grammars, not of private languages. Language is undoubtedly the same for all of us; yet for each of us, words and representations, besides being inserted in a web of syntactic possibilities dictated by the language we speak and the "form of life" we share with others, are also inserted in a more restricted and private web of syntactic possibilities that distinguish *my* or *your* use of words and representations.

Would Wittgenstein have contested this rather obvious remark? Would he have denied that every individual has his or her *idée fixe*? Whatever the answer, there is one important lesson to be drawn from Wittgenstein's late ruminations about private language. In fact, his point is not, as is often believed, that there can be no private language—in many respects, that goes without saying—but rather that private ontology and private experiences can never be that private. This is what Wittgenstein intended to say. In a nutshell, I cannot *be* while being perfectly alone. For the *ego sum* to be possible at all, the claim that I am, however ill-founded it may be, must address someone else, for I necessarily assume the *truth* of my claim; and this truth, no matter how poor of meaning it may be, cannot be totally private. Whenever a pretension to truth arises, some potential acknowledgment is required. A public arena is needed.

A grammar, from a psychoanalytic point of view, is precisely that which organizes the relationship between language and truth. Grammar enables me to claim that I truly am behind all that I say or that I truly remain the same *ego* with the passing of time. That said, no truth can be thought of as entirely private, as we learn from Wittgenstein and others. Truth implies a certain degree of necessity and universality, as Kant would have it. For Wittgenstein, it follows that the concept of private ontology is nonsense and must be ruled out. For Lacan, the consequence is less drastic and amounts to saying that private grammars must be completed with public grammars that integrate our personal certainties about being, our private (phantasmatic) ontologies, into public and more ordinary (though equally phantasmatic) ontologies. As a result of this integration, a connection is made between the *ego* and the *nos*; thus, each of us becomes "an *I* that is *We* and *We* that is *I*," as Hegel famously put it.[17]

Here, I will analyze how a connection is made between the *ego* and a special type of *nos*, the political *nos*. This type of collective subjectivity, or first-person plural, is foundational to modern societies. Clearly, the *nos* can be of different natures, and this holds for the past as well as the present. In the premodern period, the social bond was basically of a religious nature; and even today, "we" can be a church, or a religious sect, or a charitable association (not to speak of other kinds of groups and collectivities, from NGOs to football fans). In our time, however, whenever we talk of society as a whole, or of society as such, "we" cannot be disjoined from the political *nos*. Our societies are indeed secular societies. In the modern era, the social bond that integrates every individual *ego* into a collective *nos* is, first and foremost, of a political nature. And the modern political *nos* presents some peculiarities on which I will concentrate in the first part of the book, after clarifying the epistemic tenets of the psychoanalytic approach to political history in Chapter 1.

One of the chief features of modern first-person societies is that when we look at them from the perspective of the political *nos*, a certain amount of homogeneity among people seems to be required; otherwise, society could not be sufficiently united. Yet, when we look at them from the perspective of the *ego*, a certain degree of heterogeneity seems to be equally required; otherwise, the individual would disappear into the collectivity. Thus, it appears that a modern process of political subjectification, through which a modern society comes into being, pushes us in two opposite directions: on the one hand, it pushes us toward the homogenization of One *populus*; on the other hand, it pushes us toward the heterogenization of Many *egos*. How can a compromise be made between these two requirements, both of which are necessary for democracy to develop and for the project of individual *and* collective emancipation to take root? Hermann Heller and Ernesto Laclau discussed this topic extensively. The former put a stronger emphasis on social homogeneity, the latter on social heterogeneity. By analyzing the shortcomings of their arguments in Chapter 2, I will highlight the need for a theory that accounts for both tendencies of modern societies: homogenization and heterogenization.

Another significant feature of first-person societies is that the interplay between the *ego* and the political *nos* is always governed by law and rights. The secular age is the "age of rights," as Norberto Bobbio says.[18] Yet, as Michel Villey remarks, modern rights are not like the *iura* of which Roman law had spoken for centuries. In the modern period, rather than being things that can be granted to someone, rights are considered features, qualities or properties of the individual, of the *ego* who holds them. Modern rights, often characterized as subjective rights, are the "rights of man." They are human beings' properties. As Crawford B. Macpherson observes, this concept of rights became widespread in free-market societies, in which people were accustomed to the idea that they were endowed with some human properties that could be used and enjoyed but also transferred to others after signing a contract. Among those human properties, there was labor in the first instance—a natural property of man that had been commodified. Then, within a short period of time, those human properties came to include rights as well, the natural rights that "each man hath," as Hobbes put it. Thus, as I will point out in Chapter 3, a brand-new view of man, seen as the owner of himself, was instrumental in promoting a new concept of rights and preparing the ground for the revolutionary doctrine of the "social contract." In capitalist societies, people found themselves in a position to imagine that they could transfer their human properties to someone else: to the employer in some cases, to the sovereign power in others.

Unfortunately, after transferring their natural rights to the sovereign power, people were deprived of a number of freedoms that they counted among their most valuable human properties. And the problem arose as to how they could recover from such a loss. After some time, the solution was found: popular sovereignty. The sovereign power was to be seen as legitimate only if it protected the people's "unalienable" rights and gave voice to the people's own will. In this manner, one could continue to be oneself, a human being, while passing one's natural rights on to the sovereign power, which had become the people's own power at that point. In a Lacanian perspective, it is arguable that this passage involves the activation of a grammar. Only grammar combines private and public autonomy,[19] integrating the *ego* into the *nos* and individual rights into popular sovereignty so that heterogeneity among people, our own individuality, can coexist with a sufficient degree of homogeneity; this is the *sine qua non* for the survival of *one* society. As we will see in Chapter 4, this result can be attained in various ways, depending on which of the two poles of political subjectification—the *ego* or the *nos*, heterogeneity or homogeneity—happens to be privileged. The historical circumstances in which the political *nos* comes to the fore are decisive in that respect. I will illustrate this with two examples— the French Declaration of the Rights of Man and of the Citizen and the US Declaration of Independence—that gave birth to two "liberal democratic peoples" grounded in different grammars. Interestingly, the French and the American Revolutions reached the same goal, political subjectification, in *opposite* ways. I will insist on this asymmetry between America and Europe, which is often underrated by historians and political theorists. While Europe became the land of nations and nationalisms, America became the home of an altogether different type of patriotism, which I call (nonnationalist) separatism.

If modern societies are so lively and open to change compared to previous societal forms, this is because the first-person plural does not overwhelm the first-person singular; rather, a compromise between them is negotiated. This kind of compromise is what we usually call democracy. Differences among political grammars, and among democracies, are due to the different types of compromises reached between the *ego* and the *nos*. Broadly speaking, as Marcel Mauss notes, all citizens merge into the nation, but rights and duties of individuals are bound to diverge, at least partially, from those of the community as a whole.[20] A process of homogenization is launched, but true homogeneity remains out of sight. From a grammatical point of view, this means that the process of democratization—and the related process of political subjectification—tends to integrate the *ego* into the political *nos* but cannot achieve this goal once and for all. Typically, democracy aims to convert the "rights of man" into the "rights of the citizen" but never achieves perfect identity between the former and the latter. A gap remains between each human being and the nation, or the political *nos*, that bestows civil rights on the people. Every *ego* becomes a "citizen" while being a "man," who holds natural rights still unknown to the political *nos*. Hence three consequences of the greatest importance.

First: The political *nos* appears as a definite set—that is, the set of all citizens who have civil and political rights—but this set is always captured into a larger and indefinite set—that is, the set of all human beings endowed with natural rights. Each *ego* is a member of both sets, and it is only thanks to this dual membership that each one of us can be a citizen and a human being, or a "man," at the same time. What is the name of the larger set? Does it take the same shape for all political subjects? As I will argue in the second part of the book, the larger set is actually construed in different ways, depending on the political grammar in force. Within the framework of European nationalist grammars, it takes the form of an entity that I call *humanity*. Within the framework of the American separatist grammar, it takes the form of another entity, which I call *mankind*. These entities, both of which attest that we are human beings before being French or American, represent the reverse side of the political *nos* and are integral to political grammars, as they form the background against which everybody can restate his or her individuality—namely, the persisting distance between the *ego* and the political *nos*—by claiming some rights that fellow nationals do not reckon among the rights of the citizen.

Second: Such irreducible distance between the *ego* and the political *nos*, or between the rights of man and the rights of the citizen, is the quivering heart of modern democracies and the inexhaustible source of emancipatory fights. Whenever a democratic mobilization takes place in modern times, a promise is made, the promise that the distance between man and the citizen will be bridged at last. Yet that promise can never be kept. Thus, modern democracies lead to compromises (or "compromise formations") that need to be revised and amended on a regular basis. There always remains some distance between the *ego* and the political *nos*, between the holder of natural rights and the holder of political sovereignty. By the same token, there remains a distance between society and the state that embodies the people's sovereignty but should also allow human beings to achieve their true nature and attain happiness. As Mauss writes, a modern society is "a society materially and morally integrated, with a stable and permanent central authority, with determinate borders, whose inhabitants possess a relative moral, mental and cultural unity and consciously adhere to the state and its laws."[21] But this entails, as Mauss goes on to explain, that a modern society can withdraw consent at any moment and challenge the state and its laws instead of bowing to them. Indeed, modern societies are never at peace with themselves and with the state in which they wish to reflect themselves. Quite the contrary, these societies strive relentlessly to perfect the state and its laws for the sake of something that vibrates in all citizens but cannot be traced back to the state—humanity, mankind.

Third: The discrepancies between man and the citizen, the *ego* and the political *nos*, society and the state, are the cause of never-ending frustration. But what if someone objected that modern societies can be healed and that democracy can keep its promise? Historically, this objection is not an abstract possibility but a concrete reality called *fascism*. For, contrary to common opinion, fascism is not a reaction against democracy or an utterly antidemocratic ideology. As a matter of fact, fascism is a more complicated phenomenon. The first thing to note is that fascism is a political disease that infects only modern democracies. The reason for this is that fascism marks the moment when people are fooled into believing that modern democracies can get rid of all failures and compromises. This is how many politicians and intellectuals saw fascism in Italy and Germany a century ago. At the time, fascism was not seen as a betrayal or a refutation of democracy but rather as a way of bringing democracy to completion. Fascism was equated with true democracy and sharply contrasted with fake democracies—that is, "liberal democracies." The entry *Fascism* written for the *Enciclopedia Treccani* by Giovanni Gentile and Benito Mussolini made this point clear: "Fascism is the most candid form of democracy."[22] Yet fascism turned into a political nightmare. How was such a radical misconception possible? To answer this question, I will further elaborate on the notion of political grammar and elucidate how modern democracies can be smoothly transformed into *pseudo-democracies*.

To begin with, it will be necessary to go over the idea of liberal democracy. As I will argue in Chapter 5, Michel Foucault's inquiries into the birth of biopolitics and "the liberal art of governing" help us to get to the heart of the matter. Adopting an original approach to political history on which I will briefly expand, Foucault stresses that the modern democratic state qualifies as both a *factum* and a *fictio*. The state is a fact insofar as it rules over people and bestows freedoms on them. At the same time, the state is a fiction insofar as "we the people" believe that it does not effect our freedoms but simply recognizes them. In the age of modern democracy, whenever "we the people" bow to the state, the tacit assumption is that "we the people" are bowing to ourselves, as though the state were an extension of ourselves.

But who are "we the people"? Democratic constitutions take the answer for granted, while scholars still quarrel over the nature and existence of peoples, which many are inclined to call into doubt. A good way to avoid being paralyzed by this sort of ontological dilemma is to change the line of questioning: do people always make the same sort of assumption when they claim to be *one* people? As I will explain in Chapter 6, this seems not to be the case. Drawing on Lacan's theory, I will show more specifically that the political *nos* in Europe stems from a metaphorical assumption, whereas in America it stems from a metonymic assumption. The difference between these assumptions, which are conducive to distinct forms of political "representation,"[23] lies in the way in which the political *nos* integrates the *ego* into the smaller set of the *populus* and into the larger set of either humanity or mankind. Everywhere, the citizen is a man. Therefore, not only is every individual a member of two sets, the finite set of the *populus* and the indefinite set of human beings, but each individual is also a point of intersection between the two sets. Interestingly, the intersection between the two sets can be shaped differently, either by way of metaphor or by way of metonymy. As a result of this, the indefinite set of human beings looks different, and the citizen turns into an idiomatic specimen of man. In Europe, the political *nos* acquires a metaphorical surplus value that renders the "nation" and all of its citizens an epitome of humanity as such. In America, instead, the political *nos* appears as the spokesperson for a metonymic leftover, mankind, and this explains why America is not a "nation" like all others. I will illustrate the disparity between political metaphors and metonymies and other grammatical discrepancies between the New World and the Old World with the help of historical examples.

With this in mind, it becomes possible to look deeper into fascism and to do so from an entirely new perspective. The language of set theory is particularly appropriate for this purpose. This language was employed by Lacan and other psychoanalysts—notably, Ignacio Matte-Blanco—as a tool for understanding psychotic delusions. Unsurprisingly, the same language proves useful for understanding political psychosis as well. When studying fascism, the problem one has to face sooner or later is the following: if fascism is a form of "extreme nationalism,"[24] as most students of fascism maintain, what makes nationalism so extreme in some cases? From a grammatical point of view, the answer lies in the delusional identification of the finite set of the *populus* with the indefinite set of humanity. In many respects, the case of Nazism is paradigmatic, and I will elaborate on it in Chapter 7. The German *Volk* morphed into the Aryan race under the assumption that the German *populus* was not only a metaphor but also a literal incarnation of humanity, of the true nature of human beings. Hence the ideological vehemence and the democratic involution of the Nazi regime, characterized by a number of notorious distortions. Among them were the conflation of the metaphorical and literal layers of language, which pushed the Nazis into believing that the political surplus value of the German nation could be translated into the literal and scientifically substantiated supremacy of the Aryan race; the political exploitation and subjugation of certain branches of science, especially the life sciences; the invention of a paranoid newspeak that was supposed to convey the Revelation of Truth; the absolutization of the *Volk*'s sovereignty to the detriment of individual and minority rights; and, after the Wannsee Conference, the methodical extermination of all those who could not identify with humanity as such because they were not members of the Aryan race.

Today, we may wonder whether fascism is rearing its head again in Europe and elsewhere. Furthermore, we may wonder whether a *new* kind of fascism is now threatening Western democracies. If we see fascism as a form of pseudo-democracy, the answer is not obvious. For most people, it is clear that Western democracies have been adulterated by the ascent of "neoliberalism," or ultraliberalism. What is less clear and needs to be emphasized is that the ultraliberal revolution represents the exact opposite of the ultranationalist revolution of the 1930s:[25] the old fascist absolutization of popular sovereignty is turned into an equally delusional absolutization of individual and minority rights; the political exploitation of science is replaced with the scientists' (especially the economists') coercion of politics; the superempowerment of a single political party gives way to the disempowerment of all parties, which are forced to surrender to the neutral authority of a technocratic university. In Chapter 8, I will examine these and other features of present-day democracies, arguing that a new collective subject is coming to the fore nowadays, one that abjures previous allegiances and is shaking our societies to their foundations. For reasons that I will specify, I call this new actor of modern politics the human population. The burden that it puts on us is nothing less than a delusional inversion of our Cartesian being: *ego non sum, nos non sumus*. This means that political subjectification is now achieved through a process of desubjectification that is nonetheless framed by a particular grammar. I will clarify the meaning of the above definitions with the help of concrete examples, from the process of European integration to the alleged "end of modern societies,"[26] all of which prove that the most distinctive trait of our time is the "undoing of the demos."[27] At the same time, I will explain why the long-term effect of this grammatical evolution is the resurgence of nations and nationalisms, which reappear as specters from the past, contrasting the neoliberal depoliticization of society with a highly infectious repoliticization.

As I will point out in my Conclusion, the theory of political grammars opens a new perspective on current political debates and allows us to conjecture about future developments, especially in Europe. That said, the main ambition of the book is to reset the scholarly—rather than the political—debate over nations, nationalities, and nationalism. As Craig Calhoun has remarked many times throughout his writings:

> The problems of collective identity formation are commonly ignored by democratic theory. They are, however, endemic to modern political life. . . .
>
> . . . We lack a theory of the constitution of social selves which will give descriptive foundation to the prescriptive notion of self-determination. We are poorly prepared to talk about national identity or nationalism. . . .
>
> The nineteenth-century discourse of nationalism still shapes much of our vocabulary for thinking about these issues—and identifying the subjects of democratic projects.[28]

One can hardly deny that current investigations into political selves continue to be heavily influenced by nineteenth-century debates, as Calhoun writes. (Rawls's reference to Mill is just one example among many.) But Calhoun himself does not fathom the root of the problem.

To put it bluntly, the problem is that we cannot make any progress in this field unless we stop talking about "national identities." This concept is quite common in scholarly literature but extremely vague, not to say deceptive, mostly because it does not draw a clear line between the cultural and the political spheres of social life. Hence the fatal, yet frequent, confusion between the cultural resources of a certain community and the political activation, or mobilization, of those resources. The theory of political grammars centers around this paramount difference between national (cultural) identities and political mobilizations—which always bring to the fore political *subjectivities*.

In recent years, other political theorists have been concerned with the subjective moment of modern history. Among them are Étienne Balibar and Ernesto Laclau, whose works have been a source of inspiration for this project.[29] Both of them have insisted on the strong correlation between the issue of modern subjectivity and modern democracy. Moreover, both of them have seen psychoanalysis as helpful in analyzing that correlation.[30] I will illustrate the similarities and discrepancies between their views and mine throughout the book.[31] The specificity of my approach lies in my deeper commitment to psychoanalysis. For Lacan, subjectivity is not a substance, as Descartes argued, nor is it a nonentity, as Hume objected. Rather, subjectivity should be seen as a process, which is more than nothing and less than something. In other words, subjectivity means subjectification: a process whereby the invariance of the first-person perspective is secured, but the subject's identity cannot be found. Consider the *cogito*. I think, therefore I am, but I do not know who I am. Thus, I am a subject, yet I have no definite, discernible identity. Thanks to the fact that I am a subject, however, I can ask myself who I am; I can try to identify myself in one way or another. This paradigmatic example shows that subjectification comes first, subjectification lays the basis for identification, and subjectification—in Lacan's view—implies the activation of an unconscious grammar that ensures the invariance of the *ego* who is wondering about its identity. No such quest for identity would be possible if the subject did not remain invariant over time and kept on searching for the identity of the same *ego*. But no such invariance of the subject, in turn, would be possible in the absence of a grammar, as Lacan explains.

Now, think about a psychological trauma. From a psychoanalytic point of view, an event turns out to be intolerable to someone when it obstructs the process of subjectification. When a trauma occurs, what is undermined is not the subject's identity, which is far from being a consolidated reality under normal conditions, but rather the subject's capacity to be on the trail of its identity. What is jeopardized by trauma is subjectivity itself—that is, the process of subjectification and the grammar underlying this process. This means that whenever a trauma occurs, a new grammar—not a new identity—is required to get out of the crisis. Grammar makes it possible for the traumatized individual to come to terms with the unprecedented situation.

When studying political subjects or selves, this remark serves as a warning. We must pay close attention to those collective traumas and historical points of no return from which political grammars and subjects originate: wars, turmoils, revolutions, and all other moments when people experience some unbearable suffering and lose touch with themselves for a while. As soon as they can open their mouth again, all they can say is *nos sumus, nos existimus*. And they usually shout it out loud.

Part I

Discourse and Grammar

1

The Clinical Approach to Political History

Modern science studies the real by way of two distinct paradigms of inquiry: the experimental and the clinical. These paradigms differ in many respects, but from both perspectives, the real appears as that which *recurs*. For experimental research, something—typically, a natural process—is considered real if it recurs under certain circumstances that can be replicated *ad libitum* through appropriate technical procedures. A scientific experiment demonstrates that a natural process is real by showing that it regularly results from the same operations. In this manner, scientists study *how the real works*. We should not conclude from this that by ascertaining what is real, we know what is true. For modern science, the truth and the real are not the same thing. After realizing that something is real by means of suitable experiments, we cannot automatically determine what is the ultimate truth disclosed by those experiments or by a certain type of *iterability*.

When scientists conduct experiments, they associate data with a truth-value and a plausible meaning provided by previous conjectures. But this is the contribution of scientific theories, not of experimental research. Although they fuel one another, these two branches of science fulfill different needs and respond to different questions. The former answers the question about the truth of the real, whereas the latter answers the question of what really recurs. Since the questions are of a different nature, the answers, too, are of a different nature, even though they appear to converge from time to time. In short, modern science is cross-eyed. One eye looks at the truth, the other at the real. Conjectures made by theoretical physicists inspire the work done by experimental physicists, who otherwise would be groping in the dark. But physics experiments never prove once and for all that a certain theory is true. As a matter of fact, scientific theories and experimental research aim at different targets: experimental research aims at describing the real in terms of *operational* results, of data characterized by iterability; scientific theories seek to provide meaningful and putatively true readings of those data. Since no such readings are ever assumed to be the *truest* of all, we may say that the a priori axiom of modern science is precisely the division between the truth and the real, which keeps scientific inquiry alive.

Turning from experimental to clinical investigation, the axiom remains the same, but the research paradigm changes. Both experimental and clinical scientists study the real, or iterability as such. Within the framework of clinical research, however, they no longer study how the real works but rather *how the real does not work*. Indeed, if the real in general is that which recurs, it is possible to look at it from two opposite angles: the real as a regular functioning and the real as a regular dysfunctioning.

Experimental regularity (how the real works) and clinical regularity (how the real does not work) cannot be treated in the same way. Given that clinical scientists concentrate not on the successful operations of the real but on its failures, they do not approach the real by means of experimental manipulations that attempt to produce some recurring results. The clinical approach is *historical*, not operational. The reason for this is that clinical failures are nonfunctional lapses, nonoperational shortfalls. As such, they cannot be *put to work* through experimental procedures because the experiments in question should *not work* in order to reproduce real dysfunctionings. No experiment can make a dysfunctioning function or a nonworking process work. For this reason, clinical data and experimental data should not be conflated.

Experimental research and clinical research are not mutually exclusive. But even when they cooperate, they do not speak the same language, nor do they speak about the same thing. The former examines the functioning real, which regularly begets some results. The latter examines the dysfunctioning real, which fails to work and collapses. The regularities at stake in the two cases are different. Think about medicine that combines clinical and experimental researches. What is real in the living? Both illness and health are real, as both recur. But we cannot think of illness as the mere absence, or the negative, of health. Both illness and health are positive, albeit alternative, configurations of the real. Importantly, illness is *ambiguous*, and clinical data are equivocal, whereas experimental data are always unequivocal. They either confirm or refute a certain conjecture. Thus, experimental data represent *the real that is disambiguated by a (hypothetical) truth*. Clinical research, instead, does not require any previous theory about the true meaning of the real. When we adopt a clinical approach, we observe a particular configuration of the real—that is, a recurring dysfunctioning—and we take note of the fact. Then, we join a certain dysfunctioning with another. The complex or the aggregate of some concomitant dysfunctionings give form to a "clinical structure."

In light of the above, clinical data and structures may be defined as *the real in search of a meaningful truth*. To begin with, let us apply this definition to the field of medical science. Within the frame of medical research, both approaches to the real—the clinical and the experimental—are necessary. The clinical approach allows us to study the real of illness, gathering and organizing data about organic dysfunctionings. The experimental approach allows us to take things a step further and explore the real of health—namely, the operational functionality of organisms. Illness and clinical data are always ambiguous; they do not possess any clear meaning and are somewhat allergic to truth. By taking a drug, however, we can get rid of this allergy. If the drug works, we pass from the ambiguity of illness to the clarity of health. The true—better said, the putatively true—*meaning* of the clinical structure appears as soon as the *real* of the clinical structure disappears. Instead of a truthless real, another real shows up thanks to our technical manipulations and medical treatments. In other words, the true meaning of illness cannot be attained unless we cause the real of illness to disappear. To achieve this result, we move from clinical to operational patterns of research—for instance, medical treatments that aim at exploring and testing the real of health. As soon as we make this move and we obtain the desired evidence, the real of illness is no longer real because it stops recurring. As Georges Canguilhem put it, "Health is the truth of the body," whereas illness is the "untruth of the body."[1] More precisely, health is the operational real of the body, the real *disambiguated by a medical truth*. Illness is the real deprived of truth, the real of the body *in search of a medical truth*. Illness appears every time the body stops working, thereby losing its truth.

Let us now turn to psychoanalysis. The epistemological foundations of psychoanalysis are wholly clinical. Psychoanalysis cannot combine the clinical and the experimental approaches to the real. From a psychoanalytic point of view, it would be preposterous to say that "health is the truth of the psyche." No doubt human subjectivity, or psyche, is real. It is real because it consists of regular, recurring clinical structures. But the fact is that in this case, it is impossible to pass from *the real that is in search of a meaningful truth* to *the real that is disambiguated by a (hypothetical) truth*, because subjectivity itself is nothing but the search for a clear and unequivocal truth. Subjectivity is nothing but a clinical structure. When Sigmund Freud confessed that he could not trace any boundaries between normality and pathology, he was already emphasizing this point.[2] Our psyche is obscure by its own nature, and the unconscious knocks on our door every time we attempt to expunge all opacities.

What does it *mean* to be a "subject," to speak and act in the first person? Psychoanalysis not only confronts us with this problem; it also investigates the many ways in which each one of us *fails to solve* it, the many ways in which our subjectivity *does not work* and human ambiguities thus turn into clinical data to be organized into clinical structures.

A key notion of Lacanian psychoanalysis may be of some use at this point: fiction. There are many kinds of fiction. For example, it is not true that Captain Ahab was killed by the whale, nor is it true that Leopold Bloom went to Paddy Dignam's funeral on June 16, 1904. These are literary fictions that do not purport to be true accounts of actual facts. But the unconscious is filled with fictions of an altogether different nature—that is, *true fictions*. The subject of these fictions is the "subject" itself, or the first person. Some significant examples of true fictions come from the life and history of collectivities. Think of nationalism. In many respects, what we usually call a "nation" is nothing more than a fiction, a nationalist mythologem. But even though there are no such things as nations, or we do not buy into the objective existence of such entities, we cannot deny that the myth of the nation can produce real effects and alter the course of events provided that people *believe* they are ancestrally related or share the same destiny. When this happens, people speak and act chorally *as if* they were one nation, undisturbed by the fact that this ontological unity among them cannot be proved objectively. This is, very briefly, how a true fiction impacts our lives: it convinces the first person, whether singular or plural, that *I am* or *we are*. Here, as Lacan says, "truth shows itself in a fictional structure."[3] It is worth noting that, in saying this, Lacan did not mean for us to conclude that truth is always shaped into a true fiction. Every time he says, "truth here reveals its fictional ordering,"[4] he is talking about a particular truth, the truth that speaks *in the first person*. "I, truth, speak."[5] This is the illusionist's truth that inhabits our unconscious. "That would be the height of the illusionist's art: to have one of his fictional beings *truly fool us*."[6]

Every time the truth speaks in the first person, a true fiction comes to the fore. At that moment, a clinical structure appears, one in which the distance between the truth and the real becomes maximal. The "subject" is such a structure. Consider the statement *ego cogito, ergo sum*. This statement means nothing special for a spectator who hears it from the outside, but it nonetheless means everything for the "subject" who makes it. Since this statement means everything, however, it means too much and blurs every meaning. For this reason, according to Lacan, this statement is not true in any meaningful sense, nor is it even false. If anything, when we make it, we fall into the domain of the *Unsinn*.[7] Here, truth appears as a cause. It speaks (*ça parle*) but we cannot understand what it says. Thus, we fall prey to a true fiction that makes us *be* in some way, even though we do not understand who, or what, we are.

Again, the key to everything is repetition. When it comes to the *cogito*, the *res cogitans* cannot cease to repeat *ego cogito, ergo sum*, because as soon as she stops, she fades away together with her *cogitatio*. As Descartes emphasizes, the empty pretension to *truth* of the first person's fictional *being* necessarily results in the *real* effect of repetition.[8] Yet, it is the *effect* of repetition that enables the truth to act as a *cause*. The effect of repetition holds up the pretension to truth of the *cogito*, and it does so precisely by emptying it, by blurring its meaning. Nothing changes when we shift from the first-person singular to the first-person plural, from the *res cogitans* to the "nation." It is always the truth in the first person that speaks, releasing the same kind of effects that become increasingly real from a clinical point of view as they continue to empty the subject's statements of any understandable meaning.

In this manner, whether it is at the collective or individual level, something fictional—a "fictional being"—"truly fools us." It truly *fools* us because the true fictions we are, the *res cogitans* and the "nation," are nothing more than a myth that bluffs us into being. At the same time, it *truly* fools us because every time I claim to be a *res cogitans* or we claim to be one "nation," *I am* and *we are* in some sense. We cannot but trust the truth in the first person, despite the fact that we do not know what it says.

As I look into the subjective fabric of modern political history, I will not head toward any philosophy of history. In this, as in many other fields of research, philosophy should abandon, or at least downsize, its past ambitions. A more scientific approach to history is advisable today, and psychoanalysis is undoubtedly the most sophisticated science of subjectivity of our time. According to psychoanalysis, individual and collective subjectivities cannot attain any meaningful truth about themselves. The true fictions we are, the *ego* and the *nos*, fail to be true by their own nature. For this reason, psychoanalysis does not urge us to seek out the truth of our own being in the first person. Rather, it helps us to analyze how truth, being, and the real are knotted together. As modern science posits, the truth is not the same as the real. Psychoanalysis, Lacan in particular, does nothing but take this postulate to extremes. Being in the first person is that which emerges when the asymmetry between the truth and the real becomes maximal. At that point, being in the first person appears as that which fails to be true, without being false, but rather pulsating as it does in between the truth and the real. The truth is hollowed out and remains out of reach here, whereas the real starts going around in circles, circumscribing a hole: us. As we will see, what keeps the show going is phantasy, that is, the way in which the real—the clinical structure—stabilizes over time. As Lacan says, "the real is the structure itself,"[9] and the real as bare structure, while being devoid of any meaningful truth, is syntactically organized.

2

Emancipative Grammars

Laclau, Heller, and the People We Are

Over the last century, both social homogeneity and social heterogeneity have been referred to as necessary requirements of modern democracy. In the late 1920s, Hermann Heller argued that no democratic politics was possible without a certain amount of social homogeneity. More recently, Ernesto Laclau has claimed the opposite: a certain degree of social heterogeneity is the *sine qua non* of democratic, emancipatory politics.

LACLAU ON SOCIAL HETEROGENEITY

According to Laclau, society does not exist in and of itself. If anything, society is the product of ever-changing political representations, and what preexists the latter is just a collection of scattered elements, a shattered social field whose wholeness, coherence, and homogeneity must be reestablished at every political-historical turn. In this perspective, political activity consists in bringing together a number of heterogeneous social demands into a symbolic construct (the "equivalential chain" of social signifiers) and joining them together by means of a hegemonic or master signifier (the "empty signifier") that will ensure the wholeness, coherence, and homogeneity of a certain political representation of the social field (the "political discourse"). In short, this means that political activity is conjunctural and artificial. Nobody can predict our political future because politics amounts to the conjunctural and artificial synthesis of heterogeneous elements that are first combined into a whole, into *one* unified society, and then recombined to form a different whole, *another* society. In this sense, Laclau contends, politics always aims at the very "institution of the social" or the endless "reinvention" of society: "The political is, in some sense, the anatomy of the social world, because it is the moment of the institution of the social. Not everything in society is political, because we have many sedimented social forms which have blurred the traces of their original political institution; but if heterogeneity is constitutive of the social bond, we are always going to have a political dimension by which society—and the 'people'—are constantly reinvented."[1]

Without going into Laclau's theory in too much detail, let us focus on three of its aspects that Laclau himself regarded as essential. First, even though the social world is molded by political representations, something ends up eluding representation. This leftover, often likened to the Lacanian "real," is that which prevents the ontological totalization of society and attests to the underlying heterogeneity of the social field in relation to its various political representations. Second, when a certain political representation of social demands is brought into question, the hegemonic equivalential chain, which is to say the political discourse currently in force, can be shaken to its foundations. At that moment, new political discourses are more likely to emerge from the newly disconnected, or less cohesive, elements of the social field. New equivalential chains can be constructed, and new social demands can be integrated into them. Third, every political discourse is not only the *expression* of a variety of social demands but also the discursive *ground* for their very manifestation. Every new political discourse gives birth to a new "people"—namely, to a new type of society: "When these demands become more heterogeneous in the living experience of people, it is their unity around a 'taken-for-granted' group that is questioned. At this point the logics constructing the 'people' as a contingent entity become more autonomous from social immanence but, for that very reason, more constitutive in their effects. This is the point where the *name* ... does not express the unity of the group, but becomes its *ground*."[2]

The concept of political name constitutes the key to Laclau's argument, but before I turn to this notion, it is worth noting that his entire theory is based on the assumption that one can make a clear-cut distinction between nature and artifice, between the social field and the political discourse. On the one hand, the intrinsic heterogeneity of the social field always lurks behind the scenes of political history. For Laclau, social heterogeneity is the real, yet ungraspable, substance of society. It is real because it is always there, like a natural given. It is ungraspable because no political discourse can erase it once and for all. On the other hand, since social demands are *naturally* heterogeneous, they can be *artificially* united by political discourses that produce ever new equivalential connections between them. Thus, the gap between social heterogeneity and political representation, nature and artifice, can be bridged. But this is where the problems start. If social demands are intrinsically—ontologically—heterogeneous, how can they huddle together? What force is powerful enough to keep them together as parts of the same equivalential chain? In Laclau's view, this force emanates from the magic of politics.

At this point, political names come into play. These unique signifiers are indeed able to create "the society," "the people," "the unity of the group," out of heterogeneous elements. Therefore, it is as though political names were endowed with a special force or energy. It is this force that forges a society, turning the Many into One. The element that takes on the role of the master signifier that towers over the entire political discourse is precisely the political name that imposes order on the many signifiers of popular demands, inaugurates a new form of political hegemony, and starts presiding over *one* people— think about Perón or Atatürk, who are among Laclau's favorite examples. Only a political name of this sort can become the "nodal point," as Laclau calls it, of the equivalential chain. It is a political name that in each case stands out from the rest of the signifiers. But why do the others accept its hegemony? *E pluribus unum*: how is that possible?

To solve the riddle, Laclau complicates the picture and introduces the idea of an affective, "cathectic" investment that is necessarily mobilized through the political discourse. The object of such a passionate investment is nothing but the object to which the political name refers. Adopting a Lacanian terminology, Laclau describes it in terms of the *objet petit a.* To cut a long story short, we may conceive of it as the leader's voice or gaze (given that voice and gaze typify Lacan's *objet petit a*). Unfortunately, Laclau does not explain why or how certain objects—whether voices or gazes—succeed in eliciting the cathectic investment. Instead, he confines himself to saying that from time to time, certain signifiers gain the status of political names and certain objects gain the status of cathectic objects. But why and how are *these* names and objects selected from among all of the possible things that might play these roles? No answer can be found in Laclau's works.

Perhaps he did not consider this a genuine problem and thought that what seems to be a vice in his theory should be understood as a virtue, for it confirms that politics is artificial, conjunctural, and basically unpredictable. When it comes to human affairs, contingency has the last word. Nevertheless, we may wonder whether Laclau can thus avoid reducing political discourses to *hypnotic* constructs. In other words, following his line of reasoning, can we avoid kneeling before the mysterious, mesmeric power of political leaders? As Freud notes in his essay on group psychology, "hypnosis is not a good object for comparison with a group formation, because it is truer to say that it is identical with it."[3] For Freud, however, this remark was not the end but the beginning of an inquiry into the mechanism of "group formation" (*Massenbildung*). What is the secret of collective hypnosis? Why do we fall under the spell of a particular political discourse or leader? According to Freud, those questions had been left unanswered by Gustave Le Bon, who thought the phenomenon could be explained exclusively by the will and charisma of political leaders. A century later, it might be argued that Laclau has made the same mistake.

HELLER ON SOCIAL HOMOGENEITY

Heller's essay "Political Democracy and Social Homogeneity" deals with "the dynamic process whereby the state becomes and maintains itself as the unity in the plurality of its limbs."[4] At first glance, this contribution is just one more chapter in the heated altercation between Heller and Carl Schmitt, who famously claimed that "the specific political distinction is the distinction between friend and enemy."[5] Heller's point is that such a distinction is not sufficient to explain the internal unity of the state. The myth of force and confrontation with foreign countries that lies at the heart of Schmitt's theory cannot account for domestic political unity. For this unity to be possible, a common "ethical purpose" must be shared by citizens. But the idea of a common ethical purpose clearly contravenes Schmitt's definition of "the political" owing to its ethical and not purely political connotation. "Schmitt's friend-enemy antithesis is unsuitable for giving the state an ethical purpose just because, according to him, it must be understood as alien to ethical purpose, as a purely vital entity in antithesis to another strange, vital entity."[6] In Heller's view, by contrast, the assumption of an ethical purpose appears to be crucial, particularly when we consider modern democracies:

> For the formation of political unity to be possible at all, there must exist a certain degree of social homogeneity. . . . Carl Schmitt is therefore very wide of the mark when he thinks he has hit the "spiritual center" of parliamentarism. For he, taken as he is by the irrational allure of the myth of force, defines the *ratio* of parliament as the belief in the public nature of discussion. . . . In fact, intellectual history shows as the basis of parliamentarism the belief, not in public discussion as such, but in the existence of a common foundation for discussion. . . .
>
> . . . There is a certain degree of social homogeneity without which the democratic formation of unity is impossible. The democratic formation of unity ceases to exist when all politically relevant sections of the people no longer recognize themselves in any way with the symbols and representatives of state.[7]

To summarize: Heller thought that democratic institutions function correctly when people hold certain beliefs and "symbols" in common, from which a relative homogeneity of the social field can be inferred. Thus, democracy is not just a synonym of democratic institutions such as parliaments and electoral procedures. For Heller, democratic institutions do not exhaust the meaning of modern democracy. In point of fact, democracy requires a common ethical purpose, which neither Schmitt nor Hans Kelsen considered essential for democracy.

Indeed, Kelsen maintained that certain legal-political institutions—elections, parliamentarism, and the party state—are the sole conditions of democracy. For him, there is no need to conjecture that a sovereign "people" stands at the origin of modern democracy, as Schmitt believed, nor that a democratic "people" is suffused with a certain degree of social homogeneity, as Heller believed. In the end, the "people" in the first-person plural (*nos*) is not a real entity according to Kelsen. In a democracy, there are only single individuals (*egos*), who are entitled to vote and choose their representatives. Any further definition of the "people" is a mythologem to be done away with.

Heller disagreed with Kelsen's drastic conclusion. Although he did not embrace Schmitt's polemological nationalism, he was firmly convinced that democratic institutions undergo an extreme crisis every time social homogeneity and the "unity" of the people start to wane. For him, therefore, modern democracy is contingent not only on parliamentarism but also on something that represents "*the basis* of parliamentarism"—namely, the shared ethical purpose that ensures "the existence of a common foundation for discussion." But what did Heller mean by ethical purpose? What is social homogeneity? First of all, he says, it is a kind of "social-psychological state":

> Social homogeneity is always a social-psychological state in which the inevitably present oppositions and conflicts of interest appear constrained by a consciousness and sense of the "we," by a community will that actualizes itself. This relative equalization of the social consciousness has the resources to work through huge antithetical tensions, and to digest huge religious, political, economic, and other antagonisms. One cannot say definitively how this "we-consciousness" is produced and destroyed. All attempts to find the impulse for this consciousness in a single sphere of life have failed and must fail. All that we can rightly know is that in each epoch a correspondence between social being and consciousness—in other words, a societal

form—emerges. It is always the sphere in which the consciousness of the epoch is most at home that is decisive for social homogeneity.[8]

Before exploring the mystery of what Heller calls the "we-consciousness"—or, a few lines later, "the social-psychological equalization of consciousness"—let us examine more carefully his disagreement with Schmitt, on the one hand, and with Kelsen, on the other.

In contrast to Schmitt, who placed a heavy emphasis on the *external antagonism* between the people's political unity and foreign enemies, Heller pays more attention to the *internal antagonism* between fellow citizens that characterizes the life of democratic societies. Such an internal division is due to a number of "oppositions and conflicts of interest" that undermine the people's unity but are nonetheless "constrained" and tempered by social homogeneity. "Social homogeneity can never mean the abolition of the necessarily antagonistic social structure."[9] Thus, curiously, Heller contends that social homogeneity is essential for democracy not because it is conducive to universal consensus and uniformity but because it makes room for division and social antagonism. In a democracy, a certain degree of social homogeneity is that which allows the whole of society to live through "oppositions and conflicts of interest." By the same token, those "constrained" conflicts propel the process of "social equalization," as they push people into forming coalitions and fighting for better conditions without breaking the social bond. "Democracy's existence is dependent to a much greater degree than any other political form on the success of social equalization."[10]

Given these premises, it is no surprise that Heller dislikes Kelsen's theory of democracy. For Heller, one cannot reduce democracy to the "equality of conventions"—namely, to those rights, laws, and formal procedures that Kelsen saw as foundational to modern democracies. The formal equalization of all citizens is not enough to keep democracy alive. Social equalization is needed as well. And social equalization implies, once again, a certain degree of social homogeneity. "Without social homogeneity, the most radical formal equality becomes the most radical inequality, and formal democracy becomes the dictatorship of the ruling class."[11] As Heller points out, formal democracy reigns supreme in the United States, a country where the "equality of conventions can somewhat reduce the awareness of economic inequalities." More generally, as he goes on to explain, formal democracy "turns political democracy into a fiction, preserving the form of the system of representation while falsifying its content."[12] Hence Heller's conclusion: formal democracy, such as Kelsen's parliamentarism, lays the groundwork for social disparity and "can make *summum jus* (supreme right) into *summa injuria* (supreme wrong)."[13] It goes without saying that this result is far from democratic.

But then, what is democracy? Given Heller's socialist credo, one might answer that, for him, democracy consists ultimately in transforming a formal *Rechtsstaat* (state of law) into a social *Rechtsstaat*, thereby opening a path that leads from formal-legal equalization to material-economic equalization. Yet Heller himself would not have subscribed to this answer without specifying that no economic equalization can be obtained in the absence of a preexisting social homogeneity. As a matter of fact, it is only against the background of a common symbolic framework and a shared sense of belonging that the way leading from formal to material equalization is indeed open. Only on the basis of a "psychological equalization of consciousness" can democratic antagonisms foster "social equalization." That said, what does he mean by psychological equalization, or "we-consciousness," or social homogeneity? Does Heller give any clear definition of these notions?

Unfortunately, he does not. On the one hand, he traces social homogeneity back to the language and political history of a given community. Thus, while keeping his distance from nationalism, which he sees as one among many forms of "we-consciousness," he ends up reviving an old leitmotif in German (nationalist) culture: *Sittlichkeit*. In Europe, he writes, "the most important factors of social psychological equalization have been common speech and a common culture and political history."[14] On the other hand, he realizes that we encounter a problem here. Even though the notions of social homogeneity and of "we-consciousness" are the keys to understanding modern democracy, he writes that "one cannot say definitively how this we-consciousness is produced and destroyed."[15] In other words, when we speak of social homogeneity, we do not know exactly what we are talking about. All we know is that various kinds of "we-consciousness" have appeared in the past.

POLITICAL GRAMMARS

The theories of democracy developed by Laclau and Heller, however defective they may be, help us to tackle the crucial issues of social heterogeneity and homogeneity, but before going over these notions, it is worth stressing a point made by both Laclau and Heller: modern democracy is a means to emancipation.

(A) Modern political history is indeed a long sequence of struggles for emancipation. Modern people became modern the day they began to break old political chains, thereby enfranchising themselves. People who were enslaved and subjugated by others began to free themselves and proclaim their private and public autonomy, yelling at the rest of the world that they were masters of their own destiny. Viewed in this light, modern history amounts to a process of reappropriation—of the people, by the people, for the people. And this process of reappropriation or emancipation reveals itself to be intertwined with a process of collective subjectification. To gain autonomy, people had to assume that they were a new political actor, a new collective subject (*nos*) taking its first steps on the stage of history. As Jacques Rancière explains:

> Politics is a matter of subjects or, rather, modes of subjectification. By *subjectification* I mean the production through a series of actions of a body and a capacity for enunciation not previously identifiable within a given field of experience, whose identification is thus part of the re-configuration of the field of experience. Descartes's *ego sum, ego existo* is the prototype of such indissoluble subjects of a series of operations implying the production of a new field of experience. Any political subjectification holds to this formula. It is a *nos sumus, nos existimus*.[16]

Perhaps the Cartesian formula for political subjectification is not as universal as Rancière believes, but the parallel between political subjects and the Cartesian subject surely sheds light on some significant aspects of modern political life.

The first thing to note is that modern subjects, whether individual or collective, arise from an immemorial past. The reason for this is that I cannot declare *ego sum, ego existo* without assuming that my own being is already there before I make this statement; likewise, we cannot say *nos sumus, nos existimus* unless we assume that our own being is already there before we make this statement. Here the subject's existence is entirely contingent on what Lacan calls "anticipated certainty," which is critical to the process of modern subjectification and which explains why the Cartesian universe, revolving around the formula *ego sum, ego existo*, and the Freudian universe, revolving around the formula *Wo Es war, soll Ich werden*, are the recto and verso of the same universe. The concept of anticipated certainty means that something is already there before I say in the first person (or doubt)[17] that I am, but as soon as I (the first person) try to grasp this something, I get lost. All I can do is to be on the way to becoming the subject that I *was*. My present and self-conscious *ego* is baffled by an *x—Es, id, ça,* "the core of our being"[18]—that precedes my own presence and self-consciousness. *Ego sum*, my ontological self-appropriation, takes root in *Es war*, a kind of self-disappropriation.

This ontological complication is of the greatest importance, not least because it shows that the subject's statements must be coupled with the subject's *listening* to those statements. As Lacan put it, *ça parle*, "it speaks." In the end, I am not truly myself when I speak, because something as yet undefined (*Es, id, ça*) takes the floor. I am, however, becoming myself when I listen to that something and endeavor to appropriate its statements. Put slightly differently, the subject is that which listens to itself speaking. It follows that the subject is never stabilized, since it cannot catch up with its own statements. Listening, which should drive the subject back to its being, comes too late. There is always a minimal yet abysmal interval between listening and speaking, and this interval pushes the subject's being into a past that cannot be put into words. Whenever the claim is made, *ego sum*, the subject slips away. The *ego* is not here and now, as it arises from the place where it was, *Es war*. Thus, even though *ego (sum)* is disturbed by *Es (war)*, the latter is nonetheless integral to the former. The subject is split. And nothing changes when we pass from the first-person singular, *ego*, to the first-person plural, *nos*. The same gap between speaking and listening baffles the subject.

In view of the above, the notion of a *political unconscious* imposes itself, for the unconscious originates precisely in the subject's division, in the interval between speaking and listening. Because of that division, not everything is possible. I am not free to do or say whatever I please. Indeed, when I listen to myself speaking, I listen not only to one single utterance at a time but also to iterations, repetitions, and through repetition a grammar, as distinct from discourse, gradually crystallizes. Repetitions close off some paths and open others. Step by step, they restrict the space of representation, the range of discursive possibilities and symbolic capabilities. In this way, the subject's listening—through which repetitions are solidified and grammars develop—starts to function retroactively and to condition the subject's speaking.

When it comes to political subjects, this process must be clearly highlighted; otherwise, theory will be tarnished with unclarities.[19] Take, for example, Laclau's notion of political discourse: for him, a political discourse is the "articulation" of a number of social signifiers, and articulations obey two logics, the differential and the equivalential. But the problem is that everything is possible within the space delineated by those logics. In theory, any kind of discursive articulation can be produced, and the question arises as to why a certain articulation prevails and becomes hegemonic. To solve this riddle, Laclau resorts to the magical power of political names. In my view, things are more complicated; in particular, attention should be paid to political grammars. When we listen to a statement, it often happens that we do not consider it part of our political discourse. Hence, in agreement with Laclau, we may say that a political discourse consists of a restricted range of discursive possibilities. But for this restriction to be possible, a political grammar must be in force, irrespective of whether a charismatic leader stands before us. Grammars ensure that the boundaries of discourses are fixed. Grammars legitimize some statements and delegitimize others. And we absolutely need to conjecture that such grammars are in place, or else we could not tell the difference between one political discourse and another, nor could we tell which statements are part of our political discourse and which are not.

(B) Grammars shape our listening, but they do not disclose the secret of our *identity*. A grammar does nothing but situate a certain *subjectivity*. In a first approximation, identity may be defined as the goal of every process of subjectification: *ego sum* . . . this or that person with these particular features; *nos sumus* . . . this or that people with these particular features. Subjectivity is, instead, that which appears as soon as an *ego sum* or a *nos sumus* is uttered, thus giving rise to the questions Who am I? Who are we? Subjectivity is the question, identity the answer. And political grammars are simply the way in which our political subjectivity emerges together with the question of our identity. In short, a *nos sumus, nos existimus* appears well before any identity can be thought of. But how can people become a political subject in the absence of any identity? First of all, it should be noted that this is what usually happens.

Think about nations: nowadays, most scholars would deny that nations amount to real entities with a clear—historical or natural— identity. Nevertheless, there are people who believe that they are one nation, and this belief is more than enough to transform them into a political subject. Despite the fact that their national identity remains veiled, these people are able to merge into a political *nos*. Again, how is this possible? Heller's notions of "common speech and a common culture and political history" do not clarify the matter because they imply that the *nos sumus, nos existimus* reflects a positive entity, identified by objective features that substantiate the people's claim. By contrast, the notion of antagonism is more helpful. In fact, it is always by *opposing* something or someone that many scattered individuals manage to become one people. In other words, the process of political subjectification and the process of political emancipation are exactly coextensive. To oppose someone else, one need not present one's credentials. No identity has to prove true. Every time the gauntlet is thrown down, the question arises: Who are we? At that point, the quest for identity can begin. But the fact remains that a political subjectivity is already in place at that moment.

It follows that the boundaries traced by political grammars are conflictual in origin. A process of political subjectification opposes us to someone else without requiring us to have any identity. We do nothing but mobilize against a common antagonist, thereby establishing ourselves as a self-emancipating subject. As we will see later on, such mobilizations can be fueled by internal or external antagonisms—antagonisms in Heller's sense or in Schmitt's. But whatever the case, antagonism turns out to be a distinctive trait of modern political subjectivity and of modern emancipatory democracy. As Charles Tilly rightly emphasizes, "the histories of France, Britain, and other European countries negate any conception of open struggle as irrelevant, antithetical, or fatal to democratization. On the contrary, those histories show that all of Europe's historical paths to democracy passed through vigorous political contention."[20]

(C) Given that grammars do not disclose our identity, they cannot become the object of any self-consciousness or "we-consciousness." Rather, they shape the *we-unconscious* of modern people. Indeed, political grammars give form to the unspeakable lack (*manque à être* in Lacan's jargon) of political subjects, the lack that prompts their endless subjectification, while obstructing their identification. The structure of this lack is that of a collective delay. *Wo Es war, sollen Wir werden.* Where *id* was, there we shall be. Owing to the gap between speaking and listening that is constitutive of their ungraspable *being*, modern political subjects are always late, as it were, and strive to recover themselves from this delay that makes them *be* while pushing their own *being* into an immemorial past. Modern political subjects, like all modern subjects, suffer from a serious ontological disease.

(D) This same ontological disease affects democracy. If, taking our cue from Heller and Laclau, we agree that modern democracies attempt to homogenize, or equalize, the people in spite of all "conflicts of interest" (Heller) and "social demands" (Laclau) that attest to the people's persistent heterogeneity, then we are forced to concede that modern democracies never achieve their ultimate goal. Rather, they represent durable yet congenitally unstable compromises between homogeneity and heterogeneity. That said, we do not need to *naturalize* the people's heterogeneity to account for the unsteadiness of our democracies, as Laclau does, nor is it necessary to *naturalize* the people's homogeneity to explain the relative stability of our democracies, in the way Heller does. Instead, we can posit that homogeneity and heterogeneity are two sides of a Janus-faced process of subjectification that lies behind any process of democratization. When people initiate this process, they always follow two different—almost divergent—paths. On the one hand, they claim that they are one people, speaking and acting in the first-person plural (*nos*). On the other hand, they claim that they have some basic rights that belong to each and every individual (*ego*). Thus, on the one hand, they stress collective autonomy and the people's homogeneity; on the other hand, they insist on individual autonomy, which is the source of the people's heterogeneity. As we will see, popular sovereignty, or public autonomy, and subjective rights, or private autonomy, are both at stake in emancipatory struggles. Collective self-affirmation and individual self-affirmation are the two omnipresent leitmotifs in modern mobilizations. But the point is that these leitmotifs are never independent of one another, because they constitute the two themes of a single sonata, the two sides of a process whereby the *ego* and the *nos* emerge as two opposite faces of the same first-person society. Modern democracy is the name for such a process, through which we come to share one collective subjectivity while remaining riveted to our individual subjectivity. For this reason, modern democracy should not be merely understood as a set of institutional rules and arrangements, as Kelsen and others believed. Democracy is also, and above all, a "social-psychological state," as Heller put it.

(E) We are now in a position to give a more accurate definition of political discourse. As Laclau himself makes plain, a political discourse does not consist solely of speech acts but also involves other kinds of symbolic activities.[21] For example, concerts, festivals, sports, and recreation, all of which contributed to the "nationalization of the masses" in nineteenth-century Germany, should be numbered among the manifold elements of a political discourse.[22] Importantly, however, what held these elements together was not a political name or an empty signifier, as Laclau would have it; the reason they merged into a single political discourse is that a single political subject, the newborn German "nation," presented itself as lying behind them. And the rise of this particular political subject coincided with the activation of a particular political grammar: German nationalism.

3

Human Properties

Villey, Macpherson, and Our Right to Be

Lacan contends that the subject of psychoanalysis and the subject of modern science are one and the same: "The subject upon which we operate in psychoanalysis can only be the subject of science."[1] This connection between psychoanalysis and modern science, both of which rely on the Cartesian ("conjectural") *ego*, is one of the tenets of Lacan's theory.[2] In the modern age, however, not only did a new science emerge; a new type of law was developed. We may wonder, then, whether there is any relation between the subject of the unconscious and the subject of modern law.

VILLEY ON SUBJECTIVE RIGHTS

Michel Villey has insisted on the break between modern law and Roman law. For Romans, the word *ius* did not mean rights in the modern sense of the word but rather *suum cuique tribuendum*, what is due to a person: the judge was asked to decide what is mine and what is yours. *Ius* was something—a *res*—that had to be assigned to someone.

> From the perspective of ancient Romans, rights were things. . . .
>   . . . Those who quarreled over the possession of things asked the

judge to evaluate what was due to everyone, how things were to be
allocated to people. . . .

. . . According to the *Institutiones*, *ius* is not a feature of the subject, nor does it signify freedom of action (because freedom cannot be
divided into many portions). *Ius* is that portion of things which must
be assigned to one person.[3]

In Roman civilization, as Villey goes on to explain, the notions of *ius*
and of *ars iuris* were coupled with a concept of law different from ours.
Iura were things; law was basically moral law. It was the unwritten law
of *mores*, customs, and time-honored traditions: "What is law? Ultimately, it is the unwritten law (*agraphos nomos*). In the classical age, it
made no sense to speak of law in terms of written rules. At the time,
law was the order of nature, the *structure* of social groups."[4] Within
this context, it was therefore possible to specify the *iura*, the rights
that belonged to a particular individual; yet the whole of society, re-
flecting the whole of nature, had primacy over all individuals. In a
certain sense, individuals had no existence outside of their placement
within society and the cosmos. In other words, no "subject of rights"
existed in those days. The idea that free individuals are endowed with
(natural or moral) rights was totally unknown.

With the advent of Christianity, the ancient structure of the universe
was turned upside down by the birth of a God who had the power to
impose whatever He pleased and to alter the course of events—*Potentia
Dei absoluta*, as Duns Scotus calls it. Following the irruption of the
Christian God, another concept of law emerged. Law was no longer seen
as an expression of unwritten *mores* but rather as a command given by
an omnipotent God—*Potentia Dei ordinata*, as Duns Scotus calls it. As
Villey emphasizes, this was a turning point in history. It was then that
all human beings facing God's absolute power became free individuals
who could accept or refuse God's *potestas* and commandments, thereby
accepting or refusing the *potestas* of God's representatives on Earth.
Under these assumptions, people changed their approach to law: for
them, law no longer reflected "the *structure* of social groups." Rather,
law began to mean *lex*, an order given by God or by His representatives on Earth: "William of Ockham agrees with Duns Scotus. The *Ten
Commandments* are not natural law. . . . They have been *given, posited*

by God. But Ockham goes even further. While Scotus understands the commandments of the first tablet as being rational and necessary, Ockham's skepticism calls the entire Decalogue into question. God could change hatred into virtue; God could oblige us to worship false divinities. No 'reason' can restrict God's 'absolute power.'"[5]

This new theological creed, marked by Franciscan voluntarism, paved the way for a new understanding of law based on the concept of "subjective rights." In this perspective, the first individual to have rights was God, who has the supreme right to do whatever He pleases, *potestas absoluta*. As Ockham writes, "the origins of legal order cannot but be the will and power of one individual being, and this is the individual being who rules over human creatures, namely God."[6] Having said this, God was not the only one who had the right to act and not act according to His will. Human individuals, too, had their rights, their powers, their liberties. And they could decide whether or not to use them. For instance, they could choose to renounce their property rights, *potestas appropriandi*, following the example of Saint Francis. Or they could assert their rights and liberties. Whatever the case, by making use of their rights in one way or the other, human beings were now faced with a decision on two fronts. First, they had to decide whether or not to obey God's commandments; second, they had to decide whether or not to follow the orders given by God's representatives on Earth. In short, going down this road, people were pushed into a brand-new world in which the legal-political order of human communities was no longer embedded in the unwritten moral order of the ancient cosmos. At that point, the legal-political order of human communities appeared to be guaranteed "by a system of *powers* (one subordinate to the other) and positive *laws* (decreed by powers)."[7]

From Franciscan theology to Thomas Hobbes is but a step: all we need to do is abandon the belief that God is the source of law (*lex*). But this entails a theoretical revolution. If all individuals are endowed with the *potestas*, power or freedom, to obey or not to obey the positive laws issued by a secular *summa potestas*, or sovereign power, then individual freedom becomes that which renders sovereignty effective in the absence of any supranatural justification. After God has been deposed, sovereignty remains possible because people bow to the sovereign, not because they all believe in God's authority. Thus, confession gives way to pure obligation. Within secular societies, a sovereign power is in force only as a result of its being obeyed, and human liberty, that is the power to obey or not to obey, becomes the natural ground for the artifact of sovereignty. As Hobbes says, "lex enim vinculum, ius libertas est, differuntque ut contraria."[8] Law is obligation; right is freedom. Positive law issued by the sovereign (*lex*) and the natural liberty of individuals (*ius*) are placed at opposite ends of the political spectrum. But *ius* comes first and lays the foundations for *lex*. For it is our free choice not to be free that puts the obligation into effect. This is where the social contract enters the frame, as Hobbes famously argues. Before this contract ratifies our obedience, no positive *lex* can be put into force and the only thing that matters is the natural, boundless *libertas* or *ius* of every individual. *Ius in omnia*: "Subjective liberty is boundless. Where prohibition and obligation (not to speak of common law) are missing, everything is *permitted*. Liberty can be restricted only by the innate Reason of individuals. But liberty is indeterminate, *limitless*, in and of itself. This liberty is the right that Hobbes bestows on every human being ('what each man hath'). This liberty is the right of man."[9]

Three conclusions can be drawn from the above: (1) *Ius* is not a thing (*res*) but a feature or a quality belonging to every individual, *libertas*. "For Hobbes, a right is not something that must be given to someone, but rather an essential *feature*, a *quality* of the subject."[10] This means that *ius* is to be seen as a natural property of all human beings, not as a property to be allocated to someone. This natural property now appears to be essential to the definition of man. (2) By transforming *ius* (right) into a natural property of individuals, *libertas*, Hobbes makes two different languages overlap: the language of rights and the language of property. *Ius* is that which "each man hath." Thus, rights and properties begin to look like two sides of the same coin: human properties. If rights are properties, then the right underpinning all other rights is the right to property. Owing to this strong correlation between rights and properties, a natural ownership of rights, *libertas*, is thought to be coextensive with a natural right to ownership, *ius in omnia*. As Villey says, "Hobbes' language synthesizes (in the domain of politics) two terms, *ius* and *proprietas*, that remained disjoined in ancient Rome."[11] (3) But what do we possess when we possess our natural right, *libertas* and *ius in omnia*? In the end, for Hobbes, we possess nothing other than our right to possess everything we need for self-preservation; that is, we do not possess anything apart from our right to preserve ourselves and to possess ourselves. As Villey observes, Hobbes's "right of nature" is an unqualified right to self-propriety and self-appropriation: "Does the right of nature have any *object*? Does it refer to anything out there that might specify its meaning? . . . This seems not to be the case. The right of nature . . . relates to the subject, and not to external objects, as it emanates from the subject."[12] This conception of the right of nature, as Villey shows, underlies and at the same time undermines Hobbes's theory of the social contract. By means of a contract, Hobbes says, people "convey" (*transferre*) their natural right to the sovereign power; they transfer their *ius* to the *summa potestas*. But how is that possible? If *ius* is no longer a thing (*res*), how can people pass it on to someone else?

MACPHERSON ON POSSESSIVE INDIVIDUALISM

Villey's analyses of Western legal thought have been sharply criticized.[13] Yet his argument about the proprietary characterization of modern rights can hardly be disputed. Subjective rights are the great innovation of modern law and are to be seen as *human properties*.[14] Rights are among the people's properties. Property is among the people's rights. As Emmanuel-Joseph Sieyès points out, the notion of "real property" (*propriété réelle*) and that of "legal property" (*propriété légale*) mirror one another.[15] In the modern era, it is impossible to possess an object without having the right to possess it, but it is also true that having a right amounts to possessing something. Furthermore, given that *ius* does not name any external object but rather refers to an intrinsic feature of the individual, to have a right ultimately means to possess oneself rather than to own an external object, or to possess oneself *in the form of an internal object*.

Crawford B. Macpherson's investigation of "possessive individualism" sheds further light on the matter. In his essay on the fathers of modern political theory, he emphasizes the "social assumptions" that were taken for granted by those thinkers. In seventeenth-century

England, people were beginning to unshackle themselves from the constraints of old feudal societies. Most individuals were now becoming market competitors, buyers and sellers of commodities of all sorts. Importantly, among the latter were not only land, money, and goods but also life, liberty, and labor, which were not objects, properly speaking, but rather features of all human beings, or human properties. In fact, the beginning of the modern era marks the birth of wage labor. People were learning to regard their own labor as a new kind of possession.

The result was a change in legal practice. New arrangements were required to regulate all economic activities taking place in a possessive market society. Old legal devices could not cope with present necessities, nor could any inherited political order contain the social storm produced by the rapid development of capitalism. The solution for this unprecedented situation could not be the law in any of its customary connotations. The solution, the good one, was contracts:

> In a market society, where property becomes an unconditional right to use, to exclude others from the use of, and to transfer or alienate, land and other goods, a sovereign is necessary to establish and maintain individual property rights. Without a sovereign power, Hobbes said, there can be no property, and he was right about the kind of property characteristic of a possessive market society. . . .
>
> . . . Hobbes presented this as a need in any society. It is not so in every society, but it is so in a market society. And it is an especially pressing need, requiring a strong sovereign power, when a possessive market society is replacing a customary society, for then customary rights have to be extinguished in favour of contractual rights.[16]

Thus, at the dawn of the modern age, the idea of a social contract establishing the "contractual order" of "contractual societies"[17] based on "contractual rights" gradually became the cornerstone of a new legal-political order. The development of market societies and the development of legal-political language went hand in hand. People now owned both external and internal properties. External properties were money, land, and goods. Internal properties were human qualities and capacities such as life, labor, and rights. Given these conditions, people learned to relate to themselves and to others differently. Their relations and dealings were now inspired by the idea that all individuals are the proprietors of themselves and can do whatever they please with their own properties, whether external or internal. This sort of *usus sui* (my definition) lent impetus to capitalist societies. The logic of the contract, which until then had been confined to material transactions, started to regulate human transactions as well. First, it seemed possible to transfer the property of one's labor by means of contract. Then, it seemed possible to transfer the property of one's rights by means of contract. The former type of contract established sound legal foundations for new labor markets; the latter established sound legal foundations for a political system apt to ensure the smooth functioning of possessive market societies.

Needless to say, such a deep transformation of human life affected the way in which human beings saw themselves. And it is scarcely surprising that a new understanding of human beings found its first representatives among the revolutionaries of seventeenth-century England who were among the most radical ("puritan") heirs of Christian theology: the Levellers. These people, who were then witnessing the turmoil aroused in their country by the bewildering growth of a possessive market society, were well aware of the fact that Christian freedom was to be thought of as a human *potentia*, as a power to do or not to do that individualizes each one of us and belongs to all human beings. Yet, unlike Franciscan theologians, they believed that the emphasis was to be placed not so much on the individualistic as on the proprietary characterization of freedom. Human beings were the natural proprietors of their own freedom, and *for this reason* they were free individuals. As Macpherson explains, the Levellers were thus among the first to state clearly the passage from a Christian to a capitalist view of human freedom. For them, freedom was equal to self-propriety, to the use and enjoyment of oneself: *usus sui.*

Unfortunately, this notion of freedom made room for different degrees of freedom and serious disparities between human beings. In the era of wage labor, not everybody was given the freedom to enjoy his or her own person and capacities. If necessary, people could sell and transfer their human properties, for instance property in one's labor, to others. By no means were they obliged to do so. They were free to accept or refuse wage labor. Nevertheless, if they accepted it, they could not avoid losing their freedom, at least partially. They were less free than they were before. Moreover, it was through a contract and a transfer of the same type that man could pass his natural *ius* or *potentia* on to the sovereign power—and with the same result: a loss of *usus sui*:

> The fundamental quality of the Levellers' individualism is found in their concept of human freedom as a function of proprietorship. The essential humanity of the individual consisted in his freedom from the will of other persons, freedom to enjoy his own person and to develop his own capacities. One's person was property not meta-phorically but essentially: the property one had in it was the right to exclude others from its use and enjoyment. Property in one's labor, even more precisely than the broader property in one's person, was property in the material sense, for it was an alienable commodity. The criterion for full freedom was the retention of the property in one's labor, and the condition for its retention was the possession of material property as well.[18]

For the Levellers, therefore, "full freedom" was not at everybody's disposal. And at stake was not only man's freedom but also his very *being*. In one of the most impressive passages ever written in modern political theory, the opening of *An Arrow against All Tyrants* (1646), Richard Overton made the point very clear: "every one, as he is himselfe, so he hath a self propriety, else could he not be himselfe." This passage is quoted several times by Macpherson and not without reason.[19] One is struck by the disarming limpidity of Overton's words. If human freedom is the natural endowment of all human beings, then by transferring their freedom to others, people lose their own *being*, at least partially. On the contrary, when people hold on to their freedom and self-propriety, they remain in full possession of their own *being*:

> Not only has the individual a property in his own person and capacities, a property in the sense of a right to enjoy and use them and to exclude others from them; what is more, it is this property, this exclusion of others, that makes a man human: "every one as he is himselfe, so he hath a self propriety, else he could not be himselfe."

> What makes a man human is his freedom from other men. Man's
> essence is freedom. Freedom is proprietorship of one's own person
> and capacities.
>
> This proprietorship, it should be noticed, was not thought of as
> passive enjoyment. . . . Men were created to improve, and enjoy by
> improving, their capacities. Their property in themselves excluded all
> others, but did not exclude their duty to their creator and to them-
> selves.[20]

Three conclusions can be drawn from the above. First, *to be* human, *to be* oneself, now means to possess human properties. To be them-selves, people must actively affirm, or reaffirm, their own *esse* in terms of *usus sui*, as Overton argues. Second, even if individuals renounce *usus sui* by transferring their human properties to others, they do not cease to be. In that case, they are less human than they were before, but they continue to relate to their human properties—wage labor being the epitome of this alienated relation to oneself. Indeed, people can regain full possession of their human properties at any time, and to some extent it is tacitly assumed that they will do this sooner or later, for this possibility proves that they still *are*. Third, in the capitalist age, an entirely new man comes to light, a man who is in a position to own himself and to regard himself as an object of self-propriety (women were not counted among the proprietors, with the result that they were not considered to be human in the full sense of the word). But more precisely, what kind of object has man become? It is hard to tell. Whatever the answer, the mobilization of man's being is extremely important from a political point of view, because this coming-and-going of being entails that struggles of those in the modern age who feel they have lost their freedom will regularly be perceived as battles for the recovery of their own being. Such battles will erupt in the midst of ontological wars.

WE, THE SUBJECTS OF RIGHTS

Macpherson's essay has sparked a fierce debate among scholars and lends itself to criticism.[21] Nevertheless, some of his reflections on pos-sessive individualism together with certain of Villey's reflections on the origins of modern law help to highlight two crucial aspects of modern history, which I will call the juridical demarcation and the ontological inflection of politics.

(A) The juridical demarcation of politics is one of the major characteristics of the modern era. When modern people ask for more bread or protest against the tax burden imposed by public authorities, they do not do so just because they are starving, but because they believe that something is owed them. They claim a right—for instance, the right to enjoy better conditions or the right to property. And they claim the right to have those rights. Importantly, at stake can be either a right that has already been ratified in a certain country but has not been accorded to everybody or a right that is not yet recognized as a right of the citizen but is nonetheless purported to be a "right of man." Hence the key role that the notion of "man" plays in any process of modern political mobilization. It is man as such that is deemed to be endowed with a natural *ius*. Consequently, it is man as such that becomes involved in the process of modern political emancipation. For this to be possible, however, an entirely new man had to enter the frame. People had to undergo a huge transformation in their mode of life so as to learn to see themselves as proprietors of their own being and the owners of some human properties that could be reclaimed.

To further clarify this point, let me briefly recall the reasons for Karl Marx's contempt for subjective rights. As is well known, Marx maintained that rights are the symptom of a bourgeois, proprietary view of politics. For him, if modern history ultimately comes down to a matter of rights, then this is because we live in a capitalist society; but when we move beyond this historical stage, we will overcome such an ideological distortion. In saying this, Marx was confirming that as long as we live in the age of capitalism, all political mobilizations must be justified in terms of subjective rights, or human properties. According to him, only after the end of capitalism—that is, the end of modernity—will we be able to change our political theories and praxes. Until that moment, all political transitions must be juridically legitimized. Interestingly, this holds for the Bolshevik Revolution, too; even in that case, a Declaration of Rights of the Working and Exploited People (written by Vladimir Lenin) was issued.

Thus, the juridical demarcation of politics turns out to be a principal feature of modern history. Furthermore, the same feature allows us to understand how the individual and the collective layers of subjectivity are interwoven in modern politics. When I assert my rights, I am in fact always asserting something more than my rights. Individual rights would make no sense if they were seen as my personal, private, and exclusive rights. Rights become meaningful in a public space in which they can be acknowledged by, and shared with, others. Rights belong to the people, not to a single person.

(B) As regards the ontological inflection of modern politics, it follows from the previous remarks. In the modern age, it is man as such that is endowed with a natural *ius*; therefore, it is man's *being* that is at stake in the process of political emancipation. On these bases, politics becomes the domain of ontological struggles. People cross the threshold of politics every time they assume that their own being can be attained by recovering some human properties and natural rights that have been lost or gone unnoticed so far.

It is not clear, however, whether these human properties and natural rights really exist, and this is not a minor problem. Imagine, for example, that I am married and that I nonetheless claim my right to marriage. In that case, the right I claim does not refer to my current marriage. If anything, it refers to what I wish I could do in the future, and in a country where divorce is not permitted, I could not claim that right once I get married. Yet even in that case, I could insist that the right to marry more than once (or more than one person) is a natural "right of man," irrespective of whether or not that right is protected in my country. In this way, I could restate that right, which refers to what *I wish I could be*, not to what *I am*.

In short, natural rights point to our *potential* being. In the modern era, we *are* because we hold a number of subjective rights, or human properties, but these rights never refer to what we actually are. Rather, our rights transform our own being into what we wish we could be. Thus, our rights deprive ourselves of our own being in some sense. Hence the well-known riddle: What are the "rights of man"? Are they natural properties of human beings? Do they belong in the realm of "nature," whatever our definition of *nature* may be? Or are they moral properties, which belong in the realm of "values," "imperatives," and "obligations"? Over the centuries, philosophers have sought to solve the riddle, but nobody is in a position to decide which of the two answers is correct because both are correct in the end. The "rights of man" are neither natural nor moral because, contrary to David Hume's thesis, they are natural and moral at the same time.

(C) Lacan's theory of unconscious phantasies can be of some use here, for it relies on a rather similar view of man's being and human properties. To explain this theory, Lacan resorts to the formula: $ <> a.[22] Here, $ is the subject, a is the lost object of drives, and <> is the phantasy by means of which the subject aims at recovering that lost and cherished object. As Lacan argues at length, the subject of the unconscious is always driven by some phantasy to assume that its own being lies in self-propriety. Indeed, the lost object of drives is counted among its properties. It is *my* object, *my* treasure, and not one among many: this object is that which makes me what I am, or so I suppose each time. This is the object of which I must take full possession to truly possess myself. Unfortunately, that object is missing. The subject of the unconscious is precisely the subject that desperately looks for it. As a result, Lacan avers, I feel deprived of my own being. Only by recovering that object would I be able to possess myself and enjoy my own being *qua* self-propriety.

As should be evident from this short résumé, Lacan's theory of phantasy accounts for the same equivalence between *esse* and *usus sui* that takes center stage in capitalist societies. Here, to be oneself and to possess oneself amount to the same thing. But phantasies, like modern rights, do not enable us to be and to possess ourselves in any satisfactory way. Phantasies do nothing but nourish our desire to be and to possess ourselves by recovering the lost object of drives. Yet that object is lost by definition. That object is what I *ought to be* rather than something that I actually am. That object is the sign of an ontological lack (*manque à être*). I am congenitally separated from my own being. And phantasy (*phantasme*) is simply the way in which such a structural splitting of the subject reveals itself.

The same logic applies to modern rights, with the same ontological outcome. When I assert my right to do or to have something, I claim my *right to be*—my right to be married, for instance, or to be a Catholic. Thus, the logic of modern rights does not imply that there is a real coincidence between myself and my genuine being, or my true identity. Quite the opposite. This logic entails that I am split from my genuine being, or my true identity. The result is that I relate to my own being while lacking it and striving to regain it. Viewed in this light, *modern rights are analogous to phantasies*. Both rights and phantasies tie the subject and being together by keeping them separate. Both delineate the place of modern subjectivity, that is, the place where I ought to be—*wo Es war, soll Ich werden.*

(D) At this point, we are in a position to better understand the nature of subjectification from a psychoanalytic point of view. First of all, subjectification and identification should not be conflated. In some respects, subjectification paves the way for identification. But it paves the way to a *failed* identification. This is what the formula of phantasy says: a phantasy (<>) arises in between the subject ($) and its own being (*a*), thereby preventing the subject from attaining its own being. Thus, not only does the subject materialize itself through the question of being (*Who am I? What am I?*), but it also manifests its own being by failing to answer that question. In this way, the subject keeps on *subjectifying*, while pushing its own being and true identity into the realm of the unavailable. A phantasy is that which allows this kind of ontological entertainment. To return to modern law, one may say that the same sort of entertainment is offered by rights. Indeed, rights make us be by dividing us from our own being. When I claim a right, I am striving *to be* different, *to be* truly myself. Rights are claimed as a means to identify oneself. Yet they *fail* at such an identification and are even, in some sense, designed to fail because they encourage us to take a further step toward our true identity, then another, then another, *ad infinitum*. As we will see, the whole process may be called *political subjectification*. Through that process, we come into existence not only as individual subjects but also as collective subjects, not only as solitary agents but also as joint actors in the arena of history. How does this happen concretely?

(E) The notion of political grammar serves to solve this mystery. A political grammar does not appear on the side of the *ego sum* or on the side of the *nos sumus*; rather, it appears somewhere in between. A political grammar is a grid, as it were, that underpins the process of modern subjectification, whereby the individual subject comes into being by failing to identify as a collective subject. It does not follow that there are two subjects, the individual and the collective, for there is only one subject. But the fact is that the process of modern subjectification results in a split subject, an individual-and-collective subject. The modern subject as such is, to some extent, a political subject. As Lacan noted, "the unconscious is politics."[23] Put slightly differently, our private ontologies need to be integrated into a broader scheme. Whenever I claim that I am, I have to make this claim in front of someone other than me—for Descartes, this Other was God—who is asked to recognize that I am. Otherwise, I cannot make this sort of claim. When Descartes dreams of being perfectly alone, his ontological certainty fades away, since nobody is there to confirm his claim *ego sum*. But this means that as soon as I make this claim, I assume that the Other is, as well. At that point, we are two. Whatever my intentions, I shift from the *ego sum* to the *nos sumus*. I am (*ego sum*) if and only if someone is next to me, if and only if we are (*nos sumus*). Political grammars are nothing but the way in which a connection is made between me and the Other. A political grammar provides a way out of private ontology. It is not the philosopher's way out but the people's.

(F) To conclude: there is a patent analogy between the modern subject of the unconscious and the modern subject of rights. Both phantasies and rights hinge on the equivalence between *esse* and *usus sui*; both require the mobilization of being, which is a distinctive trait of capitalist societies. But this only proves that they are analogous to each other, for there also seems to be a difference between them. Modern rights, Villey avers, do not have, or do not point to, any object. Phantasies, Lacan replies, point to an object—that is, *objet petit a*. If modern rights *are* phantasies, it remains to be seen toward what object they push us.

4

Political Subjects

Lacan and
Ordinary Ontologies

From a psychoanalytic point of view, subjects have no true identity. In other words, subjectivity and identity are not the same thing. The subject is split. I am, *ego sum*, as Descartes argues; yet I cannot tell who, or what, I am. Long before the birth of psychoanalysis, modern philosophers had already meditated on this gap between subjectivity and identity. Kant gave it the name *praktische Vernunft*, Hegel the name *Geist*, which is how he defined the disparity between "subject" and "substance." In more recent years, the same problem has been discussed by theorists who are familiar not only with Kant and Hegel but also with Lacan and psychoanalysis (from Jacques Derrida to Slavoj Žižek, from Gilles Deleuze to Judith Butler). But what about ordinary people? Do they encounter the same problem? How do they work out the distance between subjectivity and identity in their everyday lives? To tackle these issues, we must leave the field of philosophical ontologies and head toward the domain of ordinary ontologies. First, however, it is necessary to explain in further detail why Lacan describes unconscious phantasies in terms of grammars and why the latter notion is crucial to understanding how the *ego* is fooled into believing *ego sum*:

If we can use a discourse that is free of logic, it is certainly not unat-
tached to grammar. The fact is that in grammar there must remain
something very rich in properties and consequences. A phantasy is
expressed in nothing better than a sentence which has no sense other
than grammatical, or which, as regards the formation and the play
of phantasy, is only debated grammatically—namely *A child is being
beaten*, for example.[1]

THE SUBJECT OF THE UNCONSCIOUS

According to Lacan, the subject is a *suppositum* (*sujet supposé*). Therefore, it has nothing to do with the "mind" in the conventional sense of
the word, because it does not amount to any subsisting *psyché*, *anima*,
or *res cogitans*. Rather, the subject appears as the alleged ground, or
foundation, of an act of enunciation: *ego sum*. The subject claims to be
there. For Lacan, the key point is that this *suppositio* about a subject
lying behind what is being said in the first person is never made by
some neutral observer that looks at people from the outside and that
can ascertain the latter's existence. This *suppositio* is made by the subject itself. Or, more precisely, this *suppositio* makes the subject. Every
subject results from a *suppositio sui*. But how can we claim to be subjects if we are not really out there?

Lacan's concept of *manque à être* deals with this paradox. The idea
is that human beings, namely "speaking beings" (*parlêtre*), come into
being insofar as they fail to render their own being *true* in any meaningful sense of the word. The subject that speaks in the first person is
supposed to be, and yet fails to be, *manque à être*, because it remains
divided from its own being and deprived of any true identity.[2] In view of
this, Lacan cannot be blamed for promoting an old-fashioned dualism
that would restate the objective existence of "minds." For the subject-
supposition he talks about is a subjective supposition, or "subjective
position" (*position subjective*), not an objective or objectified position.
It is not to be credited to some external spectator. *Ego sum* holds true
only for the *ego* who makes this claim.

Interestingly, from a Lacanian viewpoint, the *nos* is to be understood as a *suppositum*, just like the *ego*. *Nos sumus* holds true only for

the *nos* who makes this claim. This means that, adopting a Lacanian perspective, it should be possible to study "collective subjectivities" without speculating about the objective existence of "group minds." From a Lacanian angle, it is possible to analyze the life and conduct of a collective subject, of a political *nos*, without resorting to the fallacious idea that this subject really exists out there, as if it were a natural or quasi-natural entity. Before exploring this possibility, however, a more general question needs to be posed: how does the subject-supposition persuade us that we are? The answer is *phantasy*—an imaginary scenario that stages one's unconscious desire and expresses it in "a sentence which has no sense other than grammatical," as Lacan says.

To begin with, consider the process of individual subjectification. For Lacan, phantasies allow the first-person singular to come into existence without enjoying any true existence. Lacan's formula for phantasy, again, is $ <> a. Here, *a* refers to the fact that the subject's own being is shaped into an object, *objet petit a*. $ refers to the fact that the subject is divided from its own being and therefore lacks *objet petit a*. The rhombus <> refers to the subject's phantasy that frames the latter's separation from, and longing for, its own being. The entire formula conveys the idea that the subject comes into contact with its own being only by failing to reach it and attain its true identity. In other words, the subject fails to be, yet this is how the subject comes into being: by dreaming and desiring to be. As a result, the larger the distance between the subject and being becomes, the closer they get. However irrational this postulate may seem, there is a logic in it. To clarify it, we need to explain why Lacan conceives of phantasies as grammars.

The main reason for this is that phantasies draw borders. Better said, phantasies impose grammatical limitations on the symbolic capacities of the subject. Phantasies, of course, are not equivalent to linguistic grammars. They express desires, not universal rules of language that determine the right and wrong articulations. Phantasies are not *objective* grammars. Rather, they may be defined as *subjective* grammars. Not only are these grammars immune from a more or less exact formalization, but they also elude the alternative right/wrong dichotomy. On the one hand, what they exclude from the range of our linguistic, symbolic, and discursive potentialities is not just wrong but unavailable to each one of us; on the other hand, what they include is not just right but mandatory for each one of us. That said, even though phantasies are not perfectly comparable to linguistic grammars, they resemble the latter in that they impose strict restrictions on the subject's wording and demarcate the space of representations, thus showing the "logical structure" of the subject's language:

> When I say "logical structure" you should understand it as *grammatical*. It is not for nothing that the very support of what is involved in the drive, namely phantasy, should be able to be expressed as follows: *Ein Kind wird geschlagen*. No commentary, no metalanguage will account for what is introduced into the world with such a formula. Nothing can either re-duplicate it or explain it. The structure of the sentence *a child is being beaten* is not there to be commented on: *it shows itself.*[3]

Phantasies, therefore, are (like) grammars in the sense that phantasies draw borders or symbolic frontiers. And phantasies achieve this result by expressing desires. Because phantasies do not dictate any objective rules of language, as English or French grammars do, phantasies can draw symbolic frontiers only by inducing each one of us to crave a particular and totally unfathomable object: *objet petit a*. Since this object cannot be put into words and shuns representation, it automatically narrows the range of the subject's symbolic capacities. *Objet petit a* is all around the subject's representations, as Lacan points out; it orbits the subject's words and enunciations. For this is not an object that the subject can grasp, control, and possess but rather an object that slips through the subject's fingers and falls outside the scope of representations, thereby pushing them all into a closed inside: the space of *my* (or *your*) representations:

> Phantasy is really the "stuff" of the *I* that is primally repressed, because it can be indicated only in the fading of enunciation. . . . A sufficiently sophisticated study, that can only be situated in the context of analytic experience, must enable us to complete the structure of phantasy by essentially linking here, regardless of its occasional elisions, the moment of a fading or eclipse of the subject to the condition

> of an object. . . . The subject is, as it were, internally excluded from its
> object.[4]

Thus, we are pushed toward *objet petit a* by unconscious phantasies, or grammars, and each of us always feels starved for this object that delimits and at the same time decompletes the space of representations. Therein lies the secret of the subject's existence. Again, existence does not mean objective existence but rather subjective existence. *Who am I?* In the final analysis, I am a speaking being who speaks in the first person and whose being cannot coincide with any object whereof I can speak in the first person. I am (*ego sum*) on the side of the enunciation, not on the side of the enunciated, as Lacan puts it. Therefore, when I speak in the first person, my own being, or *ego*, cannot be associated with anything I am able to talk about. The first person's being must lie beyond all that is enunciated, beyond all that the first person says, beyond all that makes sense and can be identified through *my* (or *your*) representations. This is where *objet petit a* emerges: beyond the law of identity and all representations that follow such law. In some sense, I am I only insofar as I keep on asking myself *Who am I?* without finding an answer that reveals my identity. My own being remains in question, and *objet petit a* embodies that question.

The concept of "drive" comes into play at this point, since *objet petit a* is nothing but the object of drives. In this regard, the first thing to note is that drives are not instincts or natural needs. Drives are a manifestation of language. In Lacan's view, I am pushed toward *objet petit a* by phantasies. But the problem is that a gap opens up between my words and *objet petit a*, which is beyond representation. That object is unspeakable, ungraspable. This is the reason Lacan contends that I relate to it not by way of speaking but by listening. Indeed, whenever I speak, I not only speak but also listen to myself speaking. Listening and speaking are two sides of a single coin, language. As soon as I open my mouth, I start listening to someone or something. Who or what is speaking? It is at the level of listening that this question comes up, and it is at that very level that my own being morphs into *objet petit a*, the unspeakable object that lies at the bottom of phantasy. *Ça parle*, "id" speaks. Who? What? The subject does not merely ask this question,

Lacan maintains; the subject *is* this question; and this question is fo-
mented by drives: *ego sum* because *ego audio*. Drives are a form of
listening that fastens me to my own being.

Having said this, it remains to be seen how I can acquire a sense of
selfhood despite the fact that I cannot seize my own being and truly
identify with myself. To clarify this point, we need to further expand
on the theory of phantasy *qua* grammar. Phantasies frame the subject's
representational space. As Freud had already realized, phantasies are
(like) grammatical structures.[5] Since phantasies vary from one subject
to another, we can distinguish between different structures and different
subjects. This distinction cannot be made by detailing the meaning or
the semantic content of phantasies. It can only be made by exploring the
gamut of grammatical possibilities that each phantasy affords. Actually,
a phantasy amounts to a set of grammatical options that, in their turn,
fashion the unspeakable object of drives that lies on the grammatical
border of that phantasy. It follows from this that each phantasy, owing to
its structure, relates to a particular *objet petit a*, whose shape is outlined
by that structure. And this relation (of "internal exclusion" between the
subject and the unspeakable, phantasy and *objet petit a*) gives a steady
grammatical form to the subject's being. This relation, and nothing else,
is what I listen to when I listen to myself speaking.

It is important to recognize that *objet petit a* is not an ordinary
object. The human voice (or gaze) can be such an object, for instance,
but not every voice turns into an object of listening. Furthermore, this
voice is not the same for everybody. In short, there is nothing objective
in *objet petit a*. At first, we happen to *hear* someone's voice. Then, if
three more conditions are met, we start *listening* to that voice. The first
condition is repetition. When I hear someone's voice only once, I am
not listening to it. If that voice resounds over and over again, I begin
to listen to it. The second condition is some sort of opacity. Most of
the time, when I hear a voice, I get the meaning of it right away. That
voice is telling me something, or it is simply the sign that someone is
at home. When I listen to someone or something, instead, I am on my
way to realizing the meaning of what I am hearing, and I need to hear
more to understand what is going on. At that moment, I come upon an
opacity which I find disturbing. The third condition is a grammatical

construction around that opacity. As a matter of fact, when this kind of opacity appears and bewilders my understanding, two alternatives offer themselves. Either I stand in front of what I listen to with no idea as to what is to be done, thus falling prey to an unbearable hopelessness (*Hilflosigkeit*, in Freud's terminology); or else I put that opacity in relation with something else, with things and words I am more familiar with, thus building a syntactic structure around that opacity, without filling it with any clean and clear meaning. In the first case, I end up being overwhelmed by something I cannot domesticate. In the second case, a phantasy—or grammar—comes into effect, framing my listening and keeping me at a distance from what would otherwise be intolerable.

To put it in a slightly different way: a phantasy is like a screen that functions as a barrier between me and something that makes me suffer too much. I never see the screen as such, but it is on that screen that I see everything around me, because that screen contains all of my representations and draws a border between myself and the intolerable. Importantly, it is from the invariance of such an invisible screen that I draw the unconscious conclusion that I keep on being the same as before, that I do not vanish with the passing of time, that I am not being overwhelmed by some external, traumatic event. For this to be possible, however, what lies beyond (or all around) the screen, what is shaped by its grammatical border, *objet petit a*, must hit the screen night and day. To be myself and keep on being the same, I must relate to the same *objet petit a*, against which the same screen (or phantasy/grammar) keeps on protecting me without interruption. My own sense of selfhood, according to Lacan, stems from this invariance of *objet petit a* and of the screen that keeps it at a distance from me. In the end, the first-person perspective is the perspective (the point of view) established and preserved by that object and that screen. But this means that a kind of private grammar (a delimited and private screen) makes me the one, the self, the *ego* that I am. And this private grammar, as Lacan points out, is characterized by a certain syntactics and a certain semantics, since all that I say is framed and marked by something that I cannot put into words and that tarnishes the space (the screen) of *my* representations. This leads to the question of semantic overdetermination and syntactic organization of phantasy/grammar.

Semantic overdetermination and syntactic organization find expression in what Lacan calls "writing" or "letter": "grammar is that aspect of language that is revealed only in writing."[6] Consider, for example, a lapsus. Semantically, this is a blind spot, because the subject cannot grasp its meaning. Syntactically, instead, the lapsus coheres with a set of grammatical possibilities—for instance, free associations—that make it significant. And when we examine a lapsus more closely, we notice that this "formation of the unconscious" is either a metaphor or a metonymy. Both figures of speech go beyond the literal meaning of words. For this reason, Lacan argues, both of them can hint at the unspeakable object that lies beyond the representational space of the subject, without meaning or representing it explicitly. They just make this object orbit around—or along the border of—phantasy/grammar. At the same time, both tropes lay the groundwork for a number of grammatical combinations and permutations between representations. This is why metaphors and metonymies reveal the gamut and texture of the subject's symbolic capacities. As Lacan often remarks, grammars are "revealed in writing" by means of tropes and figurative language.

Obviously, the idea that the subject's sense of selfhood hinges on the invariance of a private grammar implies that *one* phantasy/grammar tends to become predominant in one's life. And depending on the "fundamental phantasy" that presides over one's life—this is Lacan's technical definition of such predominant, primordial phantasies—grammatical combinations and permutations tend to stabilize either along the axes of metaphorical equivalences between representations or along the axes of metonymic equivalences.[7] Various types of subject-supposition stem from these fundamental phantasies, or grammars, whose choice is entirely contingent on the circumstances that surround the birth of a subject. In any event, it is the preponderance of either metaphors or metonymies that determines the path of the subject-supposition. When a choice is made, a clinical structure—a subjectivity—appears. Lacan distinguishes three types of clinical structure: neurotic, perverse, and psychotic. Contrary to customary practice, however, I will not speak of neurosis or perversion, not least because these concepts are often mistaken for moral evaluations. Instead, I will speak of *axiomatic* and *demonstrative* subjectivities (more on psychosis later).

For axiomatic subjectivities, metaphors become predominant: the grammatical combinations and permutations of the subject's representations abide by the principle of metaphorical equivalence, and the semantic blind spot that points to *objet petit a* is of a metaphorical nature. The grammar is axiomatic in the sense that the subject is supposed to be and such a supposition takes on the role of an axiom, even though the subject cannot grasp the exact signification of the metaphors that substantiate this axiom. Hence the symptomatic value that those metaphors acquire, as well as the subject's feeling of guilt for not being able to find out the truth about its own being and satisfy its own "desire," that remains repressed and buried under the literal meaning of its own words (*Verdrängung*). This version of phantasy is the most common: $ <> a$.[8]

For demonstrative subjectivities, metonymies become predominant: the grammatical combinations and permutations of the subject's representations abide by the principle of metonymic equivalence, and the semantic blind spot that points to *objet petit a* is of a metonymic nature. The grammar is demonstrative in the sense that the subject strives to give evidence of its own being by taking on the role not of a subject but rather of an object offered to the Other's enjoyment. Here, too, the signification of the metonymies that substantiate this morphing into an object remains impenetrable to the subject. Hence the performances through which the subject blindly reaffirms its denial of being a subject (*Verleugnung*), as well as the subject's feeling of shame for its own abjection. In this case, Lacan speaks of an "inversion" of phantasy: $a <> $.[9]

RETURN TO FREUD

In the following, I will further expand on axiomatic and demonstrative grammars, and I will use these notions to analyze modern political subjects—that is, collective subjectivities that are grounded in political phantasies or grammars. Before I get to the heart of the matter, it is worth noting that Lacan never spoke of political grammars but came close to this concept when he theorized that, first, "the unconscious is related to grammar,"[10] and second, "quite simply, the unconscious is politics."[11] In the field of political theory, however, not only the idea of unconscious grammars but also the basic tenets of

Lacanian psychoanalysis are often neglected, even by thinkers who declare themselves close to Lacan. I will give two examples of this negligence, and then—after making some comments on Freud's *Group Psychology*—I will turn to political subjects.

(A) The first example is Alain Badiou. Contrary to appearances, not even Badiou has ever come to grips with Lacanian psychoanalysis. In particular, he has always overlooked the ontological implications of Lacan's inquiry into the unconscious. As a result, he has never paid close attention to notions such as drive and phantasy, which Lacan saw as key to disclosing the secret of the subject's existence:

> When Freud wants to articulate the drive, he cannot do other than pass by way of grammatical structure. This alone gives its complete and ordered field to what, in fact, comes to dominate when Freud speaks about the drive. . . . It is only in the world of language that the *I want to see* can take on its dominant function, leaving it open to know from where and why I am looked at. It is only in a world of language that the subject of the action gives rise to the question of who supports it.[12]

The reason Badiou bids farewell to Lacan is easy to explain: he dissociates the notion of the subject from the notion of being. Badiou's thesis, which he first presented in his seminal *Theory of the Subject* and then developed in *Being and Event*,[13] is that the subject may be defined as a kind of fiction or supposition, but this fiction is nonetheless grounded in an underlying ontological structure that is prior to the subject and prior to language and can be cleansed of all subjective and linguistic impurities. Under this assumption, Lacan's thesis about being *qua* subject gives way to a different ontological view and a different theory of subjectivity. For Badiou, ontology has nothing to do with phantasies or subjective grammars. According to him, ontology studies the real, which is of a purely mathematical nature. Therefore, the subject's being cannot be traced back to the ungraspable object of drives. Being, which turns into a synonym of the real here, is placed outside the subject, totally outside, where it can enjoy anew its old metaphysical prestige. Hence Badiou's allergy to Lacan's antiphilosophical temperament and, more generally, to psychoanalysis. Leaving aside the confusion between being and the real, which is a quite common misunderstanding among Lacan's readers, what is most striking about Badiou's philosophy is his neglect of the unconscious dimension of our lives. From his point of view, there is no gap, no screen, no phantasy that can prevent us from being "faithful" to the truth (or the truth procedure) that shapes our being. From a psychoanalytic point of view, by contrast, we remain at a distance from truth, and for no other reason we *are*—subjects of the unconscious.

(B) The second example is Ernesto Laclau. In *On Populist Reason*, Laclau speaks about "cathectic investments" and *objet petit a*, but he does not say a word about phantasies or grammars. The result is that he misses the point: *objet petit a* is not an object among others. This object lacks any identity. It is only grammar, or phantasy, that makes it what it is. As Wittgenstein says, "grammar tells what kind of object anything is."[14] Lacan agrees on that: "I insist that if the *objet petit a* has the function that everyone knows about, it is clear that it does not impact on us *in the same way* with different patients. I mean that it is necessary in what is going to follow, that I should tell you what an *objet petit a* is in psychosis, in perversion, in neurosis, and there is *every chance* that it is not the same."[15]

Instead, for Laclau, *objet petit a* is always the same. It is the "primary ontological category."[16] As such, it is something that we can observe and study without minding the subjective grammar that surrounds its coming and going. Whatever the context, *objet petit a* takes on the same role—that is, the role of a *pars pro toto*—which allows us to work out our problems. Indeed, there are plenty of problems in our societies, and the main problem is that there is no such thing as society. Society has no existence in and of itself. Society is not a given fact; society needs to be produced, constructed at every historical turn, Laclau contends, because society as such is fragmented and heterogeneous. Politics, for its part, has the task of making society more solid and cohesive by mobilizing passionate investments in those partial objects, *objets petit a*, by means of which society can turn into a relatively harmonious and homogeneous totality. As I have already indicated, this line of reasoning pushes Laclau into overrating the role of political leaders, who ultimately incarnate *objet petit a*. There is no need to insist on that. Now it is more important to stress that, from a Lacanian viewpoint, grammar tells what kind of *objet petit a* anything is. In other words, even if Laclau were right in describing society as lack, mimicking Lacan's definition of "the subject as lack,"[17] we should not forget that, when it comes to lack and *objet petit a*, there exist "different sorts of lack, of loss, of void which are of absolutely different natures."[18] As Lacan points out, this distinction between different sorts of lack and different sorts of *objet petit a* is crucial to understanding the differences between subjects.[19]

(C) Drawing on Lacan's theory—a theory that brings the subject down to more-than-nothing and less-than-something—it is arguable that subjects do not exist, properly speaking; they are simply *believed* to be. Subjects result from the ontological supposition that "I" *am* or "we" *are*. As regards the first-person singular, this supposition is put into effect by means of phantasies and drives. According to Lacan, drives bring the *ego* into being by making it crave an object, *objet petit a*, in which its own being is allegedly buried, or lost. "Where is the subject? It is necessary to find the subject as a lost object."[20] But what about the *nos*? Can we think of collective, or political, drives?

To begin with, the collective subject-supposition and the individual subject-supposition are two faces of the same coin, of the same subject. Since the *nos* includes the *ego*, the supposition *nos sumus* involves the supposition *ego sum*. Hence, we should speak of a *multilayered subject-supposition*: each of us is capable of saying *ego sum* and *nos sumus*; each of us originates in a double ontological supposition. This is not to say that each of us is two subjects at the same time; rather, each one of us is a split subject. That is, a *collective ascendant* inheres in our subjectivity and has a bearing on the structural splitting of the subject. This idea is as old as psychoanalysis. In the opening lines of his *Group Psychology*, Freud states that "individual psychology" and "social psychology" are closely connected.[21] There are many reasons why Freud thinks this. First of all, the super-ego is socially inflected, for it is molded into our parents' image. Furthermore, the super-ego imposes a number of moral obligations that originate in the cultural and social milieu in which both the children and the parents find themselves living. As Freud goes on to explain, this entails that the super-ego (*Über-Ich*)—or ego-ideal (*Ich-Ideal*)—is always shaped into certain "models" of collective affiliation (*Vorbilder*).[22]

Unfortunately, Freud did not examine in detail these *Vorbilder*, among which we find "race," "class," "creed," and "nationality."[23] If we regard them as forms of the *nos*, several questions arise immediately: first, how do these forms stabilize? How is the invariance of the first-person plural ensured? Second, how do the *ego* and the *nos* interact within us? Freud and Lacan are of little help here. When Freud talks about "stable and lasting group formations," he does not ask himself what makes it possible for these *Massenseelen* (group minds) to stabilize over time. Nor does Lacan answer this question when he introduces the concept of "collective subjectivities."[24] Yet both of them stress the importance of what I am calling the collective ascendant of subjectivity, and both of them emphasize that the *ego* does not lose its own individuality when the *nos* stabilizes. On the contrary, it is at that moment, after the *nos* has attained a "stable and lasting" configuration, that the *ego* actually attains "a scrap of independence and originality." As Freud observes, when this condition is not met, that is, when we are in the presence of "ephemeral groups" that hinge on the purely hypnotic relationship between leader and followers, people lose their own individuality, and "what we have recognized as individual acquirements" vanishes all of a sudden:

> Each individual is a component part of numerous groups, he is bound by ties of identification in many directions, and he has built up his ego ideal upon the most various models [*Vorbildern*]. Each individual therefore has a share in numerous group minds [*Massenseelen*]—those of his race, of his class, of his creed, of his nationality [*Staatlichkeit*], etc.—and he can also raise himself above them to the extent of having a scrap of independence and originality. Such stable and lasting group formations, with their uniform and constant effects, are less striking to an observer than the rapidly formed and transient groups from which Le Bon has made his brilliant psychological character sketch of the group mind. And it is just in these noisy ephemeral groups, which are as it were superimposed upon the others, that we are met by the prodigy of the complete, even though only temporary,

disappearance of exactly what we have recognized as individual acquirements.[25]

In his *Group Psychology*, Freud pays special attention to "noisy
ephemeral groups"—namely, "primary groups." In this book, I concentrate on "highly organized" groups,[26] in particular those grounded
in "nationality" (*Staatlichkeit*). How do nationalities emerge? How do
they stabilize over time? And how do they affect the *ego*? Based on the
above considerations, it is possible to make some conjectures:

1. The political *nos* emerges and stabilizes through ontological failure. According to Lacan, subjects come into being
   by failing to reach their own being, and they crystallize by
   continuing to fail in the same way, or by following the same
   grammar, day after day. If Lacan's theory of subjectivity is
   correct, this principle should hold not only for the *ego* but
   also for the *nos*.

2. The political *nos* stabilizes by contributing to the *ego*'s collapse, and vice versa. Indeed, if the *ego* and the *nos* qualify
   as separate persons (the first-person singular and the first-
   person plural), this is because they do not identify with one
   another but rather put their ontological claims, *ego sum*
   and *nos sumus*, in competition with each other. By mutually frustrating their ambitions, the *ego* and the *nos* thus
   initiate a process of entangled subjectification.

3. The grammar of the political *nos* and the grammar of the
   ego do not enter into a mirror-like relationship. Each of us
   is capable of saying *ego sum* and *nos sumus*, but the grammatical conditions for the two acts of enunciation can differ. Within the same split subject, the *ego* and the *nos* appear as separate persons, and the grammars that underpin
   their existence do not necessarily coincide. This prevents
   us from believing that the type of subjective position (or
   subject-supposition) that is put into effect at the collective
   level is perforce the same type that is put into effect at the
   individual level. By way of analogy, we may say that each
   individual is a Cartesian star on its own, but one that is al-

ways part of a galaxy. The star's movements inside the galaxy are autonomous from the galaxy's movements across the universe. Nevertheless, the star follows the galaxy across the universe—across history.

A political drive is precisely this kind of movement. Actually, it seems difficult to deny that some sort of pressure is exerted on us by the collective ascendant of our subjectivity. In the modern era, the political *nos* proved capable of driving millions of people to die for the sake of their "nationality." This is an example of political drive. When people speak and act under pressure from political drives, they do not know exactly the reason why they are doing what they are doing. In the end, they behave in a certain way because of what they *are*—without knowing. And when people fall prey to a political drive, they always manifest a certain degree of homogeneity, or similarity. There appears to be a subjective affinity between them, an affinity that differentiates them from foreign people. Thus, they tend to form *one* people, even though they remain distinct from one another.

THE QUEST FOR HAPPINESS

Happiness is all we want, the dream that each of us cherishes night and day. No wonder, then, that happiness has become a determining factor in modern political life. But can we achieve happiness? And how? Questions like these found expression in two of the most significant political documents in modern history: the American Declaration of Independence of 1776 and the French Déclaration des droits de l'homme et du citoyen of 1789. I will now interpret these documents as two "writings" in which two types of political grammar are revealed. As Lacan remarks, "the irony of revolutions is that they engender a power that is all the more absolute in its exercise, not because it is more anonymous, as people say, but because it is reduced more completely to the words that signify it."[27] This is particularly true of the French and the American Revolutions, through which two different political grammars (or phantasies) were put into effect and two different political subjects came into existence: "The phantasy, the $ with respect to *a* [$ <> *a*], here takes on the signifying value of the entry of the subject into something which is going to lead him to this indefinite chain of signifiers which is called destiny. One can escape its ultimate impulse indefinitely, whereas what is to be rediscovered is precisely the start."[28]

The Axiomatic Grammar

According to Lacan, an axiomatic grammar is in place when "the statements of the unconscious discourse" follow from an axiomatic assumption, or supposition.[29] Interestingly, however, the statements of the *unconscious* discourse and the statements of the *conscious* discourse are exactly the same. They do not differ at all unless we pay attention to grammar. Indeed, the statements of the unconscious discourse encrypt phantasies, and a phantasy is nothing but "a sentence with a grammatical structure."[30] What is unconscious is just the grammatical structure of that sentence, not its semantic content. This means that when people make axiomatic claims, they do not realize they are making such claims, nor are they aware of the unconscious foundations of their axiomatic beliefs.

I have already examined the analogy between individual phantasies and sentences like subjective rights. Now it is time to focus not on one *sentence* at a time but on a document that joined several sentences together, thereby laying the groundwork for a collective political *discourse*: the French Declaration of the Rights of Man and of the Citizen. In this document, we find a list of rights preceded by a few words celebrating the birth of a political subject, the French "nation," who makes a solemn promise to put those rights into effect in view of "collective happiness" (*le bonheur de tous*). The way in which rights are characterized in the Declaration of 1789 is axiomatic. This document declares them to be "natural," "unalienable," and "sacred" truths. The belief that those rights were conducive to collective happiness was no less axiomatic. But such a dogmatic conviction was far from justified.

In reality, the rights enumerated in the French Declaration could not be taken for axiomatic and self-evident truths for at least two reasons: (1) those rights had become necessary and incontrovertible truths only by virtue of a perfectly contingent historical process; and (2) the Declaration of 1789 was shortly followed by two new versions that altered the original inventory of rights, thus eliciting doubt that the latter were really axiomatic and self-evident truths. In light of this, it comes as no surprise that the newborn political subject was immediately disturbed by a feeling of failure, if not of despair. Day after day, it proved ever more difficult to deduce the true essence and mission of the French "nation" from a number of "natural," "unalienable," and "sacred" rights. On account of these and other difficulties, the task of finishing "the romance of the Revolution," as Napoleon famously put it, turned out to be an impossible one.[31] Yet the French nation came into being. Despite the fact that nobody was able to disclose the truth about the genuine nature and destiny of the newborn political subject, the French nation was brought into existence through a sheer supposition, the reverse side of which was a *symptom*, an *ideology*: "The truth has no other form than the symptom. The *symptom*, namely, the significance of the discordances between the real and what it pretends to be. The ideology, if you wish. But on one condition, which is that for this term you should go as far as to include in it perception itself. Perception is the *model* of ideology. Because it is a sieve with respect to reality."[32]

Taking our cue from Lacan's remarks about the ideological value of symptoms, we may begin to explore the mystery of 1789 by saying that the French nation came into existence that year, but in a curious manner—that is, by experiencing "the discordances between the real and what it pretends to be." The French nation was born in 1789, to be sure, but the fact is that it was born with no discernible identity. For the nation was not merely the summation of all the people living in France. Ever since the Revolution, as Marcel Gauchet points out, the French nation has been considered to be something "more than the people," and "the existing nation" (*la nation actuelle*) has been neatly distinguished from "the true nation" (*la nation véritable, transcendante*).[33] The gap between the existing nation and the true nation helps us to understand why, for example, "the revolutionary power could not stop, fix up things, and find its identity."[34] From a Lacanian angle, the gap to which Gauchet draws our attention can be described as a gap between the nation's *being* and the *truth* of the nation, and this gap sheds light not only on the birth but also on the structure that underpins the existence of the French nation.[35] At the beginning, people were just yelling *nos sumus, nos existimus*. Thus, they were rebelling against the king, who until then had been entitled to repeat, "I am France." When the French Revolution broke out, people reacted and shouted all together "We are France." But what was the meaning of that cry? Beside the fact that people could not accept the status quo anymore, was there any meaning at all? People were mobilizing and protesting vehemently; they were speaking and acting in the first-person plural, *nos*. But *who* was speaking and acting? Therein lies the question that all revolutionary subjects encounter as soon as they open their mouth. The divide between the existing nation and the true nation gave shape to this question during and after the French Revolution. How can "we the people" claim that we are (*nos sumus*) if we cannot discover and declare our identity?

From a Lacanian standpoint, a possible solution to this problem is *perception*: the French nation came into being from the moment it perceived the gap between its self-affirmation and the truth of the nation. It came into being by suffering from being unable to identify itself and by perceiving this suffering as a *symptom* of its own being. Thanks to this kind of congenital defect, the French nation was instantly coupled to a political *ideology*, French nationalism, that kept the true fiction of the nation alive for centuries. The affinity between symptoms and ideologies explains this success. If the symptom marks "the discordances between the real and what it pretends to be," then it can be said that the French nation was the *subject* of such a symptom from the outset. Indeed, from 1789 onward, the people of France have been tormented by the discordances between the supposition that there was such a thing as a French nation and all of its failed definitions, interpretations, and identifications. Under such circumstances, however, these people have also found themselves in a position to wave the flag of the French nation, the subject of their ontological qualms, without interruption. As a result, the nation could survive and prosper, albeit burnt by the enigma of its own nature and destiny. The goal of collective happiness remained unattainable. The true identity of the nation remained veiled. Hence those hectic responses to the nation's decline that became quite common among French people and are a distinctive feature of modern nations in general: "The nation is not living up to its destiny," "The nation is not doing what ought to be done," "The nation is falling apart," and so forth. Whatever the historical contexts may be, these grievances always point to the inherent instability of the nation, and all of them attest to the secret inclination of modern nations, which are not going to find out their true identity one day but are doomed to fail and collapse.[36] *Who are we?* As Lacan notes, a feeling of guilt grows from the soil of this unsolvable mystery: "The symptom represents a structure. . . . Phantasy can be here what wanders around, with this privilege, this privilege of being more *inadmissible* than anything—I am reading Freud—I repeat it here for the moment: *inadmissible* involves many things. One could dwell on it. In any case . . . let us say that there is appended to it, like a cherry on a pedicle, the feeling of guilt."[37]

We may wonder, of course, what phantasy was hidden behind the French Revolution and what guilt was appended—like a cherry on a pedicle—to a political document such as the Declaration of the Rights of Man and of the Citizen. To tackle this issue, let us examine the situation that French people had to confront at the time. At the outbreak of the Revolution, the question that these people were asking each other was *What do we expect from each other?* We can venture that this question was on everyone's lips because this question expresses the problem temporarily solved by the Declaration of 1789 and its inventory of rights. By issuing the first Declaration, French people were reassuring each other that the Revolution was no civil war. If anything, this was the sign that a new community was being born and a novel system of political life was being established. Therefore, people could expect a lot from each other. Broadly speaking, they could expect happiness. More specifically, they could expect that their demands would be met. For people were now recognizing each other as equal and free "brothers" who were asking each other what they were ready to accord: rights, which ratified their mutual expectations. On these bases, the process of national subjectification could begin and develop, revolving around the two focuses of the same *ellipse*—a word that means "lack" in Greek.

On the one hand, by enumerating their rights in the Declaration of 1789, people were pledging allegiance to the French "nation," as they were recognizing themselves as French "citizens" who were granted those rights. In this way, a connection was established between the individual and the collective layers of political subjectification. Individual demands were authenticated by rights; the enactment of the latter was thought to be the task of the national community. As a result of this, each *ego* could find a place in a seemingly cohesive *nos*. Thanks to their rights, which embedded their individual being in a web of mutual expectations, and under the assumption that they were all included in and protected by the French nation, people could merge into a single political body. At the same time, the citizen's *ego* was being exalted by the logic of individual rights that the national *nos* was axiomatically imposing. Those rights certified the political soundness of mutual expectations and gave everyone a new political dignity, later described in terms of *equaliberty* by Étienne Balibar. This means that politics was now "founded on the recognition that neither freedom nor equality can exist without the other, that is, that the suppression or even the limitation of one necessarily leads to the suppression or limitation of the other."[38] Old privileges had been abolished. Citizens were deemed to be free and equal in front of the nation and in front of each other, for they had been subsumed into a *nos* that was there to watch over them and take care of their rights, without distinction.

This is where things get complicated, however. Balibar, for example, insists that *equaliberty* and the rights listed in the Declaration of the Rights of Man and of the Citizen were not contingent on national sub-jectification. As he puts it, "the statements of the *Declaration* are neither nationalist nor cosmopolitan, and, more profoundly, the concept of the citizen which they embody is not a concept of belonging. It is not the concept of a citizen of such and such a state, as cited, such and such a community, but, as it were, the concept of a citizen taken absolutely."[39] Although Balibar's thesis deserves close attention, I do not find it persuasive. In point of fact, when the Declaration of the Rights of Man and of the Citizen was issued, the French were undergoing a process of national subjectification without which no such document would have gained enough support. In the absence of the national *nos*, it would have been impossible for French people to expect anything from each other, to ask each other to recognize one's rights, or to believe that one's rights would be respected by others. For this to be possible, a shared sense of belonging to the same collective Other was needed. As Lacan would have it, the collective Other, the so-called big Other, had to be present, ruling over the small other. But this entails that this big Other, the French nation, had already come into being, that it was born, and the question then arises as to how all of this happened. What kind of *being* was at stake here? What did the French people mean by *nation*? What did they mean by *citizenship*? Surely, this word meant nationality, a shared sense of belonging.

On the other hand, it is true that the logic of nationality does not explain everything in this case, as in many others. Thus, Balibar is right in saying that something seems to elude the concept of belonging in the Declaration of 1789. Nevertheless, this something has nothing to do with the principle of human rights universalization that Balibar credits to this political document. In other words, Balibar reads too much into the Declaration, since he projects onto that document an idea that pertains to our times but not to the eighteenth century (I will return to this issue later). In reality, the problem with the Declaration of the Rights of Man and of the Citizen is not that it forces the concept of belonging. What seems to disrupt the logic of nationality ultimately confirms it. It is like the flip side of the coin. To clarify this, let us look more closely at the question that lies behind the rise of the French nation: *What do we expect from each other?* If one attends to these words closely, one notices that they can be easily misunderstood. These words can express a question, of course, but also a complaint,[40] tacitly meaning, *In truth, there is nothing or very little that we can expect from each other*. Such an expedient throws light on the dark side of the French nationalist grammar. What seems to violate the logic of nationality here is nothing but the *failure* of national subjectification, a failure that was inherent in national subjectification. Undeniably, something went wrong with the French Revolution. But what? And why did this wrong prove instrumental in giving birth to the French nation?

One of the reasons why things went wrong is because the rights of the citizens enumerated in the Declaration of 1789 specified *negative* expectations without saying a word about the *positive* expectations that French people were allowed to harbor. In the end, people were not told what they had the right to expect from others—say, better economic conditions or peace or whatever. People were told exclusively what they had the right *not to expect* from others. Hence, French people were given negative liberty—that is to say, freedom from interference by others. But nothing was said about the rest, about *le bonheur de tous*, about the way in which the nation was going to achieve collective happiness. The language of rights could not meet *such* expectations. As Karl Marx put it, "the right of man to freedom is not based on the association of man with man but rather on the separation of man from man. It is the *right* of this separation, the right of the *restricted* individual, restricted to himself."[41] It is no exaggeration to say that this limitation affects all types of modern political *nos*. As regards the French nation in particular, subsequent historical developments proved that an exacerbated and *restricted* individualism, as Marx calls it, was the inevitable outcome of the bourgeois Revolution. National subjectification based on individual rights was likely to cause an increasing social atomization, so much so that we may even ask ourselves, Why did the process of national subjectification *not* extinguish after a short while? How is it possible that the French nation did *not* explode?

Marx did not ask himself *this* question: How to explain that the French nation was somehow consolidated, instead of being wiped out, by the mechanism of negative expectations triggered by the bourgeois Revolution? Lacan's theory of subjectification enables us to look into this problem. According to Lacan, the subject—whether individual or collective—comes into being by failing to be. Failure, therefore, does not mark the end of subjectification; rather, it is the motor of the whole process. Failure fuels subjectification. Yet it needs to be organized in one way or another. That is, failure needs to be stabilized through the activation of a grammar. Indeed, a grammar is that which gives rise to a subject by letting it collapse *always in the same way*. For Lacan, such a regular, recurring collapse is constitutive of the subject of the unconscious, and it is often related to a symptom—namely, an ideology. The time has come to see how a symptom (in the Lacanian sense of the word) became constitutive of the French nation.

In this regard, the first thing we have to consider is the tension between the citizen and the nation that struck the young Marx. According to the latter, the French nation should have fallen to pieces under the burden of those subjective rights that had favored its rise. Rights joined people together while separating them from one another. Thus, national *collective* subjectification could progress only by intensifying civic *individual* subjectification, and an increasing individualism was destined to work against the project of collective *bonheur*. As a matter of fact, however, the French nation survived bourgeois egotism. So, how did the national *nos* come to terms with the citizen's *ego*? Ernest Renan was the first to provide a tentative answer: "a nation is a soul, a spiritual principle."[42] If we render this formula into Lacan's language, we have this: a nation is a symptom, an ideological principle. And whether we think of the nation as a soul or a symptom, the fact remains: the worse the failure, the stronger the principle.

But the question remains: how did failure stabilize? Or *why* did failure stabilize instead of destroying the national subject? Half of the answer lies in the way in which the nation and the citizen completed each other. Citizens had become citizens under the assumption that they all belonged to the same nation, which granted them a number of rights. The nation had become the nation under the assumption that those rights demarcated a political *nos*, which integrated every individual *ego* into a collective body. From this point of view, the citizen and the nation implied and supported each other. They were part of a single structure. Yet the citizen and the nation also rebutted each other for cogent reasons. On the one hand, citizens were given rights, which divided them from one another and from the national community at large. On the other hand, the nation urged citizens to overcome egotism in view of collective happiness. This clash had characterized the French nation, or French nationalism, from the very beginning. The individual and the collective layers of subjectification, the *ego* and the *nos*, hinged on each other, but they nonetheless refuted each other. The individual and the collective subject-suppositions were strictly intertwined, yet they remained mutually repellent. We may also describe this interplay between the individual and the collective layers of subjectification in terms of borders, or "interior frontiers."[43] The divergence between the nation and the citizen drew a line between them, and that line determined the critical frontier of the French nation, which was not a physical, exterior frontier but rather a subjective, interior frontier. Along this frontier, all citizens could claim that they belonged to the same nation, even though they were withdrawn into themselves; conversely, along the same frontier, the nation could prompt citizens to prove themselves loyal, even though the nation was doomed to be betrayed at all times.[44] Another definition of such an interior frontier is the nationalist ideology. Yet another is *fundamental antagonism*. But again, why did this permanent antagonism consolidate the French nation instead of condemning it to death?

Before giving a complete answer to this question, it is worth stressing the importance of the first half of the answer. In actual fact, the ontological clash between the citizen and the nation was not only disturbing but also beneficial to their ontological endurance. If the subject, whether individual or collective, comes into being by failing to be, as Lacan argues, then the fact that the *ego* and the *nos* hampered one another also served to reinforce both of them. For this reason, French nationalism proved tremendously effective in the course of history, not despite but because of the mutual ostracism between the citizen and the nation. All of this happened without awareness. Nobody understood that the citizen existed *at the expense* of the nation, that the individual divided the existing nation (*la nation actuelle*) from the true nation (*la nation véritable, transcendante*); likewise, nobody realized that the nation existed *at the expense* of the citizen, that it distanced individuals from their own individuality. All of this went unnoticed because the structure underlying the whole process of national subjectification— that is, the splitting of the subject at both the individual and the collective levels—remained veiled to those who were just the products of that process. In psychoanalysis, this effect goes under the name *repression* (*Verdrängung*), and what is interesting is that repression is not the opposite of perception. To the contrary, repression and perception are quasi synonyms in that repression amounts to the unconscious perception of a lack, of a flaw that lies at the core of the subject. Repression, therefore, is symptomatic by definition, given that it always coincides with an invariant perception that is ultimately the same as the symptom itself. From this angle, the question of how the French nation—or French nationalism—stabilized reads as follows: In the form of what invariant perception-repression did the French nation crystallize? What permanent symptom prevented the existing nation from falling apart in spite of all failures to achieve the true nation? The answer, the complete and definitive answer, is *homo nationalis*.

In the Declaration of 1789, no distinction was made between the "rights of the citizen" and the "rights of man," and this ambiguity was essential for the grammatical stabilization of the French nation. To clarify this point, we must resort to the notions of speaking and listening, discourse and grammar. As I have said, the statements of the *unconscious* discourse and those of the *conscious* discourse are exactly the same. The difference between *conscious* and *unconscious* does not lie in the statements themselves but elsewhere. Speaking is one thing; listening is another. When we make a statement, we find ourselves at the level of discourse. When we listen to our own statements, we are at the level of grammar. A symptom, for its part, appears every time we find ourselves listening to ourselves but we do not understand ourselves. *Ça parle.* At that point, Lacan avers, the question arises as to who is the subject (of the enunciation), and it is around this question that the subject crystallizes. Now think about the French Revolution. In the Declaration of the Rights of Man and of the Citizen, as Balibar points out, "there is no gap between the rights of man and the rights of the citizen, no difference in content: they are exactly the same."[45] But again, speaking is one thing, listening another. Even though the "rights of man" and the "rights of the citizen" cannot be differentiated with regard to their content, we can speak of our rights or else listen to them. The nation, of course, speaks about the "rights of the citizen," as it declares and grants those rights, civil rights. That said, how can the nation declare and grant the "rights of man," natural rights? If these rights are the people's natural endowment, then it is clear that the nation is not in a position to bestow them. Yet the nation does this whenever it conflates the "rights of man" and the "rights of the citizen," whenever it identifies one group of rights with the other, without grasping the meaning of such axiomatic identification, without understanding its own statements. At that point, the question arises as to who is the subject (of the enunciation), and it is around this question that the subject, the nation, crystallizes: in the form of a symptom, of a perception-repression, of a listening that conceals the subject, the nation, from itself.

This is how *humanity* came to the fore during the French Revolution.[46] Humanity gave form to the immaterial, unconscious frontier that divided each citizen from himself and the existing nation from the true nation. Nobody could actually speak on behalf of humanity, but humanity was nonetheless called to the bar. The Declaration of 1789 is all about man. Here the citizen is deemed to be a man in the first instance. But why, as someone objected at the Convention, all these "metaphysical" complications in the midst of the Revolution? Why all these speculations about man, happiness, and the sense of being human? From a Lacanian viewpoint, the answer is because there was no other way to establish the national subject. The rise and stabilization of this subject was entirely contingent on the unconscious perception-repression of an intrinsic, permanent lack of the subject, of a congenital flaw that could bring the nation into being only by making it fail and lose track of itself from the outset. Therein lies the nation's perennial appeal, as well as its damnation. If the French citizen and the French nation never met but kept on colliding with each other in the aftermath of the Revolution, this is because the citizen was a man before anything else, and the nation was burdened with the task of giving voice to humanity as such.[47] Indeed, the nation itself was born as a *metaphor*—and a symptom—of the people's humanity. The problem is that the meaning of this metaphor was impenetrable. As soon as the "rights of man" and the "rights of the citizen" were declared identical, with the first Declaration, things went awry. Hence, another Declaration was issued in 1793 and yet another in 1795. The rest, the historical drama of French nationalism, followed.

This means, among other things, that Balibar is mistaken when he credits the French Declaration with a political message about humanity that goes far beyond the horizon of nationalism.[48] For, in that document, humanity marks the unconscious borders, the inner frontiers of the French nation. No doubt the "rights of man" were the sign that French nationalism harbored universal ambitions. Yet this kind of universalism did not contravene the idea of belonging and the grammar of nationalism. In the final analysis, the drive to achieve the universal essence of humanity is a common feature of nationalism, as Balibar himself has often remarked.[49] In the past, nationalist subjects of all sorts have conflated the "rights of man" with the "rights of the citizen"; there is nothing special about the French Declaration of 1789 in that regard. What is peculiar to the French Revolution is only the transparency with which this operation was carried out. The nation and humanity were ostensibly juxtaposed. But the gap between them remained unbridgeable.

As a matter of fact, the nation cannot *mean* humanity. The disproportion between the two is too great. Nevertheless, a metaphorical connection between the nation and humanity is perfectly apt to keep the process of national subjectification going. This is why the discrepancy between man and the citizen is not the end of the story from a nationalist point of view but rather the principle—the ideological principle—that governs human history, or at least national history. The nation points the way to humanity. Such axiomatic pretension is the guiding star of nationalism, even though the promise of achieving humanity can only be broken over and over again. In any event, it was thanks to this promise that the French nation could rise like a phoenix from its own ashes at every historical turn. Promise and failure were the two sides of the same coin, of the same lack, of the same ellipse. The political refrain was mesmerizing: *France bears humanity.* The countermelody, *la comédie humaine,* was no less captivating.

The Demonstrative Grammar

According to Lacan, phantasies are not necessarily shaped into axioms. Sometimes, they take the form of demonstrations. Take, for example, the American Declaration of Independence of 1776, in which we find a list of charges against the king of Great Britain that describe his "repeated injuries and usurpations, all having in direct object the establishment of an absolute Tyranny." By enumerating the Crown's "abuses and usurpations" and denouncing the king's contempt for the common "opinions of mankind," the thirteen colonies were giving a *demonstration* of their need to gain independence from Great Britain. By the same token, they were presenting themselves as "one people" and declaring their "separation" from the "British brethren." As the opening lines of the Declaration of Independence solemnly proclaim, "When in the Course of human events, it becomes necessary for one people to dissolve the political bands which have connected them with another, and to assume among the powers of the earth, the separate and equal station to which the Laws of Nature and of Nature's God entitle them, a decent respect to the opinions of mankind requires that they should declare the causes which impel them to the separation."

The goal of the US Declaration is not perfectly clear, though. On the one hand, it announces the birth of a new political subject, the American people, and illustrates "the causes which impel them to the separation" from another political subject, the "British brethren." On the other hand, it overtly rejects any kind of national affiliation. In fact, the US Declaration pleads for the insurrection of American people but never explains why those people were to be seen as "one people." The only reason for this seems to be "separation" itself. What was bringing the "united Colonies" together was their insurrection, the war against Great Britain, the dissolution of national bonds. At first, therefore, it looks as though American people were undergoing a psychotic crisis at the time. They were rebuffing their previous political subjectivity and exposing themselves to the risk of a radical desubjectification.[50]

Curiously, the word *union* does not even appear in the US Declaration, nor does it become a key word in the Constitution of 1789, which does nothing but detail the juridical and institutional system of the "Union." By contrast, the very idea of union had enraged the public debate before the final, and troublesome, ratification of the Constitution in all the US states.[51] Furthermore, neither in the Declaration nor in the Constitution does the word *nation* contribute to a better understanding of how "the people" of the United States of America saw themselves. In both documents, *nation* never refers to the United States but only to "foreign nations." After a few decades, the Civil War revealed how complicated it was for America to regard itself as one "nation." As Stanley Cavell has keenly remarked, still today the American "union"—not to speak of the American "nation"—cannot be taken for granted:

> Of the great modern nations which have undergone tragedy, through
> inexplicable loss of past or loss of future or self-defeat of promise, in
> none is tragedy so intertwined with its history and its identity as in
> America. . . . Its Revolution, unlike the English and French and Rus-
> sian revolutions, was not a civil war; it was fought against outsiders;
> its point was not reform but independence. And its Civil War was
> not a revolution; the oppressed did not rise, and the point was not

the overthrow of a form of government but secession and union; the point was its identity. And neither of these points was settled. . . .

. . . Since it asserted its existence in a war of secession and asserted its identity in a war against secession it has never been able to bear its separateness. *Union* is what it wanted. And it has never felt that union has been achieved.[52]

The reason America has never achieved union, however, is not to be found in some unique *national* tragedy, as Cavell seems to believe. If anything, such an endless search for union is the sign that a particular political grammar gave birth to America, a grammar that is completely different from nationalism. We may call it a separatist grammar. No doubt, when the War of Independence began, the thirteen colonies were claiming their right to separate themselves from the British nation. But they were doing so without claiming to be a nation. Interestingly, they did not conflate the rights of man with the rights of the citizen. The American Declaration of 1776 was based on the assumption that people have three "unalienable Rights," the rights to "Life, Liberty and the Pursuit of Happiness," *regardless of national affiliation*. For the founding fathers, these were the rights of "mankind," of all human beings, and Americans had these rights *despite*—not because of—the fact that they were British citizens. But what about the rights of the citizen? Here, too, the American conception of rights diverged from the European conception. In America, the rights of the citizen were seen as *protecting* the rights of man. Thus, the "unalienable Rights" magnified in the Declaration of Independence somehow implied civil rights, but no identification between the former and the latter was possible. The two families of rights were placed on different levels.

A detailed list of civil and political rights came along with the Constitution in 1789 and the Bill of Rights in 1791. But again, all of these rights were ascribed directly to "the people," and it is no mere chance that the word *citizen* never occurs in the Bill of Rights. All civil and political rights of Americans were considered deducible from the precivil and prepolitical rights of man. They were not understood as being bestowed by a nation. They were deemed to an emanation, so to speak, of the "unalienable Rights" listed in the Declaration of Independence. This means, once more, that American revolutionaries conceived of civil and political rights as *derivative* rights. These rights served to reinforce the *primary* rights of "the people," the rights to "Life, Liberty and the Pursuit of Happiness," and to safeguard the latter against political adulteration.

In light of the above, it comes as no surprise that neither the Declaration of Independence nor the Constitution paved the way for national subjectification. Given that rights in America were not vouchsafed by gracious permission of the nation but had been the means by which "one people" had gained independence from a foreign "nation" and established new authorities, a process of national subjectification was not on the horizon. And indeed, neither the Declaration of Independence nor the Constitution said a word about collective happiness. In the end, American constitutional rights did nothing but amplify the preconstitutional right of all "the people" to pursue individual happiness. The idea that one's happiness depended on the other's happiness was at odds with the spirit of the revolution. In America, every man had—and still has—the right to pursue happiness on his own terms.[53]

Based on these premises, however, it was difficult to make sense of the fact that "the people" had become "one people"—*E pluribus unum*. How was that possible? Worse still, was that really possible? The question had many practical implications. As Edmund S. Morgan remarks, "although independence had determined that Americans were not part of the people of Great Britain, it had not determined whether they were one people or many, or whether the sovereignty of the people, say, of Virginia was exhausted in the creation of an independent government of Virginia."[54] By proclaiming their independence, the thirteen colonies were thus facing a problem of a particular nature. Americans had bid farewell to a community of "brethren" that was already a nation—Great Britain. Moreover, they were hostile to the idea of contrasting the British nation with a new nation, their own nation, for a number of reasons—above all, ethnic, religious, and cultural diversities among the people of the thirteen colonies.[55] So, how to become a political subject, a unified sovereign power? From a Lacanian standpoint, the answer is demonstration. War itself was a demonstration, and the same can be said of the Declaration of Independence. But a demonstration of what?

In a nutshell, it was a demonstration of the fact that Americans were separating themselves from another nation without being a new nation, a political *nos*, a collective subject. As strange as it may seem, this is how Americans started a process of political subjectification: by denying such a process. And this is how they solved the problem of their union from the very beginning, long before the ratification of the Constitution. Indeed, when Americans opted for "separation" and brought the whole intrigue to the attention of a "candid world," they chose to present themselves as an object, not as a subject. They rose up against the Other, Great Britain, not by claiming to be a different subject but by presenting themselves as victims of the Other's abuses. The thirteen colonies rebelled by yelling at the rest of world that they were not a nation but the demeaned target of the Other's *jouissance*. Drawing on Lacan's theory, we may describe this "subjective position" as "an inverted effect of the phantasy." Here, "it is the subject who determines himself as object."[56]

This amounts to saying that America was born through an inversion of political phantasy: the grammar of nationalism was turned inside out. On the one hand, so long as Americans were pursuing their separation from the "British brethren," they were actually performing as "one people" in the arena of history and giving evidence that they were a political *actor*. On the other hand, they were not taking themselves for a political *subject*. They were merely acting *as if* they were a political subject, but at the same time they were denying being such a subject, as they regarded themselves as nothing more than the object of the Other's offenses. Thus, they were taking on the role of a political actor deprived of political subjectivity. From the outset, by reducing themselves to a group of despised and mistreated martyrs, Americans were disguising themselves and their place in the world. For Lacan, this attitude is never the sign that subjectivity has been erased; rather, this is the sign that a grammar is being activated, one that gives birth to a particular type of subject: "This dimension is defined, specifically, by the fact that the subject assumes the position of an object, in the most accentuated sense that we give to the word *object*, in order to define it as this effect of falling and of waste. . . . This forms part of a production, of a scenario, which has its sense and its advantage and which, incontestably, is at the source of a gain of enjoyment."[57]

In the early stages of America's separation, such a "gain of enjoyment" resulted from the unmasking of the Other's enjoyment, from the
demonstration that Great Britain had treacherously taken advantage of
colonists. And the key element of such demonstration was the notion
of man's happiness. Every American had the right to pursue his own
happiness, for every American was a man in the first instance. Hence
the script that the American Revolution followed, according to which
man's will-to-happiness was to be contrasted with the nation's will-to-
happiness, Great Britain's happiness. Man's happiness: for this reason,
Americans had waged war on Great Britain; and for the same reason,
none of them cherished the dream of collective happiness. If Americans were "one people," this was not because they dreamed of being a
nation and wondered about the true identity of "the people" but rather
because they were the victims of the Other's dream and enjoyment. By
rebelling, they were denouncing and rebutting that dream. As a result,
by no means could Americans consider themselves a nation. America's
plea for independence was based on the categorical denial of being a
national *nos*. At the outbreak of the revolution, American colonists
regarded themselves not as a *nos* but as a disgraced object at the mercy
of another *nos*. That said, in spite of such a denial of being a *nos*, and
ultimately *through* that denial, American colonists became, for all intents and purposes, a collective subject, a political *nos*. At first glance,
this success may seem inexplicable, but when we look at it through
the lens of psychoanalytic theory, the mystery of America becomes
less impenetrable. There is, indeed, some similarity between America's
collective subjectification and the demonstrative subjectification that
sometimes takes place at the individual level, triggered by a *denial* (*Verleugnung*) of the same sort. This similarity helps us to understand the
origins and the nature of American "exceptionalism," as I will argue at
length from now on. The first thing to note is the emphasis on man's
individual happiness, which is not a detail but a permanent feature of
American history. Another thing to note is the restless *questioning* of
man's happiness. America praises the "Pursuit of Happiness," but what
is man's happiness? In America, there can be no axiomatic, collective
answer to this question, because every man has the right to answer and
pursue happiness on his own terms. Thus, the pursuit of man's happiness

fosters an ever-increasing divergence among "the people," who all go their separate ways. Yet such a growing divergence separates all of them, "the people" of America, from all other peoples, thereby turning them all into "one people." What is man's happiness? America originates in this question. "It is from this point, from the locus of *objet a*, that the pervert *questions*—by questioning what is involved in the function of *jouissance*. By never grasping himself except in a partial fashion, and, as I might say, in the perspective of *objet a*, the pervert remains subject throughout all the time of the exercise of what he poses as a question to *jouissance*."[58] In light of this, the main difference between European nationalism and American exceptionalism already stands out. In Europe, the "nation" came into being through the question *How can we achieve happiness?* In America, "one people" came into being through the question *What is man's happiness?* A new type of political affiliation was established this way. A disguised political subject arose out of the people's rebuttal of all forms of national affiliation and of all axiomatic assumptions about collective happiness. And this partly explains America's idiomatic approach to civil rights, interior frontiers, and the problem of nationality.

First, civil rights. Within the framework of a nationalist grammar, the rights of the citizen are identified with the rights of man, under the axiomatic assumption that rights will bring about *le bonheur de tous*. Since happiness is never achieved, however, the identity between the rights of the citizen and the rights of man must be retouched and redefined day after day. The history of the French nation and of all other nations can be summarized as follows: the closer civil rights to natural rights, the closer the existing nation to the true nation. Unfortunately, the deciphering of national identity never reaches an end, as the nation never identifies with humanity as such. Nevertheless, the more noisily the existing nation fails to be a true nation, the more loudly the nation's promise resounds. In this sense, the nation is a symptom, an ideological principle. Within the framework of a separatist grammar, instead, the rights of man, those stated in the Declaration of Independence, come first, whereas civil and political rights, such as those listed in the Bill of Rights, come after. In America, therefore, civil rights are not identified with natural rights. The idea is not that the nation bestows natural rights *qua* civil rights but rather that Americans are members of a separate society that enacts the natural and archiconstitutional rights of man, the primary rights of mankind, by means of civil and constitutional rights, the derivative rights of Americans. Since man's happiness remains open to interpretation, however, the enactment of man's right to happiness remains open to interpretation as well. This is why derivative rights can be defined as incomplete and infinitely amendable *paraphrases* of man's primary rights. As the Ninth Amendment says, "The enumeration in the Constitution, of certain rights, shall not be construed to deny or disparage others retained by the people."[59] Importantly, it is only through such amendable paraphrases that the original rights of man can be brought to the fore in America. It is only through derivative rights that primary rights come to life. Thus, the two families of rights, while not being conflated, are closely intertwined, and "one people" is the product of their correlation.

Second, interior frontiers. As seen above, a kind of psychopolitical border between the citizen and the nation was drawn during the French Revolution. Along that border, the citizen and the nation could turn into each other by virtue of *internal exclusion* from each other. In America, things are the other way around. "The people" were singled out as "one people" and became members of a separate "union" by virtue of *external inclusion*. America entered the arena of history not because people assumed that they belonged to the same nation but rather because they all managed, instead, to demonstrate that they did not belong to any identifiable nation. From the very beginning, the process of American subjectification hinged on a *denied* identification of the American "union" rather than a *failed* identification of the American "nation." But denial is not the opposite of failure. A denial (in the Lacanian sense) is just another way to show, or to stage, the failure of any possible identification. This kind of denial allowed America to be born. America came into existence by contrasting the promise of collective identification and happiness with the elusive, unidentifiable happiness of each and every man. Adopting the same stance, America has continued to find its way into the world ever since: to this day, whenever "the people" rise up against a national *nos* or a political power that is oppressing them, Americans are wont to confuse themselves

with these abused people for no other reason than the latter are dis-
avowing their previous political allegiances and identifications. Such
is the fundamental antagonism that characterizes the American *nos*,
whose interior frontiers constantly shift from one "separation" to the
other. And therein lies the unconscious political drive of a separatist
subject. Concretely, this means that America is never, or almost never,
at peace. Either the denial of collective identification occurs within the
boundaries of the American "union" seen as a duplicate of the British
oppressor, and the result is the Civil War; or the denial occurs abroad,
with the result that America imaginarily expands, taking the defense
of "the people" who are being tyrannized by some "foreign nations."
On these bases, one can begin to understand why Americans are so
tempted to claim a rather extraordinary right, the right to *extraterritorial sovereignty*, the right to consider themselves at home when they find
themselves abroad.[60] When this happens, they are taking themselves
for "the people" at large.[61]

Third, nationality. Although *nation* never refers to America in the
Declaration in 1776 or the Constitution in 1789, Americans have
often defined themselves as a "nation" over the past two centuries. The
question of whether this definition makes sense has been at the origin
of endless disputes—from *The Federalist Papers* to Barack Obama's
appeal for "nation-building at home."[62] Here, I will confine myself to
one simple remark concerning the Stars and Stripes, which is among
America's most cherished and revered symbols. It would be misleading to think that this national flag is merely the symbol of political
unity, for the Stars and Stripes is much more than that. In the eyes
of Americans, this flag represents the rights to life, liberty, and the
pursuit of happiness of man, of the people, of human beings, *regardless of their national affiliation*. In other words, the Stars and Stripes is
the symbol of an original, persistent confusion between America and
"the people" that fight for freedom and happiness all over the world.
In saying this, I am not denying the obvious: the Stars and Stripes is
first and foremost the national flag of America. But this is because
America is "the land of the free," not because America is a true nation
whose identity will be brought to light by the existing nation one day.
America is the place where people have been freed from the burden

of attaining such a true national identity. Hence the *fetishistic* value of the Stars and Stripes, which is an ersatz flag of mankind in general. To give some examples: remember the role that the American flag played during the first moon landing, and Neil Armstrong's unforgettable words: "That's one small step for a man, one giant leap for mankind." Or think about the magical aura that surrounds the American flag in a number of Hollywood films that glorify American heroes who have just saved the world from the Nazis, from terrorists, from aliens. At the end of the movie, the Stars and Stripes waves on the screen and celebrates the victory of mankind, not only of America, over some treacherous and oppressive Other. From a psychoanalytic point of view, it is also from such small details that one can infer the exact value that the Stars and Stripes acquires for Americans—leaving aside the magniloquent statements about the "empire of liberty" that spangle the history of this country. For Americans, the Stars and Stripes is ultimately the emblem of a New World that is separate from the Old World of nations. In this world, people do not consider themselves as nationals in the European sense of the word; rather, they see themselves as the champions of mankind.

But what is *mankind*? Is it the same as *humanity*? First of all, it is worth noting that humanity hints at the *essence* of human beings, mankind at the *totality* of human beings. That is, humanity is an *intensional* concept, mankind an *extensional* concept. Humanity refers to the true sense of the function *human-beings*, mankind to the domain of that function. Neither the sense nor the domain can be determined exactly. As for humanity, its sense remains obscure and baffling. As for mankind, it is like a surface along which the psychopolitical border of America shifts. Because this border changes position, mankind changes appearance.

Let me clarify this with an example. A separation can occur everywhere along the surface of mankind. Wherever "the people" rise up against some oppressor, there appears to be separation. Wherever "the people" rebel and "appeal to Heaven," there appears to be mankind. Now consider the Vietnam War. From the point of view of some Americans, the Vietnamese were separating themselves from the communist oppressor. From the point of view of others, the Vietnamese were separating themselves from the American oppressor. As a result, "the people" struggling for freedom and the "unalienable Rights" of man were seen from two opposite angles, and this opposition modified the domain of mankind according to one's point of view. In America, there were those who believed that mankind included the American army and excluded the Vietcong army, and there were those who believed the opposite. The two fronts fought each other. Yet America found itself on both sides of this political battle. Both the "silent majority" and the antiwar activists saw themselves as true patriots. Conservatives argued for America's interventionism. Protesters sought to redeem "America's soul," as Martin Luther King Jr. put it. But the same political grammar underpinned their discourses. And in both cases, a *metonymy*—that is, a *pars pro toto* relation—was being established between Americans and mankind. Conservatives spoke on behalf of "the people," just like antiwar protesters. Both factions stood in for mankind, whose face varied from one front to the other.

It follows that mankind is no less elusive than humanity. Ultimately, these entities are the objects of two different political drives and grammars, both of which condemn the people to a feeling of failure for not being able to remove all ambiguities that stain their own words and behavior. In the case of nationalism, failure results in a feeling of guilt, as I have said. The citizen is accused of not doing enough in view of collective happiness. The nation, in turn, is accused of breaking its promise. When it comes to separatism, shame becomes predominant. Again, the Vietnam War is an instructive example. In America, both the people who approved the war and those who opposed it felt ashamed of what they were witnessing. Shame was everybody's sentiment, not only in the aftermath but also during the course of the war. Some were ashamed of what the Vietcong were doing (in tacit complicity with American protesters). Others were ashamed of what American troops were doing (with the American government's endorsement). Both groups, however, were ashamed, and beyond that, both found themselves claiming that they felt ashamed in the name of America, because both groups were repeating the refrain that all Americans unconsciously sing when they proudly stare at the Stars and Stripes: *America stands in for mankind*. But how is mankind to be understood?

What is the meaning, namely the domain, of mankind? Whatever the answer, that refrain remains written in scarlet letters on the patriot's chest, confusing "the people."

TWO ADDENDA

(A) In the following, I will further expand on political grammars. But before that, let us draw some conclusions from the above considerations. As I have already explained, there appears to be a structural analogy between rights and phantasies. This means that the structure of rights can be compared to the structure of phantasies: $ <> a. When it comes to subjective rights, $ refers to the individual subject who is claiming a right, and the rhombus <> refers to the right that the subject is claiming. But what about *objet petit a*? What is the object of rights? We are now in a position to address this crucial issue. As a matter of fact, it is not at the level of the individual subject-supposition but at the level of the collective subject-supposition that subjective rights point to an object. This is why I have stressed that the two levels of the subject-supposition form a single—*multilayered*—subjectivity.

Indeed, the object of subjective rights varies according to the political grammar in play. From a nationalist standpoint, that object is humanity. From a separatist standpoint, it is mankind. In both cases, the collective subject-supposition is framed by phantasies: $ <> a. Here, $ refers to the political subject, whether nationalist or separatist; the rhombus <> refers to the political grammar, whether axiomatic or demonstrative; and *objet petit a* refers to the object pursued by claiming one's rights, which is either humanity or mankind. Since a demonstrative grammar consists in the "inversion" of axiomatic grammar and hinges on the denial (*Verleugnung*) of subjectivity itself rather than the repression (*Verdrängung*) of the subject's lack, the axiomatic grammar can be illustrated through the formula $ <> a, whereas the demonstrative grammar can be illustrated through the inverted formula a <> $, as Lacan suggests.

In light of this, it becomes clear that individual rights are not just analogous to phantasies; they are exactly the same as phantasies. Yet these individual phantasies point to an object only on condition that they merge into those larger constellations that I have termed political

grammars and that are collective phantasies. What is pursued by claiming one's rights within the framework of a political grammar is nothing
less than one's own *being*, which takes the shape of either humanity or
mankind. It follows that political grammars—or ordinary ontologies,
as we may call them—have a strong impact on the way in which people
conceive of their rights, individually, and of their own will, collectively.
In other words, an axiomatic political subject and a demonstrative political subject cannot see individual rights in the same way, nor can they
see the people's sovereignty in the same way; therefore, they cannot
enforce democracy in the same way. Thus, although the main tenets
of modern political life seem to remain always the same, they actually
acquire different characteristics in different places.

(B) Nationalism is not the only axiomatic political grammar that can
possibly exist. Socialism is an axiomatic alternative to nationalism.
When it comes to socialism, the question is no longer *What do we
expect from each other?* A socialist subject discards this question and
the nationalist logic of mutual expectations in favor of a logic of mutual debts. As a result, the question becomes *What do we owe to each
other?* A complaint is integral to the new logic, too, but this complaint
is not made by people who suffer from the persisting gap between
the existing nation and the true nation because these people do not
believe in the national promise anymore. Rather, they demand that
the debtors pay the debt, and the debtors are those individuals who
have not met the others' expectations for too long and have turned
the national promise into a farce. When the consequences of such a
behavior become unbearable, a new fundamental antagonism arises,
opposing those who have been disloyal and those who feel betrayed.
Emphasis shifts from the *civil* rights of all citizens, which are still
among the prerogatives of traitors, to the *social* rights of people—the
working class, the proletariat—that have been left to their destiny. For
the latter, the goal is no longer to achieve a true "nation," now stig-
matized as an individualist form of society, but rather to achieve a
true "society" based on mutual trust and real cooperation.[63] National
identitarianism, transcending class divisions, is contrasted with socialist internationalism, spanning national boundaries for the sake of

a strong solidarity between workers.[64] New watchwords become widespread. Yet *humanity* continues to occupy center stage. Indeed, the socialist subject, just like the nationalist subject, aims for the betterment of the human condition, and both ideologies assume axiomatically that rights—whether civil or social—enable human beings to achieve their humanity. For this reason, there is only one step from nationalism to socialism. The two grammars remain close to each other, and there is a constant interplay between them.[65]

That said, socialism and nationalism cannot be placed on an equal footing. In some sense, socialism is a by-product of nationalism, because the logic of mutual debts presupposes that mutual expectations have been betrayed. *Justice* in the socialist sense of the word presupposes that *justice* in the nationalist sense of the word has proven illusory. This explains in part why socialists are often tempted to defend the nation, the fatherland, when the latter is in grave danger. Take, for example, the rallying cry: "We are defending the fatherland in order to conquer it!"[66] A leading figure in the Social Democratic Party of Germany launched this slogan in 1914, but his overt rebuttal of socialist internationalism did not shock anyone at the time. For socialism is a *response* to nationalism and cannot survive the death of the nation.

There is one more piece of evidence in support of the view that socialism is grammatically subordinated to nationalism: America. If a demonstrative grammar consists in the "inversion" of axiomatic nationalism, as I said before, it follows that a separatist subject proves allergic not only to nationalism but to all kinds of political axiomatics, for mankind—not humanity—plays a pivotal role in that context. Hence the scarce relevance of class-conscious movements and socialist parties throughout American history. No logic of mutual debts can catch on in the absence of a preexisting logic of mutual expectations.[67]

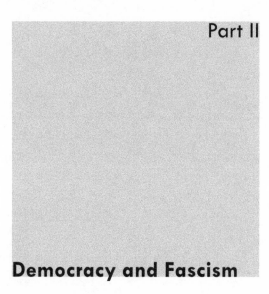

Part II

Democracy and Fascism

5

The Freudian Paradigm
of Critical Theory

1. When considering social phenomena, we can adopt either an operational or a clinical approach. In the first case, we study the pathologies of societies, in the second case their physiology. When we opt for a clinical approach, we draw attention to the diseases of society. When we choose an operational approach, we examine the healthy functioning of society.

2. Critical theory usually adopts a clinical approach to social phenomena, but there exist many paradigms of critical-clinical theory. I will discuss three of them: the Marxian, the Nietzschean, and the Freudian. These definitions refer to three trends of thought that argue for different types of interplay between truth and history.

3. According to the Marxian paradigm, every social dysfunction manifests a *historical function*. For this reason, social analysis is conducive to a philosophy (or an alleged science) of history. Truth takes center stage here. Canonically, the truth of capitalism is communism. This is not, as is often believed, a normative statement about the optimal arrangement of society but rather a clinical prognosis. After detecting social sufferings and disorders, one reads them as symptoms of the true, unstoppable course of history. Since capitalism is marked by

contradictions, so the narrative goes, it is *necessarily* condemned to self-destruction. That is to say, the truth of history is always already in action and will have the last word. As Marx himself points out, "We call communism the *real* movement which abolishes the present state of things."[1] Although this idea lends itself to countless formulations and interpretations, I will not expand on the quite obvious limitations of such an alethic version of critical theory.

4. According to the Nietzschean paradigm, social dysfunctionalities do not conceal any historical functionality but a *radical dysfunctionality* of history as such. In short, there is no truth in history. Beyond or behind social sufferings, we cannot detect any truth, only sickness. Therefore, we can study the diseases of society and give an account of their origins by means of genealogical investigation, but we cannot treat them. Any happy ending of history is out of the question here because we enter a different world, which is not the world of history, properly speaking, but rather the world of *historicity*.

4.1. Among the many representatives of Nietzschean critical theory, I will single out two: Theodor W. Adorno and Jacques Derrida. For both of them, history is sick and devoid of truth; history is a sequence of disturbing imbalances. But to argue that there is no truth in history, and that the historicity of history pulls history to pieces, we must keep on speculating about history. Thus, Adorno and Derrida share the belief that history as such has no truth, but they also attempt to understand the logic of the strange allergy to truth that actually prevents history from disappearing into thin air. For them, truth and history are unrelated to each other; this is what is implied by the notion of "negative dialectics" in Adorno's works and by the idea of "deconstruction" in Derrida's thought.[2] But what is the reason for such unrelatedness? How can we know that history is alien to truth? For both thinkers, the answer is *Wirklichkeit*: were it not for the *effectiveness* of negative dialectics or deconstruction, we could not contend that history as such is devoid of truth. Hence, negative dialectics and deconstruction are not to be seen as abstract ideas, as the products of an overfertile imagination. In fact, negative dialectics and deconstruction are always already at work. These are not empty words, for negative dialectics and deconstruction designate the concrete *modus operandi* of history. It is only through negative dialectics or deconstruction that history *historicizes* itself, thereby disrupting its own development, undoing itself, and tearing apart any truth. Negative dialectics and deconstruction are therefore inherent in history; they *actualize* the historicity of history, while carrying out the "non-identity" of history with itself (Adorno) or the tragic "aporia" of any historical passage (Derrida). Viewed in this light, negative dialectics and deconstruction appear as logical *and* historical cages. These notions unveil the secret logic of historicity that pushes forward and simultaneously ruins the course of history. In the last analysis, it does not matter whether this logic is defined as a logic of "disintegration" (Adorno) or as a logic of "dissemination" (Derrida). What matters most is that this logic marks the limits of history. Here, the Hegelian dream of a final reconciliation between truth and history is turned upside down, ending in a Nietzschean nightmare in which truth bids farewell to history. We cannot think of any true achievement of history. Old philosophies of history must give way to a new *philosophy of historicity*.

4.2. The paradoxes created by these "reflections from damaged life" are not innocuous. If history is governed by the logic of disintegration or dissemination, then the very existence of history must be called into doubt. In other words, from the point of view of Adorno and Derrida, it is legitimate, not to say mandatory, to conclude that history *is not*. Worse still, it is mandatory to conclude that nothing *is*. Indeed, the logic of historicity, taken to its extreme, not only forbids any ontological faith in history but also undermines any other ontological pronouncements. Adorno's and Derrida's antiontological voracity goes far beyond that of, say, Karl Jaspers, who conceded the end of philosophical "ontology" but continued to trust the being of being. For Adorno and Derrida, nothing can stand up to the logic of historicity that disintegrates and disseminates all kinds of identity and all kinds of entity. In the end, if history is not, this is because nothing is. Nonidentity and aporia prevail over the being of being, of truth, of everything. But then, what are we talking about when we speak of history in terms of historicity? As soon as we ask this question, "utopia" (Adorno) and "messianicity" (Derrida) emerge as the inevitable corollaries of any philosophy of historicity. History is not. Nonetheless, history is always about to be. In many respects, this makes no sense; yet this confirms that every philosophical statement is affected by nonidentity and aporia—that is, incongruity. If one reads Adorno's and Derrida's works carefully, there can be no doubt. For them, it is as though history is waiting for its own redemption; and it is only because of this utopian or messianic waiting *of* history *for* history that history falls to pieces and becomes unsubstantial without vanishing into thin air. Because of this theoretical complication, we cannot confine ourselves to saying that history is not. We must add that history is *not as yet*. All we can say about history is that history *might* be one day. But is that enough to protect theory from the risk of inanity? Given the premises of the whole argument, the answer is no. The logic of historicity forces us to dismiss any true hope in history and understanding of ourselves until the day when the Messiah will come back. Hence the overwhelming despair that exudes from the philosophy of historicity: history cannot attain any end, because history has never begun. History is like a cage with neither entrance nor exit. In Nietzsche's words, "I am all the names of history,"[3] but I am *not as yet*. We are *not as yet*.

5. According to the Freudian paradigm of critical theory, we should *neither* repudiate all articles of our ontological faith, as recommended by the partisans of the Nietzschean paradigm, *nor* defend a specific ontological credo, as recommended by the partisans of the Marxian paradigm. From a Freudian standpoint, history is not the ordained manifestation of truth, nor is it nullified by the utopian or messianic spectralization of truth. Rather, history sets the stage for "historical truths," as Freud would have it.[4] History is the realm of *true fictions*. In this view, people think that they know who they are; people believe that they can grasp the truth about themselves, but they actually come into being only by failing to reach and embody that truth. We *are*, yet we never manage to be truly ourselves. Being and truth quarrel inside us.

5.1. I will now mention a telling example of Freudian critical theory. Before that, it is worth insisting on the reason why Freud's name is paradigmatic in this context. The reason is that Freud was the first to realize that our subjective being—being in the first person, whether singular or plural—is made of oneiric stuff and that there is nothing but that stuff; there is no true being beyond that oneiric being, which is our sole and unique experience of being. For Freud, then, it is not a question of discovering the truth about our being. Nor is it a question of drowning in nontruth and nonbeing, waiting for the final redemption of history. The antiontological postulate of the Nietzschean paradigm—*being is not as yet*—is at odds with the paraontological postulate of the Freudian paradigm—*being fails to be true.*[5] Drawing on Kant's characterization of truth in terms of necessity and universality, we may say that, for Freud, our being should materialize our truth but fails to match the latter's requirements of necessity and universality. Our being thus comes to reflect a delimited historical truth, which is delimited and historical precisely because our being is always infected with contingency and particularity. We *are*, but we fail to be true to ourselves every time that we *are*.

5.2. This idea is not the exclusive prerogative of psychoanalysis. Consider Michel Foucault's "critical ontology of ourselves." Although Foucault loved to present himself as a "happy positivist," some of his works demand a deeper understanding. One of Foucault's tacit assumptions is that being is not static, that we are not obliged to surrender to the necessity and universality of being, that there is no regime of truth that governs our being always and everywhere. For Foucault, being changes. Yet being should not be conflated with change as such or becoming (as Gilles Deleuze often seems to imply). From Foucault's point of view, being changes or becomes only in a particular way, and that is the failure of being. Being collapses, as it were, and this is how being becomes apparent. Being regularly breaks down under the burden of truth. This means, first of all, that we *are* insofar as we fail to embody the truth of our being. We cannot be truly ourselves, but this is how we come into being. Seen in this light, failure is a conservative principle. At the same time, however, this means that failures can pave the way for new unpredictable configurations of our being. Failures and suffering, in fact, become intolerable from time to time. At that moment, they turn into a transformative principle.

5.3. Among the many ontological disorders Foucault has analyzed, biopolitics is probably the most controversial. One can hardly find two people that define biopolitics in the same way. For Foucault, biopolitics concerns not only our "life" but also our "freedom."[6] For this reason, he does not confine himself to studying Nazi eugenics or the neoliberal approach to human behavior. Foucault looks into the history of modern societies from the eighteenth century onward. His investigation into biopolitics has approximately the same scope as Marx's investigation into capitalism. Although Foucault never endorsed Marx's theory about the *true* evolution of capitalist societies and the final advent of communism, he agreed with Marx that modern societies suffer from congenital contradictions.

5.4. Modern societies are based on the idea that free individuals "authorize" the state, which in its turn bestows freedoms on them. Biopolitics, according to Foucault, deals with the paradoxes generated by this assumption.[7] On the one hand, the state is thought to be the result of a contract freely entered into by all individuals; thus, it seems that individual freedom is at the origin of the state. On the other hand, the state is urged to grant, secure, and even enhance individual freedom; thus, it seems that we actually receive our freedoms from the state. But which comes first? The state or human freedom? As Foucault notes, it is impossible to tell. If we say that the state comes first, then we must renounce our claim to some original, natural freedoms. If we say that freedoms come first, then we must explain how we can owe the state such freedoms, which are deemed to preexist the birth of the state. This dilemma, Foucault maintains, pushes modern people into accepting a kind of compromise-formation. On the one hand, modern individuals demand that the state *protect* their freedoms and restrict the scope of governmental activities; on the other hand, they learn by experience that the state multiplies interventions in order to *produce* freedoms through proactive measures of "securement." The doctrine of liberalism on the one side; the practice of biopolitics on the other. Although the two sides of modern politics are not congruous, they coexist all the time. But the two ingredients of the social contract—the state and individual freedoms—keep on refuting each other. As regards individual freedoms, the question arises as to what the true meaning of the people's original, natural freedoms might be. In theory, individual freedoms should be understood as an essential endowment of all human beings; in practice, they appear to be a more prosaic and contingent reality, protected but also overshadowed by the Leviathan. In sum, individual freedoms remain an open issue, being both confirmed and countered by the state's activism. As regards the state itself, which ought to restrict the scope of governmental activities but has to widen it for the sake of the citizens' freedoms, it ends up struggling against itself and, more often than not, disguising itself. Hence the development of a particular "art of government" that gradually leads to the establishing of a huge shadow state, formed of parastatal authorities, or state-authorized agents, charged with the task of governing us on behalf of the state. For Foucault, this biopolitical drift—of which today's "neoliberal" and deregulatory policies are the most extreme illustrations—does not condemn modern societies to death. Quite the opposite. Neither individual freedoms nor modern states are annihilated by the contrast between the liberal *fictio* of the state-built-upon-the-contract and the biopolitical *factum* of the modern state, or by the people's failed attempts to combine them into a steady and harmonious compound. If anything, those failed attempts consolidate individual freedoms and modern states, which come into being and prolong their survival through such failures. In other words, by contradicting and frustrating each other on a regular basis, individual freedoms and modern states do not destroy but rather transform one another without disappearing. Day after day, *they become us*, while preventing us from being true to ourselves.

5.5. This is not the end of the story, however. I say this because, first, modern states are not immortal. Today, they are challenged by international and supranational institutions of various kinds that are changing the way in which we see ourselves and our societies (more on that later). Second, the reduction of historical truths such as the state-built-upon-the-contract to so many true fictions that fail to be true proves that a historical truth is nothing more than a contingent truth, poor of necessity. When the people's suffering becomes intolerable, all historical truths are doomed to give way to alternative truths. And third, the intrinsic instability of all regimes of truth is that which allows us to take a critical stance toward them. This does not entail that we can find a way out of our historical world and enter a new one overnight.

6

The Two Paths to Modern Democracy

1. For a modern democracy to be possible, two basic conditions must be met. First, "we the people" must become the key players of the political game. Second, the state must ensure that everybody plays the game by the rules. Together, "we the people" dictate the rules, and then each of us must follow them. The state is charged with the task of putting those rules into force. Thus, the state governs and controls each of us; nonetheless, "we the people" have priority over the state, because we are collectively *sovereign* over the state. In modern democracies, there is nothing that can step over the people's sovereignty. Not even the state is allowed to do this. Hence the structural, permanent tension between the state, which rules over the people, and the people, who rule over the state.

1.1. Modern democracies arise out of secular societies. These are first-person societies that can speak and act in the first-person plural, wondering how to relate to the states that mark out their territorial boundaries. Such societies no longer revolve around time-honored traditions and beliefs. Quite the contrary: people who live in a secular age are wont to call into doubt all previous conventions and dogmas, for they consider themselves free, independent, and autonomous individuals. In the modern age, every single person turns into a sovereign *ego*, so the problem is how to integrate many scattered individuals into a cohesive society, a *nos*, that preserves the *ego*'s autonomy. The main obstacle to achieving this goal is the state itself, which rules over the people and which the latter see as a limitation on their own freedom.

1.2. The idea of the social contract stems from these premises. Since people aspire to live together in peace, they give their conditional assent: by way of contract, the state is authorized to rule over them but simultaneously cautioned against contravening the primal autonomy and authority of those who subscribe to the contract and thus merge into *one* society, counterposed to *one* state. As a result, the *factum* of the modern state is contrasted with the *fictio* of the state-built-upon-the-contract, and the state *qua* institutional fact is expected to approximate the state *qua* social fiction.[1] The state ought to defend the people's interests and conform to the people's expectations as much as possible. This is not easy. The whole of modern political history revolves around this problem.

1.3. The problem lies in the self-contradictory logic of the social contract. The subscribers to the contract yield to the state's power but are also recognized as the authors and initiators of the state that governs them only on the grounds of their free consent. Thus, on the one hand, "we the people" are the sovereign creators of the state. This much the contract stipulates. On the other hand, "we the people" transfer our sovereignty to the state. Such is our will, as the contract attests. From this it follows that "we the people" are sovereign, yet we are obliged to bid farewell to our sovereignty. Indeed, after authoring the contract, "we the people" can relate to ourselves and our sovereignty over the state only *through* the state itself, that has been recognized as the *summa potestas*. Hence the problem: how can the people's sovereignty be preserved once the contract has been signed? Put slightly differently, how can the people not only *possess* sovereignty in theory but also *exercise* it in practice?[2]

1.4. As I have explained, questions like these were elicited by the spread of capitalism and the rise of free-market societies. At the dawn of the modern age, people were getting accustomed to the idea that human beings are autonomous individuals who are sovereign over themselves and free to make exchanges and establish contractual relations with one another by selling and buying more or less everything—including land, money, and labor. Against this background, even the relationships between those free individuals and the state could be rethought in terms of contractual transactions. But how to do it right? One may call this the *liberal problem*: how can the state be contractually established so that free and sovereign individuals do not lose their freedom and sovereignty over themselves after the social contract has given birth to the Leviathan?

1.5. At first, there were just two options. Once the sovereign power had been constituted, people could reaffirm their sovereignty over themselves by identifying collectively with the Leviathan, or else they could reclaim their individual freedom and query the Leviathan's authority, thereby loosening the latter's grip day after day. Before I go into further detail, it is worth stressing that neither of these options could provide a real solution to the liberal problem because that problem was ultimately of a fictional nature. It reads as follows: how can the *factum* of the modern state be combined with the *fictio* of the state-built-upon-the-contract? Whatever the answer, this problem condemned modern people to reconcile the irreconcilable: factual obligation and fantasized freedom, *de facto* heteronomy and *de jure* autonomy.

1.6. In light of the above, modern democracy can be defined as a failed compromise between a *factum* and a *fictio*, between states and people who are thought to be free, autonomous, and sovereign over themselves. Given that modern societies must coexist with states, these societies fail to be truly, completely democratized. Nevertheless, their recurring failures nourish a process of endless democratization. In the end, it is only because first-person societies regularly bump into the state's power that they are compelled to find ever new arrangements and modernize themselves over and over again, keeping the democratic and emancipatory promise alive. As history shows, this process of stormy democratization can take different directions. People can be willing to identify with the state, or they can be willing to distance themselves from the state. In the former case, I will speak of axiomatic democracy, in the latter case of demonstrative democracy. Since both options seek to solve the liberal problem, both are conducive to *liberal democracy*. In either case, failure is the key to success.

2. *Axiomatic democracy* is typified by nationalist democracies. In general, nationalism strives to affirm the people's sovereignty and wants it to coincide with the state's sovereignty. From a nationalist viewpoint, the state is authorized if and only if the "constituted power" obeys the "general will"—that is, the "constituent power"—of the people who consider themselves to be *one* nation. If the state does not comply with the people's "general will," then people regard themselves as a nation that is oppressed by the state (sometimes a foreign state). The nation, therefore, complains about this situation and protests against the intolerable distance between society and the state, between the nation's "general will" and the state's arbitrary power.

2.1. For nationalists, the problem is how to establish the true *unity* and *generality* of the nation's "general will"—that is, how to change many individual voices into one choral voice. Nations encounter this problem whenever they come to the fore, and the solution varies little from nation to nation. To overcome diversities among people, all disparities and discrepancies must be compensated with a more fundamental unity, the nation's unity, that transforms all the people into a unanimous political subject. Yet this entails that the word *nation* says more than what it means. Indeed, this word is two-faced for nationalist people: it refers to a certain community (*natio, gens*), to be sure, but it also points to something else. On the one hand, the "nation" names a particular and diversified group of people; on the other hand, it hints at a further element by virtue of which those people are understood as being the members of one society, one nation. This grounding element, which validates the people's union, is nothing less than the people's *humanity*. From the perspective of a nationalist subject, it is thanks to our humanity that "we the people," the *existing* nation, become one nation, a *true* nation.

2.2. *Naming* and *hinting at* occur at different levels. At the discursive level, when people speak of their own *nation*, this word functions as a name for the existing nation or society, marked by a patent heterogeneity. At the grammatical level, instead, when nationalists listen to that name, the "nation" tacitly hints at the true society, which, unlike the existing society, is marked by a hidden homogeneity. This is how the true *unity* and *generality* of the nation's "general will" are obtained, even though nobody is aware of that. As is well known, no rational justification for the nation's homogeneity can be given by people who pledge allegiance to the national flag. Nonetheless, all of them assume that the true nation *is* beyond and below the existing nation, and such an axiomatic assumption does nothing but add a metaphorical surplus value to the "nation," which thus begins to signify more than what it means. Literally, the word means what it names—that is, the existing nation. Metaphorically, the same word hints at the true nation. At that point, humanity comes into play. It is only because people see themselves as having some human properties in common that they see themselves as equal to, or homogeneous with, each other. For nationalists, the "nation" *is* insofar as it brings the people's humanity to light, and the true nation is charged with bridging the distance between the existing nation and humanity as such.

2.3. This axiomatic assumption lies at the heart of all versions of nationalism: civic, religious, and ethnic. Nationalism is always based on the unconscious belief that humanity *equalizes* nationals. For a modern "nation" to be possible, it is necessary that the "nation" shines the light of humanity into the sky of history, and the national metaphor serves this purpose. This is not without consequences, however, because humanity irradiates the nation too much, as it were, and nationalists are blinded by the national metaphor. Drawing on Kenneth Burke's theory of metaphor,[3] we may say that the national metaphor conflates two perspectives—the existing nation's and the true nation's perspectives—but nationalist people cannot make sense of it, for they cannot bridge the divide between the literal meaning and the semantic surplus value of the "nation." As soon as the national metaphor is put into effect, a gap opens up between the existing nation and the true nation, between what is visible—the society as it stands—and that which is supposed to *be* beyond and below what is visible—the people's humanity. Nationalists cannot say who they are, or where they stand, at that moment. In psychoanalytic terms, they step onto the stage of history as a split subject. At the discursive level, the "nation" continues to name the existing society. This is what people *speak about*. At the grammatical level, the "nation" starts hinting at the people's humanity that renders them a true nation. This is what nationalists *listen to* when they refer to themselves in the first-person plural. The two perspectives do not overlap but are nonetheless conjoined by way of metaphor. The result is that as soon as nationalist people open their mouths, they get lost and grope in the dark. The "nation" appears as a riddle that excites and at the same time bewilders everybody. Through the national metaphor, the "nation" comes into existence, but it does so only by calling its own identity into question. Hence the *deflationary trajectory* of all modern nations, which come into being only by failing to realize their own truth.

2.4. The national metaphor is the key to understanding how many people merge into *one* nation. The national metaphor says (without saying it explicitly) that citizens are human beings before being citizens. But this entails that individuals become citizens of *one* nation thanks to the same metaphor. Indeed, the people's insertion into the national society is because they possess human properties—namely, rights, which are both civil (the rights of the citizen) and natural (the rights of man). From a grammatical point of view, this makes perfect sense, given that the national metaphor embeds man in the citizen. From a discursive (or logical) point of view, however, this makes little sense, and leads to all kinds of problems, because nobody can tell exactly how to construe the identity between man and the citizen, bring it to completion, and achieve collective happiness. Still, all versions of nationalism hold on to this unresolved ambiguity. On the one hand, people are recognized as nationals and belong to the nation because of their very humanity, which is spelled out by their natural rights. On the other hand, people discover their own humanity through the nation itself, which grants human rights in the form of civil rights and takes—or mistakes—natural rights for national rights. This unending confusion, or interchange, between civil and human rights, national and natural properties, is a distinctive feature of modern nationalism, whether civic, religious, or ethnic.[4]

2.4.1. *Civic nationalism.* I have already discussed this matter at length. The ambiguity between human and civil rights, between the "rights of man" and the "rights of the citizen," is clearly attested by some of the most relevant documents of the French Revolution, such as the Declaration of 1789 and subsequent versions. As Étienne Balibar has noted, French revolutionaries did not make any distinction between human and civil rights,[5] but the identity between natural and national rights, between man and the citizen, remained a foggy issue. Thus, a metaphorical—rather than a logical—connection between the former and the latter was made. The citizen turned into a metaphor of man, and by the same token, the French nation turned into a metaphor of humanity, under the assumption that the French nation was the shortest, if not the only, path toward enforcing the rights of human beings and achieving their true nature. Day after day, failure after failure, this assumption continued to nourish the *promise*: our humanity will be truly achieved the day when our society will be truly nationalized.[6]

2.4.2. *Religious nationalism.* In seventeenth-century England, the notion of "birthrights" was equally ambiguous. As Georg Jellinek points out, it is difficult to say whether this notion designated *natural rights* or the *inherited rights* of Englishmen. For Jellinek, this is the sign that the concept of natural rights was still unknown back in those days and that this concept started to play a critical role only a century later—first in America, then in France. From a grammatical point of view, however, Jellinek's conclusion seems a bit hasty. In fact, the ambiguity of English "birthrights" cannot be downgraded to a mere linguistic opacity, not least because this ambiguity did not disappear with the passing of time but was confirmed and even strengthened, as though an entire political grammar had crystallized around it.[7] No doubt this ambiguity was not enough to generate a political grammar. For this to be possible, the confusion between inherited and natural rights had to be integrated into a nationalist axiomatics centered on a national metaphor. At any rate, that ambiguity was a first step toward nationalization. Charles II and the Cavalier Parliament did the rest after the Restoration. Through the Corporation Act of 1661, the Act of Uniformity of 1662, and the Test Acts of 1673 and 1678, they gradually introduced a confessional-political dogmatics that prepared the ground for the Glorious Revolution and subsequent developments. The nature of the modern "nation" becomes apparent when one looks closely at this historical moment. The new dogmatics fixed the boundaries of a new society, the Anglican nation, by assuming *axiomatically* that national allegiance could not be distinguished from religious allegiance—to the clear detriment of those not professing the Anglican faith. The advantage for the vast majority of people was that, under this religious-and-national diktat, they could consider themselves homogeneous with each other for the simple reason that they now considered themselves *more human than others.* Indeed, the new Protestant axiomatics had changed them into the only nation that worshipped the true God, and Britain thus appeared to be nothing less than the reincarnation of Israel, the people of God, later glorified by George Frideric Handel in some of his most popular oratorios.[8] After decades of battles, the lowest common denominator among Englishmen had been found by turning Great Britain into a holy metaphor of humanity as such, of a true and truthful humanity; and by virtue of this religious-and-national privilege, Britons were entitled to a number of "birthrights" that were denied to others—for instance, the Catholics—and were *on principle*, not by mere chance, inherited and natural, civil and human, historically determined and absolutely irrevocable: "the true, ancient and indubitable rights and liberties of the people of this kingdom" (Bill of Rights, 1689). At that moment, what Jellinek is inclined to define as a linguistic obscurity proved to be a crucial ingredient in the process of nationalization. Great Britain and humanity had exchanged rings at last, after a period of great bewilderment, because the two rings had been discovered to be interchangeable. Henceforth, the loss of "birthrights" would have entailed not only the loss of nationality but also the loss of one's humanity in the eyes of all Britons. Probably, this was the first time in modern history that nationality and humanity were united in marriage. The ceremony was religious, since it had to extinguish the fires of a bloody and long-lasting religious conflict. Yet, thanks to this religious ceremony, a modern body politic was born, one that could claim its inherited-and-natural right to dominate other peoples, to civilize-and-humanize the rest of the world—which the British nation did under the reign of a Protestant and German-speaking dynasty:

> Like all sustaining national myths, the idea that Britain was a chosen land and therefore fruitful, did not depend for its effectiveness upon being true. Poor or not, large numbers of Protestant Britons believed—believed precisely because they *were* Protestant, and because it was comforting to believe it—that they were richer in every

sense than other peoples, particularly Catholic peoples, and particularly the French. . . .

. . . As long as a sense of mission and providential destiny could be kept alive, by means of maintaining prosperity at home, by means of recurrent wars with the Catholic states of Europe, and by means of a frenetic and for a long time highly successful pursuit of empire, the Union flourished, sustained not just by convenience but by belief as well. Protestantism was the foundation that made the invention of Great Britain possible.[9]

2.4.3. *Ethnic nationalism.* The grammatical linking of the "nation" with humanity is easier said than done. Most of the time, this operation is accomplished amid violent and chaotic conflicts. Furthermore, the results are always equivocal, and therefore debatable, for nationalism is nourished precisely by the ineradicable ambiguity of the "nation." In some sense, nationalism can be thought of as a literary performance. Nationalism and literature go hand in hand, indeed, not only because of the great relevance of national literatures for any process of nationalization but also because of the literary nature of nationalist politics, which is regularly punctuated by a series of metaphors that revolve around a central, hegemonic trope—the national metaphor. Consider, for instance, German nationalism. Even in a case like this, when a national grouping is isolated from the rest of the human species on account of its ethnic diversity, the "nation" turns into a metaphor of humanity as such, of a true and truthful humanity. This is why people magnify their own nation and describe it as the *Favoritvolk*, "the regenerator and recreator of the world" (Fichte's definition), or else praise the beautiful variety of nations, all of which brings the multifaceted essence of humanity to light (Herder's interpretation of the national metaphor). Either way, people end up coupling the "nation" to humanity, with the result that they can no longer draw a clear-cut line between man and the citizen, nature and nurture. Rather, they establish a figurative link between the two and thus find themselves in a position where they can address their fellow citizens by alluding to their very humanity. "Germans, think with your blood!" There can be little doubt that when Otto von Bismarck, the archetype of the nationalist leader, issued this rallying cry, he did not take this phrase literally. Only ethnofascists—people like Hitler and his acolytes—considered these words something more than a figure of speech, as we will see later on. For ethnonationalists, by contrast, blood is nothing but a trope, hinting at something that both excites and bewilders the people. The word *blood* is, in fact, among those that are particularly apt to inflame ethnonationalist passions. Equally useful for this purpose are words such as *soil, ancestors, language,* or *customs.* Within an ethnonationalist context, all of these terms start to function as peripheral metaphors that point to a core metaphor, the national metaphor. All of them serve the purpose of entrenching a myth of common origins and a sense of kinship among fellow country-men. Hence the heavily metaphorical jargon that became so popular in nineteenth-century Germany. That said, what we should keep in mind when discussing the issue of German ethnonationalism is that no politi-cal jargon—or "symbolism," as George Mosse would have it[10]—can catch on in the absence of a political grammar. It is grammar—not jargon or symbolism—that blurs the distinction between civil and human rights, thereby making the people believe that they are invisibly homogeneous in spite of all visible disparities among them. It is grammar that turns a vague intuition into a deep-rooted axiom, welding literature and poli-tics. An axiomatic grammar took shape in Germany from an early stage of the "nationalization of the masses." The Reichsgesetz betreffend die Grundrechte des deutschen Volkes of 1848 can be seen as a first step toward the formation of a German nation.[11] All Germans were granted some "basic rights," which each of them had by virtue of being both the citizen of a German state and a German man. But this was not enough to infuse German people with a strong feeling of nationality and a unique sense of identity. Soon after the trauma of the French occupa-tion, the German Federal Army had been formed. To achieve not only military but also national unity, however, a brand-new grammar had to be forged. Germans needed to find their own way in modern his-tory, a way that could divide their own destiny from the destiny of the most hated enemy, the French nation. For Germans, any form of civic nationalism would have been a cruel reminder of years to be forgotten, the *Franzosenzeit.* Nor could religious nationalism do well in a region where Protestants and Catholics had lived together for centuries and were expected to cohabit in the years to come.[12] Thus, owing to these (and other) constraints, an ethnonationalist grammar rapidly crystallized, sealing a chain of equivalences between the core metaphor of the "nation" on one side and the peripheral metaphors of blood, soil, ancestors, language, and customs on the other.[13] The principle of *ius sanguinis* was first introduced in Prussia through the Law Respecting the Acquisition and Loss of the Quality as a Prussian Subject, and His Admission to Foreign Citizenship of 1842; it was extended to the whole country through the Nationality Law of the German Empire and States of 1871, followed by the Nationality Law of 1913. Against this background, the German *populus* could raise its head and embark on the mission that all nationalist peoples accept with enthusiasm: under the guise of the "nation," what they seek to recover and restore is their own humanity. No matter whether they believe in the civic, religious, or ethnic origins of the "nation," these peoples *believe* and are ready to die for the sake of the "nation" because the blood they spill on the battlefield is the price of being true to themselves:

> With but very few exceptions, authorities have shied away from describing the nation as a kinship group and have usually explicitly denied that the notion of shared blood is a factor. Such denials are supported by data illustrating that most groups claiming nationhood do in fact incorporate several genetic strains. But, as earlier noted, such an approach ignores the wisdom of the old saw that when analyzing sociopolitical situations, what ultimately matters is not *what is* but *what people believe is*. And a subconscious belief in the group's separate origin and evolution is an important ingredient of national psychology.[14]

2.5. Nationalism is not conducive to democracy always and everywhere.[15] A nationalist discourse can be overtly antidemocratic, and nationalist elites do not necessarily give voice to democratic demands. Bismarck, for instance, was a fierce nationalist but never sympathized with parliamentary parties or democratic institutions in general. Having said this, one can hardly deny that nationalism reveals itself to be, more often than not, an emancipatory ideology. Even though nationalism does not release democratic and egalitarian effects in the short term, it does so in the long term.[16] In other words, nationalist discourses tend to become ever more democratic and egalitarian with the passing of time. The reason for this is that nationalism, unlike fascist ultranationalism, hinges on the principle of subjective rights, and these rights belong to *all* nationals. Given that the members of a national society are human beings in the first instance and are endowed with the same human properties, nationalism *tends* to see all of them as forming a nation of equals.[17] To give but one example, Emmeline Pankhurst, one of the leading figures in the British suffragette movement, was no less nationalist than Bismarck.

2.5.1. Historically, the democratic potentialities of nationalism are difficult to refute. Suffice it to say that the history of European *democracies* is closely intertwined with the history of European *nation*, and the latter, in turn, is closely intertwined with the history of European *nationalisms*. Still today, the political mythologeme that lies at the heart of European democracies asserts that the nation is the "constituent power" that authors the state's constitution. In all European countries, the principle of national sovereignty reigns supreme: peoples are believed to be sovereign nations. In light of this, it seems no exaggeration to say that European democracies are both *national* and *nationalist*. Recent developments in Europe give further evidence of this correlation between nationalism and democracy. Everywhere on the Continent, not to speak of Great Britain, the decline of *national* democracies caused by European integration has triggered the resurgence of *nationalist* movements that reclaim the nation's sovereignty for the purpose of reviving democracy.[18]

2.5.2. As I have indicated, socialism is the axiomatic alternative to nationalism. From a grammatical point of view, socialism *opposes* nationalism. Put another way, socialism can only emerge from a national/ nationalist background. As history shows, a national/nationalist constitution can evolve into a more socialist democracy, but the opposite never happens, nor can socialism be advocated without contrasting it with nationalism. No socialist agenda is conceivable unless we assume its conscious aversion to, and unconscious collusion with, a national/ nationalist agenda. Once more, recent developments in Europe confirm such a grammatical constraint. As soon as national democracies began to fade, socialist parties started to lose ground everywhere on the Continent. At that point, they had to choose: either disappear or undergo a major transformation, thus degenerating into something else. In both cases, the grammatical hierarchy between nationalism and socialism is clearly detectable. Nationalism comes first and socialism afterward, as a response to the former.

3. *Demonstrative democracy* is a synonym of separatist democracy. By separatism, I do not mean a generic desire to establish a new and separate state, because such a desire is often cultivated by nationalist subjects.[19] Separatism, as I understand it, means a nonnationalist grammar. When it comes to separatism, metonymies replace metaphors, demonstration replaces axiomatization, mankind replaces humanity, and the problem is not how to make sure that people are sovereign over the state but rather how to prevent the *res publica* from hampering the individual's pursuit of happiness. The United States of America is the epitome of separatism.

3.1. Nationalists and separatists treat the issue of social homogeneity differently. For *one* society to be possible, as I have noted, a certain degree of homogeneity must be attained, but separatists do not meet this requirement by identifying collectively with the nation's "general will." On the contrary, they dismiss the very possibility of any collective identification. The perspective is reversed. But then, how to avoid the threat of heterogeneity? How to prevent society from falling to bits? The separatist solution is homogeneity *through* heterogeneity. In a nutshell, the assumption is that people can achieve homogeneity on the basis of a *common* denial of homogeneity. Despite appearances, this solution is not just a play on words.

3.2. Nationalist and separatist societies can be described as, respectively, the society of collective identification and the society of individual differentiation or the society where popular sovereignty weighs more heavily than individual rights and the society where the opposite is true. In the first case, individual demands and expectations tend to be integrated into the nation's "general will," and the heterogeneity of society thus tends to be repressed by the axiomatic homogeneity of the nation. In psychoanalytic terms, we may define this process as a collective *Verdrängung* (repression). In the second case, every form of homogeneity is called into question and denied on account of a more radical heterogeneity, but some sort of homogeneity tends to arise out of such a denial, which is what all members of society have in common. In psychoanalytic terms, we may define this process as a collective *Verleugnung* (denial).

3.2.1. Nationalism is characterized by the fact that the nation acquires a metaphorical surplus value. The *present* nation is thought to be a *true* nation because it becomes a metaphor of what renders the citizens equal and similar to each other in spite of all differences: their shared, albeit unfathomable, humanity. This explains, among other things, the otherwise inexplicable sense of pride and superiority of nationalist peoples: nationalists always feel that they are more human than others (imperialism and racism being notorious expressions of such a feeling). By the same token, this explains why that feeling is combined with a sense of distress, resentment, and anger. As soon as the national metaphor comes into effect, a gap opens up between the nation and humanity, between the literal meaning and the metaphorical surplus value of the "nation." Being nothing more than a metaphor, the "nation" never morphs into a literal incarnation of humanity. Hence the endless complaints about the nation's failures and the *promise*: our humanity will be truly achieved the day when our society will be truly nationalized. Nationalisms of all kinds rest on this promise, which alternately exalts and disheartens nationalist societies. Separatists, instead, see things differently. Here, there is no room for metaphors, since the very possibility of a collective identification with the nation's "general will" is dismissed. The heterogeneity of individual demands and expectations does not undergo any process of axiomatic homogenization. Yet it remains mandatory that people form *one* society. Therefore, some sort of homogeneity must be attained. How is that possible? As already suggested, the answer is homogeneity *through* heterogeneity; and metonymy, rather than metaphor, is the way to achieve this result.

3.2.2. In Lacan's view, metaphor and metonymy are figures of speech that stand out from the others because they show how subjects position themselves *in their own words*. We should recall that, from a psychoanalytic perspective, subjects come into being by failing to be, by failing to realize (in every sense of the word) the truth of their own being. As

I emphasized above, failure is the only way in which the true fiction of the first person, whether singular or plural, can be sustained. Who am I? Who are we? In the last analysis, the subject coincides with the hole that this question marks out. The subject is nothing more than a flaw. Yet this flaw is not nothingness. The *ego* and the *nos* are not mere illusions. Although the subject amounts to a hole, a grammar tends to crystallize around it, with the result that a certain hole—and with it, a certain subject—acquires stability and continues to be the same through the passing of time. The sentiment of being a *self*, relatively invariant over time, originates with that process of grammatical solidification. Grammars make subjects steady in spite of their failures. And for grammars to be possible, Lacan maintains, metaphor and metonymy must come into play. Indeed, one of the basic tenets of Lacan's theory of the subject is that metaphor and metonymy are the keystones of grammatical stabilization. These are the means by which the subject's failures can be organized and positioned in the subject's own words. A metaphor is what both underpins and undermines the subject's *identification*, thus keeping the subject from realizing the truth of its own being. The "nation" is a case in point. On the one hand, the nation appears as a first-person plural (*nos*) with a proper name. On the other, the nation appears as a metaphor of humanity, a metaphor that conveys yet conceals the true being of the first-person plural. A metaphor of this kind takes center stage in every nationalist grammar. But what about the other path, the metonymic path, to subjectification? Here, too, the subject's invariance hinges on the invariance of a hole, of a lack. The difference is that the lack does not impair the subject's identity. In this case, the subject is molded into a part, or a partialized entity, which is subtracted from the Other's identity. That is, the subject arises from a *separation* that decompletes the Other's truth and calls it into question. For this reason, separatist people do not have any identity on their own, nor do they strive for one. But then, who are they? How can they position themselves and their separation *in their own words*? To this end, metonymies—not metaphors—must be mobilized.

3.2.3. One of the best-known cases of metonymy is synecdoche, by means of which a part stands in for the whole (*pars pro toto*). Quintilian gives some examples: "a roof" for a whole house, or "the point" for the whole sword.[20] When using the word *roof* to mean "the house," we make the house *be* in our words by subtracting, as it were, the roof from the house. It is not clear why this trick works. In the twentieth century, scholars from different fields made several attempts to solve this mystery. Among them, Roman Jakobson famously conjectured about the paradigmatic and syntagmatic axes of language. It is widely known that Lacan was a friend of Jakobson's. But Lacan's understanding of metaphors and metonymies is not the same as Jakobson's.[21] For the latter, these figures of speech are to be studied from a purely linguistic perspective. For Lacan, neither metaphors nor metonymies become comprehensible unless one takes into account their *ontological* implications. As regards metonymies, the fact that an ontological implication is being made is proved by the fact that a ship *is*, or at least comes to mind, whenever we read that "a prow hove in sight." At that very moment, a ship is supposed to *be* below and under the literal meaning of the word *prow*. Another kind of supposition is made when, for instance, the "nation" names a heterogeneous group of people but also hints at that which turns them into a homogeneous entity. When this happens, a metaphor is being activated. Whether they are of a metonymic or metaphorical nature, such ontological suppositions are extremely important to Lacan because the modern subject, the Cartesian *ego*, arises from a similar supposition, the subject-supposition. According to Lacan, first, the speaking subject, the *ego*, is supposed to *be* below and under the literal meaning of the words that the subject says; second, the overall symbolic structures that frame this ontological supposition are organized into grammars, which render the subject invariant over time; third, all subjective grammars revolve around metaphors or metonymies.

3.2.4. In Lacan's view, the metaphor and the metonymy determine the "subjective position" of each of us because they create a kind of blister inside language that enables the subject to find a place in its own words, without drowning in these words. When we make a metaphor, for example, we go beyond the literal meaning of the words at our disposal by way of addition, by enriching the semantic value of a word, thereby going beyond that word and ultimately beyond the Word as such, *in our own words*. But we also go beyond the literal meaning of the words at our disposal by way of subtraction, by reducing the semantic value of a word,[22] thereby going beyond that word and beyond the Word as such, *in our own words*. As Lacan remarks, the subject-supposition hinges on metaphors and metonymies because these tropes, and nothing else, allow the subject of the enunciation (the first person) to find a place in its own words without vanishing in the words that are being enunciated. Indeed, pushing language beyond the limits of the literal meaning of words, the metaphor and the metonymy engender an ultrasemantic space in which the subject can accommodate itself and distinguish itself from what is being said. And depending on the grammar that the subject-supposition follows, either metaphors or metonymies will be privileged. The metaphorical subject-supposition is exemplified by the "nation." As regards the metonymic subject-supposition, its mechanism is yet to be clarified. Before that, it is worth noting that the metaphorical and the metonymic subject-suppositions do not compel anybody to employ only metaphors or only metonymies. Each of us uses both figures of speech in everyday life. Nevertheless, the role that metaphors and metonymies play at the grammatical level becomes more or less significant depending on the subject-supposition hidden behind the subject's wording. This means that *the unconscious* will make the most of either the metaphor's or the metonymy's ultrasemantic potentialities.

3.2.5. The metonymic subject-supposition is grounded in the *pars pro toto* relationship. The "prow" can stand in for the ship as a whole, but the "sail" can do the same, as Lacan explains with his well-known example of the "thirty sails" standing in for a naval fleet.[23] Now consider a separatist society. If this society hinges on the dismissal of any identity and the denial of any homogeneity, then what kind of equivalence between individuals can be established so as to turn them into one people? I will call it a *metonymic equivalence*. Such is the equivalence that can be established between, say, the "prow" and the "sail" by reason of their parallel *hinting at* the ship. The "prow" and the "sail" can be equalized—without being identified—merely on account of the fact that both of them are extracted from the same whole. No metaphor lies behind a metonymic equivalence. The "prow" and the "sail" are not metaphors of the ship, nor are they metaphors of each other. Each of them is nothing but a *pars pro toto* of the same entity. Within a separatist society, this kind of equivalence becomes predominant. Individuals are equalized and merge into one people because each of them is extracted from and stands in for the same whole. Each of them is a *pars pro toto* of an "x," which plays the same role as the ship in relation to the "prow" and the "sail." It remains to be seen what this "x" is. The answer is not obvious. First of all, we should keep in mind that no axiomatic homogenization of society comes into effect in this case. Many individuals turn into one people not because of their axiomatic integration into the same nation but because of their metonymic *hinting at* something from which all of them are extracted and with which none of them can identify. In a metonymic equivalence, one part (or individual) can be equalized with the other precisely because no part (or individual) can identify with the whole from which all parts (or individuals) are subtracted. So, again, what is the mysterious whole that equalizes all individuals?

At first, we may venture that this whole is society itself: one individual can be equalized with the other because the two of them are part of the same society, even though neither can identify with the latter. But therein lies the rub: if society were such a whole, then the society *as a whole* would preexist the individual and determine what an individual is—namely, a part of that preexisting whole. As a result, the idea of a preliminary axiomatic identification of society would resurface—and with it, the idea of the nation. For the nation is that which ensures axiomatically that society identifies *as a whole* from the outset. In spite of appearances, this is no minor question. In point of fact, *this* question torments separatist people, who do not seek to recover their true identity but instead strive to demonstrate their difference and separation from all foreign nations. How can this difference be substantiated? How can "we the people" deny being one nation and yet become one people? *E pluribus unum*: how is that possible? In the final analysis, this goal can be achieved if and only if a certain condition is met: both people taken individually and as the whole of society must become part of a wider sequence of metonymic equivalences. That is, both the individual and the society must be understood as being part of something else, of a larger set, of a broader "x" from which both of them are extracted. If this condition is met, not only can one individual be equalized with the other by way of metonymy, but each individual can be equalized with the whole of society without resorting to any national metaphor. For this to be possible, the chain of metonymic equivalences must be stretched out to the point at which both the individual and the society end up being included in it. But what is the whole from which both the society and the individual can be subtracted in sequence? In America, this "x" has usually taken the name *mankind*.[24]

3.2.6. It is not easy to understand what mankind is, as mankind has no clear boundaries. In some respects, mankind can be compared with humanity, since the two concepts point to the same Thing—that is, the "core of our being" (*Kern unseres Wesens*). But the shape of this Thing varies depending on the "subjective position," which can be either axiomatic or demonstrative. From a semantic point of view, we may begin by saying that mankind is an extensional function, whereas humanity is an intensional one; but this would not be entirely correct, for we should also specify that humanity and mankind are semantic dysfunctions rather than functions. Humanity is the intensional dysfunction that blurs the sense of identity associated with a particular name, typically the nation's name; mankind is the extensional dysfunction that blurs the domain of reference of a name with different characteristics, the separatist people's name. As regards humanity, we have already examined how it emerges as a semantic surplus value of the national metaphor, and how it beclouds the true identity of the nation. Now it is time to look more closely at mankind and the metonymic dysfunction that befogs the first-person perspective of a separatist people. In this regard, the first thing to note is that mankind is a whole that, being the largest of all, presents itself as a nonwhole (*pas-toute* in Lacan's terminology). The best way to explain this feature of mankind is to draw a parallel with motherhood. When does a woman become a mother? Not when she becomes pregnant but when a child is extracted from her. At that moment, the child's childhood and the mother's motherhood start to exist. Likewise, mankind comes into existence every time that an individual or a society is extracted, or separated, from it. At that moment, mankind comes into being together with the individual and the society—*through separation*. The characterization of mankind as a nonwhole follows from this premise. Indeed, every time that mankind comes into being through separation, its boundaries are violated, but this violation is nonetheless necessary for mankind to *be*. Thus, mankind emerges as a nonwhole, or an intrinsically decompleted whole, just like motherhood.

Against the background of such a boundless nonwhole—be it mankind or motherhood—metonymic equivalences start to compose a boundless chain, one that knows no interruption and can expand in all directions. From one *pars pro toto* to the other, the chain revolves around the ungraspable nonwhole from which it flows, and to which every link of the chain points while being equalized with all the others. This structure illustrates how a separatist society is formed. In a separatist society, however strange this may seem, one individual can stand in for the whole of society without identifying with the latter because both the individual and the society can stand in for a third term, the nonwhole of mankind, that renders the individual and the society equivalent metonyms. Furthermore, not just every individual but also every group of people, or sector of society, can stand in for the whole of society, because the same sort of metonymic equivalence can be established between whatever group of people and the society as a whole, which are both part of mankind. On these bases, a society can grow and diversify while remaining centered on a sequence of telescoping equivalences between individuals, social groups, and society in its entirety. The backbone of this society is always the *pars pro toto* relationship that makes it *malleable* and *incomplete*. First of all, a separatist society is malleable because metonymic equivalences between individuals, social groups, and the whole of society are subject to radical changes, as people are not forced to identify with the whole of society following the axiomatic trajectory of metaphorical equivalences (like those between the nation and blood, ancestors, language, customs, and so forth). Second, a separatist society is incomplete because it proceeds from the nonwhole of mankind that *renders society a whole by exceeding and decompleting it* all the time, thereby pushing it back to its origins: the moment of separation, of birth, that needs to be reenacted over and over again in order to let both mankind and society *be*.

3.2.7. Although this analysis may seem abstract, it sheds light on some aspects of American society, to call things by their real names. For example, *eternal inflation*: America has an innate tendency to inflate, to expand—whether from a territorial, economic, or cultural point of view. This tendency represents a major asset of American society but also a congenital defect. In fact, America is inclined to grow and evolve frantically by extending and reshaping the malleable chain of metonymic equivalences that underpins its existence. But the fact is that America also disintegrates because of that process, which ultimately increases the metonymic fragmentation and dispersion of society. As a consequence of this, it is as though America continues to find itself *in statu nascendi*. On the one hand, America inflates so as to fill the gaps that open up between the heterogeneous elements that compose it and merge, one after the other, into an ever more crowded chain of metonymic equivalences. This is how America endeavors to become *one* cohesive and close-knit society. On the other hand, the more America is stuffed with metonymic equivalences, the more it decomposes and furthers the heterogeneity of society to the detriment of homogeneity. Thus, inflation must be rebooted over and over again to keep America alive in the absence of any axiomatic union or unification. Homogeneity through heterogeneity, eternal inflation, ontological failure—all of these concepts designate the same dysfunctioning structure that compels America to remain in a situation of permanent crisis. Right at the center of this structure stands the American citizen, the champion of mankind, who is wont to mistake the exceptional, manifest destiny of America for the apotheosis of man as such.

3.2.8. The difference between separatist and nationalist societies could not be greater. In a separatist society, individual happiness reigns sovereign. In America, every individual has the right to pursue happiness regardless of the happiness of others. Every American has this right, for every American is a member of society and therefore a member of mankind, of a prepolitical nonwhole. For this reason, people do not have to tell each other who gave them this right or what this right entails exactly. In a nationalist society, instead, individual happiness cannot be disjoined from national happiness, *le bonheur de tous* that is put center stage in the French Declaration of 1789 and, more generally, in all nationalist proclamations. In this case, a homogenizing equivalence is established between the society and the nation. The nation *identifies* the society by hinting—via metaphor—at the people's humanity, with the result that the society's identification is both triggered and obstructed. Hence the problem *What is our nation?* and the related question, which is more like a complaint, *Who can ever be a true citizen?* In the end, nobody can. But the point is that this question-complaint resurfaces with unfailing regularity within a national context. Here the search for the true citizen equals the search for the true nation, and neither can come to an end. In America, by contrast, a heterogenizing equivalence is established between every individual and the whole of society. America *includes* individuals by hinting—via metonymy—at the nonwhole of mankind, with the result that America, by its own nature, cannot be identified. Hence the problem *Where does our society end?* and the related question that resounds throughout American history, *How can we huddle together?*

3.3. The notion of metonymic equivalence helps us to grasp not only the nature of a separatist society but also the asymmetry between the European and the American paths to democracy. This asymmetry is still underrated by many political thinkers. According to Ernesto Laclau, for example, a democratic society revolves around metaphorical equivalences, and a political act consists in joining a number of social demands together by means of an "empty signifier" that functions as a hegemonic metaphor. For Laclau, there is no other way to "construct" a society or a people. But we do have historical evidence for the existence of societies that are centered on metonymic—not metaphorical—equivalences, and in such societies, democracy looks different from what Laclau thinks.

3.3.1. To begin with, nationalist and separatist peoples relate to the state differently. Nationalists tend to identify with the nation's "general will," which is believed to rule over the state. Therefore, by bowing to the state, they assume that they are bowing to themselves. Separatists, by contrast, strive to loosen the state's grip on society because they rule out the possibility of any political identification. They do not bow to but rather turn their back on the state. Two different types of democracy result from these opposite attitudes. Consider the mechanism of democratic representation. In Europe, national democracies are based on the assumption that all decisions made by governments and parliaments reflect the nation's "general will," which has control over the state's legislative and executive branches. Quite a huge assumption. How is it possible that people hold such a view and identify first with the nation, then with the state? A metaphor ensures that the chain of equivalences between people, the nation, and the state holds together. The "nation" names the existing nation but also hints at the true nation. For this reason, the nation's representatives—and with them the ship of the nation-state—are believed to act on behalf of a homogeneous society while ruling over a mass of heterogeneous people. Political representatives become the living metaphors of *one* people that keeps on looking for its own truth and identity.[25] In a separatist democracy, the mechanism of political representation follows a different path. In the United States, the House of Representatives and the Senate are composed of officials that represent not only *one* people but also *many* US states. As for the Senate, every US state has the right to elect two legislators, regardless of its population. As for the House of Representatives, originally meant to give voice to American "public opinion," every US state is entitled to a number of representatives proportional to its population. Federal legislation, however, must be passed by both the House and the Senate. In practical terms, this entails that the US states are given the power to defend their own interests against the Union's interests. Here, homogeneity has no axiomatic priority over heterogeneity.[26]

3.3.2. In Europe, governments, parliaments, and national institutions more generally turn into the symbols of a unified society. Unfortunately, as soon as the national metaphor comes into effect, a gap opens up between the existing nation and the true nation; and because the nation identifies with the state, there appears to be something wrong in both the existing nation and national institutions, which are therefore urged to correct their dysfunctionings. This explains in part the congenital instability and the frequent rearrangements of political institutions that punctuate the history of most European countries. In America, by contrast, society does not identify with the state, and democratic institutions are therefore more stable compared to Europe because they do nothing but extend the chain of metonymic equivalences that underpins the society's existence. The American *res publica*, as seen from below, resembles a matryoshka. Public authorities at different levels (from local to federal) coexist and express the society's allergy to a too-strong vertical integration. The common belief is that the *res publica* has no special role to play with regard to the people's pursuit of happiness. Whenever possible, public institutions should be kept at bay so that society might flourish on its own and demonstrate the unparalleled heterogeneity of its *socii*, which mirrors the heterogeneity of mankind across the world. Hence a number of watchwords that resound in American history: the melting pot; the American New Man; private is better than public; individual freedoms must be given priority over social equality, and so on. Heterogeneity impinges on all aspects of American life—and heterogeneity is sometimes conducive to segregation and discrimination. That said, authorities can do very little to repair this and other damages caused by the people's heterogeneity because institutions are not charged with the task of homogenizing the society. The *res publica* is not there to synthesize social demands and harmonize the social field from the top down. The *res publica* must simply allow the society to branch out in all directions. When it aims for a more ambitious goal, it runs the risk of abusing its power, or so Americans think.[27]

3.3.3. I will now offer some examples of metonymic equivalence. The first one is hyphenated Americanism. As Horace Kallen and Michael Walzer emphasize, it is a fact that linguistic compounds such as African-American, Italian-American, and the like are ordinary in America, whereas compounds such as African-French or Turkish-German make no sense in Europe. There is nothing we can do about this. American and European societies follow different grammars. To be an American means to be a *pars pro toto*—more precisely, a *pars* taken from a *totum* that can be totalized only through its figurative partialization. African-Americans, Italian-Americans, and all other hyphenated Americans are Americans, no doubt about that, yet none of them is totally American, not even American-Americans, as Walzer explains.[28] In other words, the whole of America has no homogeneous identity and is fragmented by definition. The *totum* of America comes into being only when this or that *pars* is subtracted from it. When two or more parts are being subtracted, a chain of metonymic equivalences between them can be established, and this chain renders them all parts of the same whole by way of separation. Thus, African-Americans, Italian-Americans, and the like do not have any identity in common, but they nonetheless share the same metonymic relationship with the whole of American society, which in turn enters into a metonymic relationship with a wider and boundless entity, the nonwhole of mankind. As Kallen points out, America is "a commonwealth of nationalities," "a democracy of nationalities," "a multiplicity in a unity, an orchestration of mankind."[29] That is to say, America has no national identity of its own. America is a *civil society* rather than a *national society*. Or, as Walzer puts it, America is "a radically unfinished society." The existence of America is contingent on this kind of structural incompleteness, which is the reverse side of the a priori disavowal of any national axiomatics. As both Kallen and Walzer argue at length, America would not be America if it could be fully Americanized. To be an American is to know this in one way or another:

> America is still a radically unfinished society, and for now, at least, it makes sense to say that this unfinishedness is one of its distinctive features. The country has a political center, but it remains in every other sense decentered. More than this, the political center, despite occasional patriotic fevers, doesn't work against decentering elsewhere. It neither requires nor demands the kind of commitment that would put the legitimacy of ethnic or religious identification in doubt. It doesn't aim at a finished or fully coherent Americanism. Indeed, American politics, itself pluralist in character, *needs* a certain sort of incoherence. A radical program of Americanization would *really* be un-American. It isn't inconceivable that America will one day become an American nation-state, the many giving way to the one, but that is not what it is now; nor is that its destiny. America has no singular national destiny—and to be an "American" is, finally, to know that and to be more or less content with it.[30]

3.3.4. Let us now turn to the movements for civil rights of the 1950s and 1960s. It is a fact that those struggles represented a turning point in American history, and what is most striking about civil rights movements is that they spread all over the country more or less simultaneously, thereby reinforcing each other despite the diversity of motivations and targets. It was like an epidemic. People from various backgrounds— Blacks, Chicanos, women, homosexuals—rose up against discrimination and called for the banning of laws that restricted their freedoms. During the campaign, no movement conquered hegemony over the others. None of them even sought to do so. The rallying cry was liberation, but nobody cherished the dream of achieving national happiness. The idea was far more prosaic. The idea was that each and every individual has the right to pursue happiness without being refused such a possibility because of racial or sexual *difference*. In short, civil rights movements were waving the flag of social heterogeneity, not of social homogeneity. The US states (in particular the southern states that were heavily infringing on African-Americans' rights) and federal authorities (feminists were protesting against the Fair Labor Standards Act of 1938) were summoned to step back and stop intruding into the life of society. Thus, for the nth time in history, American society was asserting the people's independence and distance from the *res publica*. Protesters did not make a plea for the nation's unity (like the British suffragettes had done a few decades earlier, after espousing the cause of nationalism), nor did they have a political agenda in common. In the end, civil rights movements found themselves aligned with each other along the same political frontier not by virtue of a shared discourse (in Laclau's sense of the word) but by virtue of a shared grammar (in Lacan's sense of the word). Every movement was giving voice to a *pars pro toto* of American society, and all of them ended up forming a chain of metonymic equivalences, without identifying with each other. Thanks to this chain of equivalences, civil rights movements gained impetus and were able to exert more pressure on American public opinion. The Civil Rights Act of 1964 certified that protest movements had formed such a chain by repealing discrimination based on race, sex, and national origins *all at the same time*. As John F. Kennedy, Martin Luther King Jr., and others declared, this decision was perfectly in line with the deep inclination of American society. The Civil Rights Act had further inflated America:

> When the architects of our republic wrote the magnificent words of the Constitution and the Declaration of Independence, they were signing a promissory note to which every American was to fall heir. This note was a promise that all men, yes, black men as well as white men, would be guaranteed the "unalienable Rights" of "Life, Liberty and the pursuit of Happiness." It is obvious today that America has defaulted on this promissory note, insofar as her citizens of color are concerned. . . .
>
> . . . Now is the time to make real the promises of democracy.[31]

3.3.5. The so-called American dream is one more piece of evidence that metonymic equivalences play a key role in American society. As Kallen notes, the American commonwealth does not find its raison d'être in a national, ethnic, linguistic, cultural, or religious identity. If anything, "the common life of the commonwealth is politico-economic."[32] The American dream is first and foremost a dream of prosperity and economic success that every individual has the right to achieve, no matter how. Such is the meaning of happiness in America. For most people in this country, happiness means wealth, and business matters more than anything else. But the interesting thing is that Americans take it for granted that this holds true not only at home but also abroad— not only for America but also for mankind. For Americans, people all over the world have the right to pursue happiness *on their own* and improve their standard of living *individually*, with little or no regard for others. For this reason, all countries in the world should praise and facilitate the people's quest for prosperity and wealth—namely, free trade and free enterprise. Needless to say, such a heavy emphasis on private economic undertakings happens to disturb other—more traditional, or less liberal—peoples. Nonetheless, Americans do not care. Why so? First of all, because economic achievements are more than that in their eyes. As a matter of fact, Americans regard them as democratic achievements, by means of which the right to pursue happiness is restated by people on a daily basis. For Americans, moreover, these achievements benefit everybody, not only Americans. To give an example: Americans do not necessarily speak in bad faith when they say that they are exporting democracy while exporting their business. Most of them do not see any inconvenience in doing this because business and democracy largely coincide for them, and what is good for the American economy is deemed good for democracy across the world. Once more, a chain of metonymic equivalences underpins this unconscious assumption. In America, every individual is a *pars pro toto* and stands in for the whole of society, since both the individual and the society are part of a broader nonwhole, mankind, that renders them equivalent metonyms. Two consequences follow from this. First, each step toward happiness taken by an American can be understood as a step toward happiness taken by American society as a whole: this is what turns the American dream into a social bond, and this is how Americans are formally—not materially—*equalized*. Second, each step toward happiness taken by an American can be understood as a step toward happiness taken by mankind in general: this is what the chain of metonymic equivalences pointing to mankind implies, and this is how American democracy is figuratively—not literally—*universalized*. Thus, from an American perspective, it is mankind that inflates, moving closer and closer to happiness, every time that America inflates. Any economic-and-democratic benefit for Americans, whether at home or abroad, appears as an economic-and-democratic benefit for mankind at large. On the back stage of American subjectivity, the two points of view cannot be disentangled from each other. What is beneficial to America is beneficial to the entire world.

In Europe, of course, America's ambition to speak on behalf of mankind arouses suspicion. Carl Schmitt's response, "Wer Menschheit sagt, will betrügen,"[33] typifies Europe's propensity to doubt America's special relationship to mankind, that is a *fil rouge* of American rhetoric from Thomas Jefferson to Woodrow Wilson and beyond. In addition to this, following Karl Polanyi's lead, many Europeans may object that the right to "the pursuit of happiness" is nothing more than a trick invented by the best-off of the thirteen colonies with the purpose of protecting themselves from the worst-off's reprobation. Yet this and other biased objections are misplaced, for the United States is the place where, pace Polanyi, happiness concerns individuals, not the collectivity; and in a place like this, pace Schmitt, every individual is a human being, a *pars pro toto* of mankind, before anything else. The state, for its part, has to make sure that people find their own way to happiness and that they go their *separate* ways: "The American Constitution, shaped in a farmer-craftsman's environment by a leadership forewarned by the English industrial scene, isolated the economic sphere entirely from the jurisdiction of the Constitution, put private property thereby under the highest conceivable protection, and created the only legally grounded market society in the world. In spite of universal suffrage, American voters were powerless against owners."[34]

7

From Democracy
to Fascism

1. In previous chapters, I have described the two main entrances to modern democracy: the axiomatic and the demonstrative. Now I will focus on two fake entrances that I gather under the same label: *fascism*. As I will argue, fascism never aims for the end of democracy; rather, fascism attempts to stabilize modern democracy, which is unstable in and of itself. As I have explained, national (axiomatic) democracy is unstable because of its ineffectual repression (*Verdrängung*) of heterogeneity. Here, the "nation" establishes the people's homogeneity by way of metaphor, thereby creating a distance between the existing nation and the true nation. On the one side, the existing nation appears as a place where heterogeneous expectations and demands are shaped into the rights of the citizen. On the other side, those rights are also taken for the rights of man, which represent the homogeneous features and properties of all human beings who are considered members of a true nation. But the point is that the identity between the rights of the citizen and the rights of man remains open to interpretation because it results from a merely figurative, *metaphorical* overlapping between the nation and humanity. This is why humanity keeps on troubling the nation: humanity should eradicate

heterogeneity, but humanity and the nation do not coincide literally. Separatist (demonstrative) democracy, instead, is unstable because of its ineffectual denial (*Verleugnung*) of homogeneity. Here, all demonstrations of the people's heterogeneity lead to some sort of hidden homogenization that turns *many* individuals into *one* people. Homogeneity should be dispelled by the people's diversity, which is believed to reflect mankind's heterogeneity. But the fact is that the mirror-like relationship between the people's diversity and mankind's heterogeneity lends itself to a variety of interpretations because it is of a purely figurative, *metonymic* nature. This is why mankind disconcerts and bewilders: mankind should eliminate the risk of homogeneity, but mankind and *one* people do not coincide literally.

1.1. In sum, both humanity and mankind are signs of democracy's failures. In fact, neither type of democracy is able to fulfill its promise, which is the true homogenization of society in one case and the complete heterogenization of society in the other. Whatever the case, there appears a remainder that prevents democracy from reaching its ultimate goal. In the first case, there arises a metaphorical remainder marked by a plus, because humanity exceeds and beclouds the meaning of the "nation." In the second case, there arises a metonymic remainder marked by a minus, because *one* people is nothing but a part of mankind. Having said this, I think it is equally important to stress that modern democracy does not cease to exist because of its failures. On the contrary, if democracy remains alive and kicking, this is precisely because it never manages to fill the gaps between what it tacitly promises and what it actually achieves. In other words, modern democracy is characterized by an intrinsic dysfunctioning that nevertheless drives things—namely, democratization—forward. By contrast, when this dysfunctioning comes to nothing, democracy becomes corrupted and dies. What seems to be the true or the complete achievement of the democratic promise immediately turns into a sheer simulacrum of democracy. I define this simulacrum as *pseudo-democracy*, or fascism.

2. Before tackling the issue of fascism, we need to further scrutinize some characteristics of modern democracy. Adopting a more conventional approach to political matters, we may say that modern democracy is based on a two-pillar principle: on the one side individual

rights, on the other popular sovereignty. For modern democracy to be possible at all, both pillars are required.[1] Yet two different kinds of democracy can be established on these bases, depending on which of the two pillars is privileged. One type of democracy emphasizes popular sovereignty, the other individual rights. One aims at increasing political homogeneity, the other at increasing social heterogeneity. The preeminence of one pillar never entails the collapse of the other. In national democracies, where political homogeneity and the principle of popular sovereignty are favored, social heterogeneity and the principle of individual rights are not banished but rather contribute to keeping the nation alive. Indeed, the rights of the citizen, expressing the heterogeneous expectations of nationals, and the rights of man, expressing the homogeneous features of human beings, cannot be identified with each other once and for all. If anything, the latter *tend* to be identified with the former through a process of gradual recognition and endless emancipation that gives expression to the nation's "general will." Within the context of a separatist democracy, this kind of national identification is overtly questioned, but the principle of popular sovereignty remains nonetheless vital. The only difference is that popular sovereignty does not bring to light the political homogeneity of society here; rather, popular sovereignty serves to confirm and reinforce social heterogeneity. As a rule, people are wont to elect those candidates who can defend their own interests, or those who belong to the same social group, whereas political representatives at all levels are expected to enable people to pursue individual happiness with little or no concern for collective happiness.

2.1. An ocean divides these versions of modern democracy. On one side of the Atlantic, we find the European democracy of national sovereignty, which is based on the idea that people should identify first with the nation, then with the state, in order to achieve the dream of public autonomy and happiness. On the other side of the Atlantic, we find the American democracy of individual rights, which is based on the idea that people should be left alone, without being encumbered by too many restrictions that may impede the pursuit of private autonomy and happiness.[2] These two options offer opposite interpretations of the same two-pillar principle—individual rights, collective sovereignty—but neither, while privileging one pillar, entails the elimination of the other. Rather, both of them can be seen as inconclusive compromises between the two basic precepts of Western democracy. In the course of modern history, such compromises found expression in different constitutional charters. That said, all compromises and constitutions, as different as they may be, remain similar in many respects. Parties and parliaments, for example, are essential to democracy on both sides of the Atlantic.

3. In modern democracies, parties play a key role because they are charged with the task of perfecting the inconclusive compromise on which the coexistence of the state and the society is based. Parties are urged to make this compromise less inconclusive and to correct the intrinsic dysfunctioning of democracy through adequate legislative measures or, if necessary, through constitutional reforms. For this purpose, it is not always mandatory that parties comply with the grammar that laid the groundwork for the democratic constitution of the state in which they find themselves operating. Such a grammatical restriction applies to America but not to Europe. In America, there can be no alternative to the grammar that crystallized during the War of Independence because this kind of grammar rules out the very possibility of any axiomatic homogenization of society, which represents the democratic alternative to the demonstrative heterogenization of society. In Europe, by contrast, even though the nation-state is nationalist in origin, not all parties are nationalist because a political axiomatics such as nationalism can be challenged by alternative axiomatics such as socialism or even by the demonstrative questioning of all axiomatic authorities.

3.1. Once more, the asymmetry between Europe and America deserves closer inspection. In European democracies, social heterogeneity is repressed but not abolished, because it remains hidden behind any axiomatics. The political homogeneity of the people imposed by the national metaphor remains a sheer postulate, for the distance between man and the citizen cannot be bridged once and for all. Thus, the process of homogenization must be restarted over and over again. Whenever the national metaphor reveals its own limits and deflates, humanity must be reanimated. But, at that point, it is possible to reactivate a metaphor of humanity not only by renewing the nationalist axiomatics, as often happens, but also by means of a new axiomatics such as socialism; in this case, it is no longer the "nation" but rather the "society" that emerges as a metaphor pointing to the people's humanity. Or else, it is possible to opt for a political grammar such as liberalism, which seems to follow a demonstrative path to subjectification.[3] In America, instead, where the metaphorical homogenization of society is a priori excluded, the range of possibilities is narrower. Here, no axiomatics can catch on. Political debates are by no means less lively, but they promote systematically the metonymic heterogenization and eternal inflation of society.

3.2. Consider, for instance, definitions such as Left-Right or conservative-progressive. In Europe they make sense, less so in America. In Europe, the Left is represented by socialist parties, the Right by nationalist parties. Socialists fight against nationalists by contrasting one hegemonic metaphor—the "society"—with another—the "nation." Nationalist parties are conservative in that they hold firm on the original axiomatization of society; progressives are socialist parties that propose a *new* axiomatics or liberal parties that endeavor to introduce a *new* demonstrative grammar in Europe.[4] But what if we apply the Left-Right and the conservative-progressive antinomies to America? Are these categories still meaningful? In many respects, they are not. The American People's Party, for example, and all antielitist movements that every now and then become widespread in America are neither left-wing nor right-wing, neither conservative nor progressive. Furthermore, these categories do not reflect the actual composition of more traditional parties. The Democrats, for example, are divided into five factions today: liberals, libertarians, centrists, *progressives*, and *conservatives*. Significantly, there is no trace of *socialist* factions.[5] Similarly, no faction in the Grand Old Party is called *nationalist*.

3.3. To complicate matters further, Europe and America do not inhabit the same political spacetime. In Europe, space and time are fractured by grammatical *discontinuities*. In America, they are marked by a substantial *continuity*. The concept of political grammar enables us to highlight and explain this difference. First, it is important to note that there is, indeed, a difference. Think about constitutional history. Since 1787, the US Constitution has never been replaced with a new one. In France, by contrast, the Fifth Constitution and the Fifth Republic are now in place. Or think of the founding fathers. To this day, these quasi-mythical figures inspire and galvanize the American epic—slavery and racism notwithstanding. In France, nobody looks back on the glorious events of 1789. I am not the first to draw attention to these (and other) discrepancies.[6] But what are the reasons behind them?

3.3.1. From a grammatical point of view, America's continuity is due to the metonymic structure of American society, whereas Europe's discontinuities are due to the metaphorical nature of European nations. The key to understanding American society is the *pars pro toto* relationship. One individual can stand in for the other because the two of them are part of the same whole, American society, and both the parts and the whole are extracted from a wider nonwhole—that is, mankind. In this way, all individuals are equalized with each other, and each of them is equalized with the whole of society. A particular kind of anaclitic relationship is established: each individual clings to society, but all individuals and the whole of society, in their turn, cling to the nonwhole of mankind. Thus, a boundless chain of metonymic equivalences keeps "the people" together, and this chain is characterized by a certain redundancy. All metonymic equivalences relate to each other, as all of them appear as *paraphrastic repetitions* of the same lack of identity. In other words, one metonym becomes the figurative illustration of the other, because all of them point in the same direction. What is American society? If you look at Americans, you will find not just one but countless answers, since America is the realm of the infinite paraphrase. One metonym after the other, America grows and inflates without interruption, always revolving around the same hole that renders its spacetime continuous in spite of increasing diversification. As previously clarified, this hole is the nonwhole of mankind that exceeds and decompletes American society, thereby making room for one more link in the chain. A never-ending sequence of metonymic equivalences follows, all of which repeat one another. In the final analysis, America is the name for this inflationary continuity, which is deprived of identity, for it never comes to an end. The meaning of America is inexhaustible.

3.3.2. Europe is the place where meaning is not inexhaustible but rather beclouded. National societies are the product of metaphors, not of metonymies, and metaphors do not yield to paraphrase. Take the metaphor "love is war." Here, the word *war* has a meaning of its own but simultaneously acquires a new sense from its combination with the word *love* (as Burke says, we see love from the perspective of war). Thus, the meanings of both *war* and *love* are occluded. If it were possible to paraphrase expressions like this, poetry would not exist. By way of metaphor, Lacan avers, "sense is produced in non-sense."[7] Now take the statement "Otto Bismarck belongs to the German nation." Literally, this sentence means that Otto is a German citizen; however, if we read a metaphor into it, this sentence implies not only that Otto is a German citizen (literal meaning) but also that he is endowed with some human properties (metaphorical sense). Nobody can tell what this entails exactly, because nobody can paraphrase the idea of humanity conveyed by the national metaphor. Not even the words *blood*, *ancestors*, *language*, and the like can disclose the secret of the German nation. If anything, all of these words represent as many *antiphrastic repetitions* of the same lack of identity. This amounts to saying that each of them regularly fails to unveil the truth of the nation and makes the latter collapse. In the end, the nation can only fail to be true to its own blood, because this blood is always the blood of the existing nation, not the blood of the true nation. Hence Otto's restless complaint and reiterated appeal, "Germans, think with your blood!" He could have cried, "Germans, think with your ancestors!" or "Germans, think with your language!," and nothing would have changed, for all antiphrastic repetitions of the national metaphor consolidate the chain of metaphorical equivalences that make it deflate. They simply put the nation's disruption into words.

3.3.3. Let us return to America's continuous spacetime. As regards space, it is continuous for reasons that should be clear by now. Briefly put, within the framework of a demonstrative grammar, any *pars pro toto* relationship with the whole of society is taken, unconsciously, for a *pars pro toto* relationship with the nonwhole of mankind. Therefore, by clinging to American society, every individual clings to, and stands for, a larger and unbounded society, which is the unfathomable society of all people on Earth. This explains, among other things, America's irrepressible tendency to conflate its own interests with the interests of mankind in general, as well as the latent indistinction between territorial and extraterritorial sovereignty. As regards time, Lacan made a curious remark about the "pure past" he encountered during a trip to America, "a past that is all the more essential in that it never existed."[8] In saying this, Lacan did not want us to conclude that America has no past at all. Rather, he was emphasizing that American history seems to be frozen. In some sense, it is as though the present is already written in the past. More precisely, it is as though the present paraphrases the past. Consider the US Constitution. The letter has remained largely unaltered for more than two centuries, while the spirit is subject to endless rephrasing. What is more, at every turning point in history, America moves back to its birth and beginnings, which is why figures like the founding fathers continue to be praised and regarded as the closest interpreters of America's "manifest destiny" and "great experiment of liberty."[9] In sum, America lives in the present continuous.

3.3.4. Again, the distance between America and Europe could not be greater. Today, nobody in Paris or Berlin recalls the good deeds of Lafayette or Bismarck for the simple reason that these names belong to the past, and the past is neatly divided from the present. That is to say, time is fractured, and history is *discontinuous* in Europe. Indeed, when the nation deflates under the burden of its untenable promise of happiness, it does not vanish into thin air. To the contrary, it is at that moment when nationalism is likely to grow stronger. As I have noted, failure is the lifeblood of the nation. But national failures and collapses nonetheless entail that people take some distance from the past and start over. Whenever the nation breaks its promise, the national metaphor must be processed into a refreshed axiomatics. The myth of "rebirth" is a crucial ingredient of nationalism. Moreover, owing to this constitutive instability and structural discontinuity, people can also change direction from time to time and turn to a new axiomatics, such as socialism, or an altogether different grammar (embodied by liberal parties and, at a later stage, fascist parties). As a result, the fabric of history is torn apart. In Europe, time is always out of joint, for the present and the past are deeply at odds. The present is antiphrastic and upends all attempts to grasp the "eternal truth" of the national metaphor. Consequently, the problem in Europe is not *How shall we become ourselves?*, as is the case in America, but rather *What does it mean that we are ourselves?* And this question shapes European history into a sequence of implosions. Europe is the land of a deflating present.

3.3.5. To recapitulate: different grammars demarcate different space-times. In America, spacetime is molded into a continuous diastole that calls society into being while leaving it unfinished; in Europe, spacetime is fissured by discontinuous syncopes that call society into being while bringing it crashing down. Paraphrasis and metonymy dominate in the former context, antiphrasis and metaphor in the latter. Whatever the case, society suffers from an intrinsic ontological dysfunctioning. In America, such a congenital dysfunctioning affects the domain of reference of the political *nos*; in Europe, it affects the sense of identity of the political *nos*.

4. Nationalist deflation and separatist inflation of society breathe life into democracy. On both sides of the Atlantic, modern democracy takes the form of an *inconclusive* compromise between opposite requirements. Homogeneity versus heterogeneity, popular sovereignty versus individual rights: whichever requirement happens to be privileged, democracy is kept alive by its own failure to achieve the dream of happiness. Accordingly, happiness—and with it, democracy—turns into nothing more than a promise. But what if someone objected that happiness can be achieved instead? What if someone proclaimed that democracy can be more *conclusive* and that all tensions between homogeneity and heterogeneity, popular sovereignty and individual rights, can be overcome? This objection is what I call fascism. As we will see, there are two ways to raise and express the fascist objection to modern democracy. One consists in turning the national metaphor into a *delusional metaphor*, the other in turning the chain of metonymic equivalences into a web of *delusional metonymies*. I define the first option as old fascism and the second one as new fascism.

4.1. Fascism is often understood as being the antithesis of democracy. But the fact is that fascism is not antidemocratic. If anything, fascism is pseudo-democratic. In fact, fascism does not take a stand against democracy, as such, but only against liberal democracy. As a general rule, fascism presents itself as the most refined form of democracy and as a way to overcome all democratic crises and dysfunctionings of the past—for instance, those crises that affected many European societies a century ago, when fascist movements began to rear their heads on the Continent. Fascism is therefore a highly ambiguous historical event. As evidence thereof, fascist regimes are usually recognized for what they really are—distortions of democracy—only when they are observed from the outside: from abroad, in some cases, or else when they are over. This is the reason why it seems legitimate to ask ourselves at any moment: do we live in a fascist regime? Today, as ever, the answer is not obvious.

4.2. Since modern democracy is based on a faulty and temporary compromise between contrasting requirements, the solution to democracy's failures is to abolish that compromise in one way or another. Hence the two versions of fascism. One consists in absolutizing popular sovereignty at the expense of individual rights. The other consists in absolutizing individual rights to the detriment of popular sovereignty. The two options represent opposite exits from democracy, but both can be labeled fascist because they entail a deceptive fulfillment of the democratic promise. In the former case, the maximization of popular sovereignty should allow people to attain the goal of collective autonomy and happiness. In the latter case, the maximization of individual rights should allow people to attain the goal of individual autonomy and happiness. The first possibility has already been explored in the past. The second possibility is becoming a reality these days. Let us begin with the past.

5. Authoritative scholars have characterized fascist movements and regimes in terms of ultranationalism.[10] But, assuming that we see fascism as an outburst of "extreme nationalism," as many students of fascism suggest, the question remains as to what makes nationalism so extreme as to transform it into ultranationalism. From a grammatical point of view, this question does not just concern the historical factors that prepared the ground for the birth of fascism in Europe during the 1920s and 1930s. Of course, those factors must be taken into serious consideration. When it comes to Nazism, for example, it is well known that Germany's socioeconomic conditions after World War I were the main cause of Hitler's rise to power. At the time, Germany found itself in a situation of unprecedented despair, and the people's will to revenge

could only grow stronger, as often happens when a nation collapses. But on that occasion something went wrong, or at least something changed compared to the past. All of a sudden, nationalism gave way to ultranationalism. And therein lies the rub. What is the difference between nationalism and ultranationalism, or fascism? Is it only a matter of intensity, of greater or lesser fanaticism? Or does something else hide behind such political developments? Is the "master race" nothing more than a zealous and particularly aggressive version of the "nation"?[11] Or is it a brand-new political subject, grounded in a different political grammar?

5.1. "We are the master race." The subject of this declaration is no longer a nationalist subject, for this declaration does not promise but rather *reveals* humanity—or so the Nazis believed. The collapse of the German nation after World War I had been too heavy a trauma for Germans, who now found it difficult, if not impossible, to trust the promise of a future reconciliation between *das Volk* and happiness. Bare promises such as those made on behalf of the nation could no longer reassure them. What they were ready and willing to welcome at that moment was a word of revelation that might immediately close the gap between them and happiness, the national society and humanity. That word was uttered by the Nazis, and it was a word that replaced promises with orders. It was then that the national metaphor was transfigured into a delusional metaphor, and nationalism morphed into ultranationalist fascism. The Nazi idea was that the gap between the existing nation and the true nation could be closed without waiting too long by unveiling and detailing the literal truth about humanity as such. According to the Nazis, this truth was hidden in the German *Volk* since time immemorial and just needed to be spelled out. Notoriously, this truth had a name: the "master race," the Aryans.

5.2. The metamorphosis of a national metaphor into a delusional metaphor involves transforming old political statements about the true nation to come into statements that reveal the truth once and for all. Axiomatic statements such as nationalist proclamations, while complaining about the divide between the true nation and the existing nation, always reaffirm that the "nation" will keep its promise: humanity and *le bonheur de tous* will be achieved one day. Nationalist subjects confine themselves to proclaiming and promising that this will happen sooner or later. Thus, a nationalist axiomatics establishes a homogeneous society under the assumption of an abiding discrepancy between the existing nation and the true nation. The bridge between the two sides of the political *nos* is of a metaphorical nature here and remains open to interpretation. Every new interpretation corresponds to a new nationalist proclamation, which is going to be supplanted with another proclamation and yet another, day after day. But suppose, now, that the gap between the existing nation and the true nation has been closed all of a sudden. If that is the case, nationalist proclamations must give way to the revelation of truth, of humanity, and the national metaphor cannot but change into something else.

5.3. This is how the new delusional metaphor, the "master race," emerged. It remains to be seen why this phrase can be defined as a metaphor and why this metaphor can be defined as a delusional construct. To clarify the first point, we need to go over the notion of humanity. As I have already explained, humanity does not exist, properly speaking, and the same holds for the nation. Humanity is assumed to be the essence of the nation, the essence that allows (or should allow) the nation to be true to itself. In short, humanity is a dream, a desire, that arises within the framework of axiomatic political grammars. For humanity to be possible at all, a metaphor must come into effect. This is why Nazism remained so close to nationalism. Indeed, both the "master race" and the "nation" function as metaphors of humanity in the first instance. That said, they do not function in the same way. The "master race" was considered more than a metaphor, for it no longer hinted at some ineffable humanity, as the old "nation" did. Rather, it announced that the nation and humanity had found a way to identify with each other—literally, not metaphorically.

5.4. The "master race" is a linguistic construct with special characteristics. No doubt this metaphor was conceived as a way to bypass all failures and antiphrastic effects of the old "nation." Thus, it was meant to *undo* the old national metaphor and all peripheral metaphors related to it. At the same time, however, the new metaphor was meant to *preserve*, not to cancel, those old metaphors, as it was deemed to achieve the same promise made by the nation. When Hitler took power,

Germany's dreams and desires were the same as before—humanity, happiness. Hence the problem that the Nazis encountered: how to undo *and* preserve the national metaphor? How to do away with and yet stay attuned to the needs of the old "nation"? Before going into further detail, I want to underscore that this sleight of hand is exactly what people were craving when fascist parties began to gain support not only in Germany but all over Europe. For most people, fascist slogans were a welcome solution to the problem, and lasting crisis, of the European "nation." Year after year, war after war, nationalist grammars had been shaken to their foundations, losing their grip on the majority of citizens, until the day came when things reached a breaking point. First in Italy, then in Germany, people became enthusiastic about a radical change in their ordinary ontology. Science and philosophy of the time were ready to throw them a bone, Life. By following that bone, people lost contact with reality, and in a matter of years, ultranationalism grew up to become a biopolitical tragedy.

5.5. The attack on individual and minority rights is a typical trait of old fascism. From a grammatical point of view, there is a plain explanation for this. In national democracies, the nation is a metaphor of humanity. This entails that perfect homogeneity among people is never attained. The heterogeneous expectations and demands of individuals, those that find expression in the rights of the citizen, are taken for the homogeneous features and properties of human beings, those that find expression in the rights of man. The two types of rights are closely intertwined. Yet the intertwining remains ambiguous and open to interpretation, which is why democracy keeps on perfecting itself. With fascism, the picture changes. When the nation is no longer a sheer metaphor but becomes a literal materialization of humanity, the "master race," then perfect homogeneity among people can be reached. At that point, the rights of man can be identified, literally, with the rights of the citizen, and no further compromise need be negotiated. Nobody is entitled to claim new rights anymore. No individual or minority right can be invoked and turned against the *Volk*'s "general will." But the question continues to resound: how to change a metaphor (the nation) into something more than a metaphor (the master race)? How to elevate the former to the rank of a literal revelation of humanity?

5.6. The "master race" was two things at once: a metaphor and a literal expression. To make this miracle happen, the Nazis mobilized science, in particular the life sciences. The starting point of their lucubrations was, What does it mean to be a human being? If we conceive of humanity not as a promise but as something that we can bring to life here and now, we need to provide not only metaphors but also clean and clear statements about the true, literal meaning of humanity. For the Nazis, the secret of humanity read as follows: to be a human being means to be alive. The more alive people are, the more human they are. And the slogan "we are the master race" obviously implied that the Germans were the true children of Life, those who embodied humanity as such and were destined to outcompete all other *Rassen*. The importance of this biologistic jargon cannot be overstated. The notion of Life was the key to the transforming of the "nation" into a delusional metaphor, the "master race." And Life was both a political metaphor and a scientific concept. In other words, Life itself functioned as a delusional metaphor, or a literalized metaphor. On the one hand, Life was seen as the subject matter of scientific analyses that were to be taken literally. On the other hand, Life was seen as the subject matter of political pronouncements that could only be taken figuratively.[12] But the fact is that the Nazis made no distinction between the two regimes of enunciation.[13] The two types of expression—literal and figurative—were totally conflated, with the result that a kind of *newspeak* developed, as George Orwell would have it. Exploiting the resources of this neolanguage, the Nazis found the means to imagine that the "master race" was both the evolutionary apex of Life and the predestined winner of modern political conflicts.

6. The Nazi newspeak was framed by a new political grammar, a *revelatory grammar*, characterized by a self-contradictory logic. Let us return to the delusional metaphor. This metaphor is deeply delusional because it conveys a metaphorical sense but simultaneously seeks to erase it. The delusional metaphor aims for a literal meaning, so much so that it compels those who adopt it to take a self-indicting stance toward their own words. All political-scientific formulas invented by the Nazis bear witness to this kind of impediment. *On the one hand*, the "master race" functioned as a metaphor of Life because it was Life, and nothing else, that was meant to ensure the perfect homogeneity of

the German *Volk*. The "master race" was allegedly composed of people who shared the greatest power of Life. All of them were "worthy of living," "worthy of Life." Life, in its turn, was but a metaphor of being. In the Nazi neolanguage, all that lives *is*, and all that is *lives*. Such is the ontological supposition—the subject-supposition—that gave birth to Nazi Germany. Those who had the greatest power to *live* were the same who had the greatest power to *be*—namely, the "master race." But, *on the other hand*, although the Nazi newspeak was imbued with these and similar metaphors, the Nazis rejected them all, striving to change them into literal expressions, as though these metaphors could be traced back to scientific phrases and concepts to be tested through appropriate experiments. Hence the insane political-scientific semantics of the Nazi newspeak, filled with *hapax legomena* and magic spells produced by a delusional fluctuation between political watchwords and biological notions. *Rassenkampf, Lebensraum, Blutschande, Untermensch*—it is impossible to draw a line between politics and science here. For the Nazis, there was no difference between political metaphors and biological concepts. Yet there was order amid this chaos—a particular type of order that Lacan's theory of paranoia helps us to discern.

6.1. As Lacan explains, a delusional metaphor was critical to Daniel Paul Schreber's paranoia,[14] and in that case, too, it is as though language spoke against itself. Schreber's delusional metaphor, "God is a whore," stood at the center of a *Grundsprache*, a basic or fundamental language, which Schreber saw as a means to express the literal meaning of this theophanic epiphany. Through an impressive sequence of linguistic exploits, he sought to turn this metaphor into a nonfigurative Revelation of Truth, of the hidden "Order of the World." Because of the self-contradictory logic of the delusional metaphor, however, Schreber's attempts failed miserably, one after the other, letting an altogether different truth cross his mind. In reality, he had been the victim of "soul murder"; he had been dead since the very beginning of his delusional wordings. This is the Revelation that Schreber attained while struggling with his own words. "What is at issue is nothing less than a case of soul murder."[15] Elias Canetti was the first to see some affinities between Schreber's theopolitical delusion and the Nazi biopolitical aberration. In Canetti's view, something terrible, an unsurpassable trauma, lies at the origins of both psychotic outbreaks: in one case the murder of a soul, in the other the murder of a nation. Germany had not been allowed to recover from the consequences of the Great War. The nation could not survive defeat and failure this time:

> All the important slogans of National Socialism—"The Third Reich," the "Sieg-heil," etc.—derive directly from the words "The Diktat of Versailles." The whole content of the movement is concentrated in them: the defeat to be turned into victory; the prohibited army to be re-created for this purpose. . . .
>
> . . . The world is still horrified and shaken by the fact that the Germans could go so far; that they either participated in a crime of such magnitude, or connived at it, or ignored it. It might not have been possible to get them to do so if, a few years before, they had not been through an inflation during which the Mark fell to a billionth of its former value.[16]

6.2. Drawing on the similarities between Nazism and Schreber's paranoia, we can see some features of totalitarianism. What is *totalitarian* in a totalitarian regime is, first and foremost, language. A totalitarian newspeak is believed to be true and complete; everything can be said and known through that language, with no ambiguity—or so fascists think. Thus, a totalitarian newspeak challenges the limits ordinarily imposed by a political grammar, which normally restricts the range of the subject's symbolic capabilities and delimits the space of representation. A totalitarian newspeak has no limit and knows no restrictions. Viewed in this light, a totalitarian grammar is a grammar that denies being a grammar. For the Nazis, this entailed that the secret of humanity could be brought to light, without uncertainty. For them, humanity did not exceed the literal meaning of the existing nation given that the true nation was no longer a promise. Therefore, the present of the *Volk* and the presence of humanity could now overlap perfectly because they were both placed in the *plenitudo temporis* of a political Revelation, of an absolute Truth, represented by the "master race." As was the case with Schreber, however, this thought was doomed to expose the German *Volk* to an altogether different truth, which eventually shone in the sky above Germany. The "master race" was a metaphor before anything else, and it remained a metaphor despite all efforts to render it into a nonfigurative newspeak. No scientific concept, biological statement, or medical statistics could spell out, literally, the political Truth of the "master race." How to prove beyond any reasonable doubt that the Aryan race was truly the superior and dominant *Rasse*? On the basis of what scientific evidence could anyone draw this conclusion? Given the Darwinian credo of most scientists and the Nazi nomenklatura's commitment to the theory of natural selection, it was decided that the answer had to be found in "struggle for existence"—that is, war. And when the war came, so, too, did the verdict. In Berlin, anno domini 1945, after all hope of victory had vanished, Hitler condemned the Aryan race, including its youngest offshoots, to extinction. The "master race" had finally embraced its destiny and discovered the Truth: the subject that rejects all ontological failures, the subject that strives to get rid of all human ambiguities, is the subject that cannot be at all.

6.3. The Nazi Party was the representative political body of the master race. As such, it became the effigy of a truly human and totally homogeneous society—the racial society, the Aryan Germany. On behalf of that society, and with the people's support, the Nazi Party won the elections in 1933. Yet Nazi politicians were not merely the representatives of the German people, for the Nazi Party was more than a metaphorical representation of German society. The Nazi Party literally incarnated that society. The Nazi Party was deemed to *be* Germany, a new Germany, when it rose to power. For this reason, it could take full control of the German state and outlaw all political opponents; and for this reason, most people in Germany did not see any inconvenience in this blatant act of aggression. To clarify this matter further, think of Arno Breker's sculpture *Die Partei* (*The Party*), flanking one of the entrances to the Reich Chancellery from 1939 to 1945. This portrait of a naked young man holding a burning torch in his right hand was both a metaphorical illustration and a physical literalization of the Aryan society. On the one hand, *Die Partei* was a figurative representation of the race that expressed the Truth of Life. On the other hand, this sculpture was more than an artistic figuration in the eyes of the Nazis because it literalized the Aryan type and materialized the Aryan Man, whose traits were being detailed by Aryan scientists over the same years. Thus, *Die Partei* was, to all intents and purposes, a delusional metaphor, and it was no accident that Breker's sculpture had been installed right in front of the new Reich Chancellery. Indeed, the Nazi Party had knocked on the door of the German state under the aegis of the master race, and *Die Partei* was there to attest that the master race was not a vague promise but a high and mighty reality. Those who did not recognize themselves in *Die Partei* could only fall out with the whole of Aryan society. Those who were not affiliated with the Nazi Party were doomed to be banned from Germany sooner or later. Through *Die Partei*, the new racial society had completely identified with the German Reich, and all tensions between the people and the state, those tensions that had enlivened and burdened modern democracy over the centuries, were bound to disappear. Unsurprisingly, however, there was a downside to this version of the social compact. Aryan society could identify with the German state without room for discussion, without any further gush of social heterogeneity, only because social heterogeneity was now radically, madly, rejected. Adopting Lacan's terminology, we may speak of an act of *Verwerfung*. The German word *Verwerfung* has several meanings: rejection, foreclosure, and anathema. All of them are relevant to the analysis of paranoid delusions.

6.4. Soon after the Nazi seizure of power, all signs of social heterogeneity became anathema to Hitler and his comrades. The Nazis believed they had closed the gap between the "nation" and humanity. The rights of the German *Volk* had become indistinguishable from the rights of humanity. Therefore, all differences between people had to vanish, allowing humanity to acquire its genuine and harmonious body, fully enlightened by the rising sun of the master race. There is no need to remind the reader that this belief caused countless atrocities. But students of National Socialism are wide of the mark when they argue that these abominable crimes are to be traced back to the Nazi "ideology" or "culture."[17] For no ideology (in the conventional sense of the word) can explain the Nazi violence, the rage and discipline with which the *Schutzstaffeln* pursued the *Endlösung*. Why such a ruthless persecution of the *héteros*? The answer is not political ideology but political ontology (that is, grammar). The problem for the Nazis was not just the fate of Jewry, Gypsies, homosexuals, or communists but the fate of their own society. The problem was that in order to *be*, Aryan society had to reach the highest possible level of social homogeneity, and for this purpose, all spots of social heterogeneity had to be erased—literally, not metaphorically. As the Nazis themselves often declared, both in public and in private, the Jews were a threat to their own *being*, to Germany's existence: "We are fighting this war today for the very existence of our *Volk*. . . . My comrades literally are fighting for the existence of our *Volk*. . . . Because this in our view is a Jewish war."[18] There was nothing emphatic or purely rhetorical in these words, however horrible they may sound today. This is exactly how the Nazis saw the Jews through the lens of their political grammar. In Nazi Germany, the extermination of the *héteros* was considered the *sine qua non* for the Revelation of the master race. The more effective and complete the extermination, the brighter the Revelation. Hence the idiotic conclusion that Germany could even win the war *through* (or with the help of) the *Endlösung*: "The Germans were to walk over the corpses of the Jews, as Hitler had always predicted. The apocalypse of the Aryans would be averted as the apocalypse of the Jews began."[19]

6.5. In Nazi Germany, the annihilation of Jewry and the annulment of minority rights went hand in hand with the alleged absolutization of popular sovereignty, which is another distinctive trait of totalitarianism. As I have noted, totalitarian regimes are not antidemocratic. They are to be seen, more properly, as pseudo-democratic. Each time, they celebrate the triumph of the people's "general will," which is ultimately the triumph of the party's will, since the totalitarian party not only represents the whole of society but also materializes it. Leni Riefenstahl's documentary film *Der Triumph des Willens* gives us a sense of what was going on in Germany during the 1930s. The triumph of the Nazi Party is depicted as the triumph of the entire Aryan society, which seems to have attained perfect homogeneity. The Nazi Party and German society do not enter into a mirror-like relationship but identify, literally, with each other. When watching this film, it is hard to tell where the Nazi nomenklatura ends and the German *Volk* begins. The party's absolute sovereignty coincides with the people's absolute sovereignty, and every threat to the Nazi leaders looks like a threat to Germany itself. It is often said that this and similar documents were the product of sheer propaganda, but this remark leaves the most pressing questions unanswered: why were Germans so susceptible to Nazi propaganda? Why did the majority of them follow the *Führer* with enthusiasm? One of the reasons, probably the most important of all, is that by following him, they had the feeling that they were following themselves, reaching themselves, achieving their true *being*, and fulfilling the democratic promise. Power had fallen back into the hands of the *demos* at last. "*Wir wollen uns selbst*" (We want ourselves), as Martin Heidegger proclaimed the day when he publicly pledged loyalty to the Nazi Party.[20] These words expressed a widespread sentiment. For Germans, the *Führerprinzip* was not a way of abdicating the people's will but a way of affirming it. With the rise of the Nazi Party, the principle of popular sovereignty had been maximized, absolutized, in the eyes of most Germans, who did not see the Nazi regime as a purely dictatorial or antidemocratic distortion of German democracy. Rather, the *Volk* saw it as a solution to democracy's impasse.

6.6. In Nazi Germany, as I have said, the maximization of the people's sovereign homogeneity was pursued at the expense of individual and minority rights. The Nazis rejected all of these rights, together with any possible sign, notice, or mere suspicion of social heterogeneity. But this act of paranoid rejection caused them to experience the flow of time in a seriously altered way. Indeed, a paranoid rejection leads the subject to take something or someone that stands before him as nonexistent. A paranoid subject affirms that something *is not* when rejecting it. The problem, however, is that for a paranoid rejection to be possible, the existence of what is to be rejected must be acknowledged at first, and only later can it be rejected. Similarly, the Nazis repelled social heterogeneity, while being forced to admit that it actually existed. This is the vicious circle in which the paranoiac is trapped, and this is why, as Lacan points out, there is a great difference between rejection (*Verwerfung*) and repression (*Verdrängung*). When the neurotic represses something, he is not rejecting anything, since repression does not involve taking anything as nonexistent. On the contrary, when the paranoiac rejects (or forecloses) something, he is excluding it from the realm of reality, yet he is restating its existence all the time. As a result, it is as though the present time splits. What is to be rejected belongs to the past by definition, but this past keeps on intruding into the present and prevents the latter from truly coinciding with itself, with the presence of the present. All the paranoiac's efforts are geared toward making the past disappear into a *now*, into a moment of Revelation that should mark the advent of Truth, of presence as such. But that moment never arrives. All that remains is a delusional anger that grows with the passing of time.

6.6.1. A paranoid rejection is always coupled to a delusional metaphor. For the Nazis, the "master race" was such a metaphor. In many respects, the "master race" was still akin to the old "nation" in that both of them hinted at humanity by way of metaphor. But the Nazis could not content themselves with that; they needed to materialize humanity. Hence their tireless attempts to make the past of the nation disappear into the present of the master race so as to open the door to the advent of an everlasting, millennial presence. As Hitler declared, "I intend to set up a thousand year Reich and anyone who supports me in battle is a fellow-fighter for a unique spiritual—I would almost say divine—creation."[21] But how to accomplish this mission and reach the moment of Revelation? The sign that the moment had arrived was easy to detect: every remnant of social heterogeneity would have disappeared. Yet the moment of Revelation took long to arrive. So Hitler and his acolytes decided to reverse the order of things, as all paranoid subjects do sooner or later. Instead of waiting for the moment of Revelation, they started to produce the signs that the moment had arrived. Merciless persecutions began, in an atmosphere of excitement and anxiety. The Nazis' ferocity was certainly due to the fact that they could not tolerate any dissonances. But the state of violent mental agitation into which they fell was due to the fact that they could not tolerate the past—a past that kept on spoiling the present of the Revelation, the present of presence as such.

6.6.2. A brief mathematical excursus can help us to discern how the Nazi unconscious was structured. It is well known that the Nazis were obsessed with numbers. They counted things and people, and they did it all the time, as though they were looking for a new number that could cipher the Revelation that they could not put into words. We may call this number aleph-o, the first transfinite number, also known as the cardinality of the natural numbers. According to Georg Cantor, aleph-o names an actual infinite set. Consider the set of all natural numbers: 1, 2, 3, 4, and so on. We know that this set is infinite but it is difficult to determine what its actual size is. Now take the subset of all odd numbers: 1, 3, 5, 7, and so on. We know that this subset, too, is infinite, but again, it is hard to tell what its actual size is. We know, however, that the size of this subset is the same as the size of the set of all natural numbers. In fact, to count all odd numbers, we should use all natural numbers. Therefore, Cantor avers, the set and the subset are equipotent. The cardinality, or size, of these two sets amounts to the same number, aleph-o. The same holds for the subset of all even numbers, whose size is the same as that of the two previous sets, aleph-o. In short, the same mathematical bridge—equipotency—connects the set of all natural numbers with the subset of all odd numbers and the subset of all even numbers. Before Cantor, mathematicians had focused mainly on potential infinite sets, which could not be counted. After Cantor, the infinite becomes actual, and it is possible to equate the set of all natural numbers with the subset of all odd numbers, as both are countably infinite. Now suppose that we define the set of all natural numbers as *humanity* and the subset of all odd numbers as the *Aryan race*. In a world that follows Cantor's laws, the set of humanity can be equated with the subset of the Aryan race.

6.6.3. That said, how can we prove that the subset of the Aryan race is actually infinite? To all appearances, human races are limited and finite. How can we equate one race with the infinite set of humanity? The Nazis found a way to deal with this problem, but we need to introduce another subset to understand their solution. Imagine that we define this further subset as the *Jewish race* and that we associate it with the subset of all even numbers. What happens to the latter subset when we make the subset of all odd numbers and the set of all natural numbers—that is, the Aryan race and humanity—converge to the point that they end up coinciding? Inevitably, the subset of all even numbers evaporates at that point. If the subset of the Aryan race is infinitized, then the subset of the Jewish race is condemned to vanish. What appears to be possible from a mathematical point of view—the coexistence of two infinite subsets within the same actual infinite set—is impossible from an ontological point of view. Ontologically, not mathematically, the two subsets are incompatible. As a result, not only does the survival of one subset turn out to be contingent on the annihilation of the other, but the extermination of one will give us the impression that the other is being infinitized. The closer the Jewish race to zero, the closer the Aryan race to aleph-0.

6.6.4. There were many problems with such a correlation. For one thing, the infinitization of the Aryan race was possible only on condition that the annihilation of the antagonist subset was infinitized as well. In other words, extermination was to be thought of as an infinite, never-ending process, and there can be little doubt that the Nazis conceived of it in this manner: the witch hunt against the Jews, the Gypsies, the mentally ill, the physically disabled, and all other manifestations of the *héteros* might have gone on *in saecula saeculorum*. But there was another side to the story, which deserves close attention. What happens to the subset of all odd numbers when the subset of all even numbers is being annihilated? Whatever our wishes may be, both subsets tend to disintegrate. In the end, the annihilation of all even numbers entails the annihilation of all odd numbers. Put slightly differently, the extinction of the Jewish race could not be dissociated from the extinction of the Aryan race. The rejection of the *héteros* implied the self-rejection of the *homós* from the outset. In reality, the German "nation" had been the victim of a "soul murder" and had died long before World War II. The "master race" had simply brought this death to light by accomplishing suicide. And the Nazis had succeeded in presenting this suicide as a materialization of paradise on Earth.

6.7. The Cantorian decoding of Nazi paranoia that I have briefly sketched out casts further light on the nature of paranoid delusional metaphors.[22] Such metaphors basically aim for their own literalization, as I have indicated, and it is now clear that this process of literalization is nothing but a process of ontological infinitization by means of which the paranoiac seeks to bridge the distance between being and truth. Let us return to the Schreber case. Not only did Schreber believe that he had a special relationship with God and thought of himself as being God's fiancée and whore; he was also convinced that he was God. A specimen of humanity was thus identified with the archetype of humanity. Hence the delusional metaphor, "God is a whore." As for the Nazis, not only did they believe that they had, like all modern nations, a special relationship to humanity. In addition, they were also convinced that they embodied humanity, literally. Hence the delusional word of Revelation spread by the master race. In both cases, subjectivity—that is to say, the subject as lack, or the subject's congenital exile from truth—is mistaken for identity—that is to say, the filling of that lack, or the full presence of truth. Paranoid delusions always endeavor to articulate this highly deceptive and ill-fated "mistaking" of the subject, as Lacan would say. And all of them regularly face self-destruction. Any attempt to abolish the ontological defectiveness inherent in our subjectivity cannot but destroy subjectivity itself. With the passing of time, Schreber went completely out of his mind, spending the last years of his life in the asylum where God had forsaken him or where *he* (Schreber the God) had forsaken *herself* (Schreber the whore).

7. There are some similarities between my reading of Nazism and other interpretations of totalitarianism. Claude Lefort, in particular, has emphasized the democratic origins and the pseudo-democratic drift of totalitarian regimes, as well as the totalitarian identification of the state with the whole of society, the totalitarian dream of achieving perfect homogeneity among people, the totalitarian phantasy about the "People-as-One," the totalitarian inclination toward transforming science into scientism, and further aspects of totalitarianism that I myself have briefly examined above:

> Democracy inaugurates the experience of an ungraspable, uncontrollable society in which the people will be said to be sovereign, of course, but whose identity will constantly be open to question, whose identity will remain latent. . . .
>
> . . . In my view, totalitarianism can be clarified only by grasping its relationship with democracy. It is from democracy that it arises, even though it has taken root initially, at least in its socialist version, in countries where the democratic transformation was only just beginning. It overturns that transformation, while at the same time taking over some of its features and extending them at the level of phantasy. . . .
>
> . . . Modern democratic society seems to me, in fact, like a society in which power, law and knowledge are exposed to a radical indetermination, a society that has become the theatre of an uncontrollable adventure, so that what is instituted never becomes established, the

known remains undermined by the unknown, the present proves to be undefinable, covering many different social times which are staggered in relation to one another within simultaneity—or definable only in terms of some fictitious future. . . .

. . . But if the image of the people is actualized, if a party claims to identify with it and to appropriate power under the cover of this identification, then it is the very principle of the distinction between the state and society, the principle of the difference between the norms that govern the various types of relations between individuals, ways of life, beliefs and opinions, which is denied; and, at a deeper level, it is the very principle of a distinction between what belongs to the order of power, to the order of law and to the order of knowledge which is negated. The economic, legal and cultural dimensions are, as it were, interwoven into the political. This phenomenon is characteristic of totalitarianism.[23]

7.1. Lefort's analyses, which I find convincing, have been widely cited and discussed in recent years, and they have been criticized, too, on a number of occasions. For example, not everybody agrees that the notion of totalitarianism is sufficiently accurate from a historical point of view. Since the end of World War II, so the argument goes, this category has been used to define both fascism and real socialism, but the fact is that this category took center stage during the Cold War and was part of Western propaganda against the Soviet regime; on closer inspection, there are no strong similarities between fascism and real socialism, or at least there are more differences than similarities between them.[24] This criticism is not without basis: historically, it is crystal clear that Stalin and Hitler did not share the same view of the world; fascism and real socialism did not abide by the same political principles, nor did they have the same political agenda. But Lefort— and before him, Hannah Arendt—never denied the obvious. Rather, they intended to draw our attention to something else, to the delusional conflation between politics and the Revelation of Truth that became the hallmark of both types of "ideology," the Nazi and the Soviet.[25] Seen in this light, the notion of totalitarianism does not seem inappropriate, and even less so when we look at it from the angle of political *ontologies*, or grammars. Indeed, from a grammatical point of view, the kinship between fascism and real socialism is apparent. Both grammars were meant to convert an axiomatic metaphor, whether nationalist or socialist, into a delusional metaphor: the "master race" in one case, the "master class" (the proletariat) in the other. And in both cases the assumption was that democracy, whether nationalist or socialist, could keep its promise at last and become real: *real* socialism on the one side, *real* nationalism on the other.

7.2. "We are the master race"; "we are the master class." There are many similarities between these subject-suppositions. Both led to the elaboration of a political-scientific newspeak, the annulment of minority rights, and the apotheosis of the totalitarian party; most important, both implied that political metaphors—the "nation" or the "society"—could be transfigured into the literal Revelation of the people's humanity. This goal being achieved, all tensions between the people and the state would have been appeased all of a sudden. And this explains why, both in Germany and in the Soviet Union, the state went through a huge transformation: the final appeasement between the people and the state involved canceling any residual distance between the state and the "nation," or the "society." A new homogeneous and harmonious totality was therefore arising from the ashes of modern history.[26] In Germany, the road to this new totality was termed *Gleichshaltung*. In the Soviet Union, it took various names, such as *dekulakization* and *collectivization*. The result was that the state power was vastly expanded in both countries.

7.3. *Nationalsozialismus*: What are the reasons for this curious mixture of nationalism and socialism, of red and black colors? From a grammatical point of view, this hybridization is highly significant. Since Nazism was based on the assumption that the gap between the literal meaning and the metaphorical surplus value of the "nation" could be bridged by transforming the latter into the "master race," the Nazis were also convinced that every trace of social heterogeneity and spark of antagonism between the *Volk* and the citizen would have vanished at that moment, for social heterogeneity and antagonism were the symptoms of the nation, not of the master race. In short, the idea was that the process of democratization could be brought to an end. On these bases, not only nationalism but also the axiomatic alternatives to nationalism were doomed. That is, both nationalism and socialism were now bound to achieve the promise of humanity by simply merging into the new omnipotent grammar, *Nationalsozialismus*, that was meant to meet *all* demands coming from below, whether nationalist or socialist in inspiration.

7.4. The Soviets came to the same conclusion, starting from the opposite premise. For them, the issue of nationalities and nationalisms had been a major source of trouble from the very beginning. Stalin had taken care of this problem from the early stages of his political career. Soon after the Bolshevik Revolution, he had been appointed the People's Commissar for Nationalities. In November of 1917, he and Lenin had issued a Decree on Nationalities that bestowed the right to self-determination and secession on the peoples of Russia. After seizing power in 1924, Stalin renounced being so audacious, but he retained the idea that real socialism was not at odds with the blossoming of nationalism. Stalin, of course, was well aware of the contradiction between the socialist and the nationalist creeds. But he chose to redouble the contradiction instead of eradicating it. Just as nationalism is at variance with socialism, he started to argue, so the highest development of state power under the dictatorship of the proletariat is at variance with the "withering away" of state power at the end of history. Yet such contradictions do not represent insurmountable obstacles, Stalin maintained, because this kind of self-contradictory logic lies at the heart of history; it is the motor of history. In his view, however absurd this may seem, the dictatorship of the proletariat could only *result in* the withering away of state, just as true nationalism could only *result in* true socialism.[27] And this helps us to understand why the Soviet nomenklatura began to profess a Russian ultranationalist faith (National Bolshevism) during the Stalin era.[28] In the *plenitudo temporis* of a political Revelation, when humanity becomes true, there can be no difference between a true "society" and a true "nation," just as there can be no room for the *héteros*. Stalin's Russian chauvinism, the forced resettlement of "enemy nationalities," and the ethnic cleansing of the 1930s and 1940s prove that ultrasocialism and ultranationalism are two halves of the same whole: totalitarianism.

8

Old and New Fascisms

1. I will now focus on a new kind of pseudo-democracy. Pier Paolo Pasolini called it "new fascism."[1] In his view, both old and new fascisms undermine the fundamentals of modern democracy. Yet new fascism does not do this by absolutizing popular sovereignty at the expense of individual rights. New fascism celebrates our freedoms and absolutizes human rights to the detriment of our sense of belonging to a social-political community. Therefore, old and new fascisms strive to accomplish democracy—which is the restless ambition of fascism—via opposite routes. In the former case, the result is the birth of political subjects such as the master race, supported by a revelatory political grammar. In the latter case, the result is the birth of an altogether different subject, which is no longer a political actor, properly speaking, but a passive, anonymous entity: the human population.

1.1. Old and new fascisms can be seen as the paranoid and schizophrenic versions of pseudo-democracy, respectively. Even though paranoia and schizophrenia resemble each other in many respects, they should not be conflated. Over the past century, psychiatrists—from Eugen Bleuler to Ignacio Matte-Blanco—have insisted on the particular "bilogic" (or "double bookkeeping") that governs the behavior of schizophrenic subjects.[2] Briefly put, schizophrenics perceive the world and delusions as being compatible, thus remaining unbothered by the discrepancies between the two. By contrast, paranoid subjects seek to eliminate all discrepancies and rebuild the entire world on delusional grounds. As I noted in the previous chapter, Nazism is a telling example of paranoid politics. But paranoid politics is not the only possible form of pseudo-democracy. Another kind of democratic pathology had been adumbrated by Alexis de Tocqueville in the last pages of his *Democracy in America*:

> The first thing that strikes the observation is an innumerable multitude of men all equal and alike, incessantly endeavoring to procure the petty and paltry pleasures with which they glut their lives. . . . Above this race of men stands an immense and tutelary power, which takes upon itself alone to secure their gratifications, and to watch over their fate. That power is absolute, minute, regular, provident, and mild. . . . For their happiness such a government willingly labors, but it chooses to be the sole agent and the only arbiter of that happiness: it provides for their security, foresees and supplies their necessities, facilitates their pleasures, manages their principal concerns, directs their industry, regulates the descent of property, and subdivides their inheritances—what remains, but to spare them all the care of thinking and all the trouble of living? . . .
>
> After having thus successively taken each member of the community in its powerful grasp, and fashioned them at will, the supreme power then extends its arm over the whole community. It covers the surface of society with a net-work of small complicated rules, minute and uniform, through which the most original minds and the most energetic characters cannot penetrate, to rise above the crowd. The will of man is not shattered, but softened, bent, and guided: men are seldom forced by it to act, but they are constantly restrained from acting: such a power does not destroy, but it prevents existence; it does not tyrannize, but it compresses, enervates, extinguishes, and stupefies a people, till each nation is reduced to be nothing better than a flock of timid and industrious animals, of which the government is the shepherd.[3]

1.2. Back in the nineteenth century, the schizoid combination of factual despotism and nominal democracy that Tocqueville describes in this passage was just a possibility that he was grasping well ahead of his time. Almost two centuries later, this possibility is becoming reality. In our time, it is a fact that "each nation is reduced to being nothing better than a flock of timid and industrious animals, of which the government is the shepherd." In his essay, Tocqueville thus foresaw something like a forgery of democracy but one that has nothing to do with Nazism or with old fascism more generally. The scene set by Tocqueville is different. Here people are left alone, rather than being tyrannized by an absolute, indisputable truth. Hence, people remain free, or so they believe. In fact, they continue to enjoy their individual rights. Apparently, moreover, they still exert their collective sovereignty. Nevertheless, as Tocqueville points out, people do nothing but choose "their own guardians," as they are actually robbed of their own will, of their free agency, of "all the uses of themselves." What does this mean? How can "outward forms of freedom" and latent forms of servitude co-exist? What is the logic, or the "bilogic," that makes this result possible?

1.3. To clarify this, I will introduce a new category, the *delusional metonymy*, that proves helpful in analyzing not only schizophrenic disorders but also some features of new fascism.[4] By new fascism, I mean a new political grammar that is poisoning our societies and that materializes in various ways. In a first approximation, we may say that this grammar, unlike the others, fuels the depoliticization and a kind of increasing desubjectification of society. Nowadays, this process usually goes under the name *neoliberalism*. But there is much confusion about neoliberalism today. Just to give one example, neoliberalism is often mistaken for an economic doctrine, despite the fact that the word *neoliberalism* cannot be found in any textbook on micro- or macro-economics. So what is neoliberalism? David Harvey comes close to an answer in his well-known book on the topic, especially in the following passage: "I cannot convince anyone by philosophical argument that the neoliberal regime of rights is unjust."[5] Indeed, the problem posed by neoliberalism is this: how can our rights be turned against us, the people who hold them? How can our rights become harmful to us? Let us take this from the beginning.

2. In the beginning was the horror, Auschwitz, and what happened in the aftermath of that tragedy pushed the pendulum of Western history in the opposite direction. At the end of World War II, the general response to the Nazi camps was "never again." There remained the question of how to validate that "never again" in legal and political terms. The first answer came in 1948, when the Universal Declaration of Human Rights was adopted by the United Nations General Assembly. Since then, "human rights" have become an issue for everyone, because "everyone" is the alleged holder of those rights. But what kind of rights are we talking about? Are these universal human rights the same as the old human, or natural, rights? For centuries, interpretations of human or natural rights have varied depending on political contexts. As I have indicated, the American and the European conceptions of natural rights are rather dissimilar. In America, natural rights are seen as being the rights of mankind. In Europe, they are seen as being the rights of humanity. In America, natural rights tend to *separate* the people: every time that a natural right is being claimed, individuals are reasserting their freedom and independence from each other and from the collectivity. In Europe, instead, natural rights tend to *identify* the people: every time that a natural right is being claimed, individuals are urging the nation (or the society) to be truer to itself. Until recently, these have been the two major paths to natural rights in the Western world. Today, after the trauma of Auschwitz, things have changed. On the one hand, human rights still represent one of the cornerstones of American and European democracies. On the other hand, human rights have acquired a new value, for they have been inserted into a new *corpus juris*, which is no longer related to the people's nationality. This double coding of human rights—which are now thought of as constitutional *and* universal, context-dependent *and* context-free rights[6]—lies at the heart of the contemporary bilogic of human rights, according to which these rights belong to us by virtue of our political affiliation but also belong to "everyone" regardless of one's political affiliation. How can these two versions of human rights coexist? Can we avoid any contradiction between them? As a matter of fact, we cannot, and this impossibility is one of the remote conditions for the rise of a new type of democracy, based on a *dissolving political grammar*. The last forty years have witnessed

a dramatic expansion and a growing accreditation of this new model of democracy throughout the Western world. The virus, however, is a little bit older than that.

2.1. At first sight, there is no difference between universal and constitutional rights. In both cases, the idea is that human rights protect individuals against any abuses of power carried out by the state. Whether universal or constitutional, these rights defend us against all offenses perpetrated by or in complicity with public authorities. The only difference is that constitutional rights belong to citizens, whereas universal rights are ascribed to human beings as such, that is, to all members of "the human family," as the Universal Declaration solemnly affirms. In practical terms, this entails that universal rights can be claimed even by people who find themselves living in a country where constitutional rights are not in force, because those people, too, are part and parcel of the human family. But what is the human family? Is it a metaphor of humanity? Is it a metonymy of mankind? Or is it something else?

2.2. Article 16 of the Universal Declaration offers a general definition of family: "The family is the natural and fundamental group unit of society and is entitled to protection by society and the State." Taking our cue from this definition, we may say that the family is the true holder of universal rights. Given that all human beings are members of this "natural and fundamental group unit of society," all of them are entitled to protection and have "human rights." The phrase "the human family" should be taken literally from this point of view. But then, what about the passage right at the beginning of the Preamble in which we are told "of the equal and inalienable rights of all members of the human family"? Here "the human family" (or *one* family in the singular) stands in for *all* human families (or for "mankind," that occurs shortly afterward)—*pars pro toto*. So, which of the two readings is the good one? The literal or the figurative?

2.3. If we take the phrase figuratively, "the human family" hints at an infinitely wide society (or "mankind") by way of metonymy. If we take it literally, "the human family" is both a *pars* and a *totum*, in that it terms each of our families as well as the family of all who have the same remote ancestors or the same Father in heaven. But we cannot decide which of the two readings is correct. In fact, "the human family" lends itself to both interpretations, and this ambiguity is conducive to a delusional metonymy—namely, a metonymy that does not only establish a *pars pro toto* relationship but also formulates a *pars qua totum* equation by conflating the literal meaning and the figurative sense of a certain phrase. When it comes to "the human family," we cannot stop swinging between the literal and figurative layers of language. As a result, the *pars pro toto* tends to be literalized, ending in a delusion trope, the *pars qua totum*. The entire Universal Declaration of 1948 revolves around this bilogical wavering between *pars* and *totum*, which is best illustrated by the underlying assumption that everyone is "everyone."

2.4. "Everyone" is the grammatical subject of most articles of the Universal Declaration, as "everyone" is the holder of universal rights. But therein lies the rub. On the one hand, "everyone" is each one of us, literally; on the other hand, "everyone" refers to all human beings, figuratively. This is one more piece of evidence that the Universal Declaration of Human Rights centers on a particular trope. As we have seen, within the framework of a demonstrative grammar, every individual stands in for the whole of society, and society itself stands in for the non-whole of mankind. Thus, the chain of metonymic equivalences points to a remainder, mankind, that cannot be actualized from within the chain. Here metonymies continue to be ordinary figures of speech given that they all hint at something that remains ungraspable. Within the framework of a dissolving political grammar, by contrast, such an ungraspable remainder dissolves. The unfathomable nonwhole of mankind gives way to the *totum* of the human family, which is conflated, literally, with a *pars*: "everyone." Hence the conclusion that *the individual is the society*—everyone is "everyone." Think back to Margaret Thatcher's slogan: "There is no such thing as society. There are individual men and women and there are families."[7] With this remark, Thatcher was not saying that people do not live in society; rather, she was stating that society does not exist in and of itself. All that exists are individuals. Therefore, society is nothing but individuals. But how is it possible to claim that individuals and society are the same thing if society has no existence of its own? No doubt the *Zeitgeist* talks in riddles. In the end, it secretly tells everyone that the individual *is* (the society) insofar as the individual *is not* (the society that does not exist in and of itself).

Such is the strange assumption deeply rooted in a dissolving political grammar. Under this assumption, which I call the *meontological supposition*, the individual is the society, and the society is the individual, provided that both of them come to nothing. If everyone is "everyone," this is because "everyone" is no one.

2.5. "Everyone" is no one. The meontological supposition plays a key role in the Universal Declaration of Human Rights because the subject of rights is taken, literally, as a nonsubject that has not the right to have rights. Take, for example, the third, fourth, and fifth articles. Article 3 ensures life, liberty, and security of person; article 4 forbids all forms of slavery and servitude; and article 5 declares torture and other inhuman treatments to be illegal. As Amnesty International's surveys attest every year, there is not a place in the world where people are granted the right to have all the rights listed in those articles. The Universal Declaration, for its part, takes note of the fact and does nothing but ratify that people all over the world do not have the right to have all of those rights. In plain English, from a purely grammatical point of view, "everyone" has the right to have those rights in virtue of the fact that no one is given the right to have them.

2.6. Consider article 25: "Everyone has the right to a standard of living adequate for the health and well-being of himself." The problem is, Who decides what constitutes a standard of living that is adequate for "everyone"? If the decision is left to "everyone," it is more than plausible that no one will agree on what is truly adequate for "everyone." Put another way, the ideal of a "common standard of achievement for all peoples and all nations," as the Preamble has it, is so abstract that it can only lose touch with reality. Hence the dematerialized value and the depoliticizing effects of universal human rights. When "everyone" is in a position to claim rights, then no one finds himself in a position to claim them. "Everyone" becomes like everyone else. "Everyone," the subject of universal human rights, is thereby charged with a universal yet hopeless mission: to be someone, to be a *pars* of human society, while being "everyone," the *totum* of human society.

2.7. The difference between the new grammar of rights and those of the past lies in the fact that context-free rights, unlike context-dependent rights, do not propel political subjectification. Universal human rights are the rights of no one, because no one can turn them into the rights of someone, of a political *nos*. "Everyone" is no one. In short, the grammar of universal human rights lays the groundwork for political desubjectification. Before exploring the consequences of this momentous change of perspective, it is worth noting that the equation of "everyone" with no one ends up subjugating "everyone" to the state's authority rather than protecting "everyone" against the state's power. To give just one example, consider how the Universal Declaration conceives of freedom of movement. Article 13: "Everyone has the right to leave any country, including his own, and to return to his country." Article 14: "Everyone has the right to seek and to enjoy in other countries asylum from persecution." But what about the right to *enter* any country? Interestingly, this right is not mentioned. This means that escape from starvation is not a "human right" according to the Universal Declaration of Human Rights. If that were the case, "everyone" would have both the right to leave any country and the right to enter any country, not only because of persecution but also because of poor living conditions. This possibility, however, is not contemplated. The state, against which people should be protected, still represents the only authority entitled to watch over the people's movement and decide on their "right to life" (article 3). Again, all of this casts light on the bilogic of universal rights. In theory, these rights defend human beings against the state's power. In practice, they put "everyone" into the state's hands.

2.8. There is no need to emphasize that it is counterintuitive and utterly inappropriate to speak of fascism with regard to the Universal Declaration of Human Rights. This and other documents were thought of as antifascist, antidiscriminatory manifestos. They were meant to be a response to totalitarianism and its delusional agenda. That said, there is a delusional element to these documents, too. Indeed, the Universal Declaration paves the way for an escape from reality that is becoming ever more apparent with the passing of time. Think about what is currently happening in the Mediterranean Sea or along the US borders. Thousands of people attempt to reach other countries, and thousands of them die. Nevertheless, most of us do not feel much concern about that. This moral insensitivity is somewhat suspicious. Apathy is a clinical sign. Most of us know about these people, yet most of us do not care about them. We do not even argue for the inevitability of such brutalization, as European colonialists and American imperialists, to say nothing of black and red fascists, did. This kind of innocent negligence, this way of losing touch with reality—which is perfectly consistent with the escapism that the grammar of universal human rights nurtures—is one of the most impressive features of our time, one that should definitely push "everyone," the universal holder of universal rights, into raising the question of whether fascism or something similar is rearing its head. How can we rule out the possibility that those who believed that the dying are unworthy of life (old fascism) somewhat resemble those who are by no means struck by their fate (new fascism)? More importantly, why do we feel so apathetic and emotionless? What is happening to us?

3. Part of the answer lies in the current distortion of democracy and the related dissolution of society. We are so unresponsive because we feel more isolated than ever, as though we could no longer regard ourselves as one accountable *populus*. In many respects, what we are witnessing today is the exact opposite of old fascism. With the rise of the latter, the political *nos* and popular sovereignty had been infinitized, whereas the other pillar of modern democracy, subjective rights, had been nullified. Subjective rights had morphed into the superior race's rights. The logic of old fascism may thus be defined as the monologic of the One or of absolute homogeneity. With new fascism, things are the other way around. Rights are infinitized and heterogeneity is absolutized. Here, however, the principle of popular sovereignty is not abolished altogether. Rather, the people's will and responsibility are deprived of any effect. The true fiction of the *populus* loses strength and becomes unproductive without being removed. "We" are still there, and yet "we" are not. The logic of new fascism may thus be defined as the bilogic of the not-One (*pas-une* in Lacan's words).[8] Think of the crisis of representative democracy. As the historian Emilio Gentile has remarked, we live in times of "theatrical democracy" (*democrazia recitativa*). Our democracies continue to be nominally based on popular sovereignty, but the people are actually voiceless.[9] Nowadays, politicians do not *represent* the people's wishes and their collective demands. Most of the time, they just *pretend* to play the game of democracy with the result that democracy is diminished and reduced to one simple rule: *enjoy*

your freedoms. As for the people's sovereignty, it looks like an obsolete totem, even though its ancient rituals (elections, parliamentary debates, fights between political parties) continue to be performed.

3.1. *Democracy is all about individual rights.* This definition is misleading, as it is not clear whether it refers to universal or constitutional rights. Today, it has become customary to speak of "fundamental rights" in both cases. Fundamental rights are those rights that are ratified by constitutional *and* international law. Thus, context-dependent and context-free rights merge into the same class of rights. It remains to be ascertained whether this class is self-consistent. On closer inspection, there appear to be some significant discrepancies between constitutional and universal rights. Constitutional rights require that people subjectify them. This means that these rights are the prerogative of a *populus* that "authorizes" them in the first-person plural by "authoring" a constitution (or a similar document). Universal rights, by contrast, are ascribed to human beings regardless of the people's will. This means that they are deemed to be objective rights. These are rights in the third person, the rights of "everyone," which are at one's disposal even if no one pleads for them. These rights are neutral from a political point of view and totally disentangled from any historical context. In other words, universal rights are not contingent on political subjectification. For this reason, they are not comparable to constitutional rights. In the last analysis, constitutional and universal rights can be conflated with each other only if we take a bilogical perspective on them.

3.2. *Democracy is all about human rights.* This definition is no less misleading, because what counts the most is the subjectification of rights. A modern *populus* is a collective subject—a "political person" in Hobbes's terminology—that can speak and act in the first-person plural, thereby being able to govern. As a rule, when people govern themselves, they do not just emerge as a political subject. By the same token, they become a political object that is the target of their own legislative measures and governmental provisions. At that point, people reveal themselves to be a "multitude" (*multitudo*, as Hobbes calls it) or a "population." Since the eighteenth century, the notion of population has been, among other things, a way of marking the difference between these two aspects of the modern body politic. When people are sovereign, they are sovereign *over themselves*. Therefore, they become not only active but also passive. When they are active, they form a *populus*, as they are conveying their own will. When they are passive, they form a population, as they are complying with their own will. Now, if we take things one step further, it is easy to see that the concept of the human population refers to people that are being increasingly robbed of their will and tend to become *totally* passive. Under such circumstances, people are still governed but find it ever more difficult to govern, not least because they map their subjective rights onto universal, desubjectified rights.

3.2.1. All of this takes us back to the issue of subjective rights *qua* human properties and the issue of humanity and mankind *qua* political remainders. As I have argued, a political remainder is a political object that exudes from a political subject. This object resembles Lacan's *objet petit a* in that it encapsulates the subject's being but remains out of reach. Humanity and mankind embody this kind of object for axiomatic and demonstrative political subjects, respectively. In neither case can the political *nos* bridge the gap between $ and *objet petit a*. For the subject is never in a position to bridge the divide between subjectivity and true being, or identity. As Lacan explains, modern subjects come into existence precisely by failing to appropriate their own being, $ <> *a*. Lacan used this formula in regard to individual subjects. I, for one, contend that the same formula holds for political subjects, as well, and that it sheds light on how the political *nos* relates to itself. On the one hand, people exert their sovereign power *collectively*—and here comes popular sovereignty. On the other hand, people resist their own sovereign power *individually*—and here come subjective rights. On the side of collective sovereignty, we find $, the political *nos*. On the side of individual rights, we find *objet petit a*, humanity or mankind. Insofar as rights are the natural endowment of "man," and not just the political endowment of "the citizen," they continue to challenge the political *nos* that is expected to achieve perfect identity between the rights of man and the rights of the citizen, thereby achieving perfect identity between itself and humanity, or mankind. Hence the proliferation of rights (from civil to social) in Europe or the extension of rights to Afro-Americans and other minorities in America. In both cases, whatever progress "we the people" make, there always remains room for further convergence between the two poles of political subjectification, $ and *a*.

3.2.2. In light of the above, a political remainder appears as an object that the political *nos* seeks to reach for the purpose of achieving itself and attaining happiness. That object, however, is ungraspable because it remains at a distance from the subject, who can only pursue it without attaining true happiness. Is there any way out of such a frustrating impasse? Actually, there are two. I call both of them fascism—old fascism and new fascism. In the first case, popular sovereignty and political homogeneity are infinitized, or absolutized, in the name of a delusional subject that should literally embody the Truth of humanity. Individual rights and all remnants of social heterogeneity are anathema to this kind of subject, for they challenge a truly human and fully sovereign society. Any trace of passivity is doomed to disappear. Hence, for example, the hectic hyperactivism of the "master race," which could only command but not obey. In Nazi Germany, the people were no longer subjected to anyone, *not even to themselves*. Indeed, the tacit assumption was that the distance between them and the Führer, between being and representation, between *a* and $, had been bridged once and for all. Those who still had to obey were seen as nonexistent, as the *dying*: the Jews, the Gypsies, and all other inferior races.

3.2.3. Today, we live the exact reverse of that nightmare. Viewed as a choral response to Nazi crimes, the Universal Declaration of Human Rights has absolutized, or infinitized, subjective rights. As a result, those rights have morphed into desubjectified, or fundamental, rights. Against this background, "we" tend to evaporate, for "we" regard ourselves as having rights that hold sway irrespective of who "we" are. Those rights are thought to be valid anyhow, whether or not "we the people" claim them. Those rights are beyond our will, and this is the reason those rights can be turned against us. In this context, in fact, "we" no longer find ourselves in a position to command but only to obey. For "we" no longer exist. "We" are there only to claim all together that "we" are not there.

3.3. From this it follows that, first, we are slowly becoming a human population to be administered by a good shepherd; second, owing to political desubjectification, all mechanisms of democratic representation are now seriously impaired; and third, we are going through a process of delusional hyperobjectification, which is the exact opposite of the process of delusional hypersubjectification that characterized old fascism. In the latter case, a revelatory political subject came into *being* by passing through the door of humanity. In the former case, a dissolving political subject comes into *nonbeing* by passing through the door of mankind. Such delusional subjects—the revelatory and the dissolving—originate in opposite grammars, which represent the delusional versions of axiomatic and demonstrative grammars, respectively. A revelatory political subject arises from a delusional metaphor—for instance, the master race—that literalizes an axiomatic metaphor—for instance, the nation. Hence the metaphorical-*and*-literal amphiboly in which this type of hypersubjectified subject is trapped. A dissolving political subject, instead, arises from delusional metonymies that literalize demonstrative metonymies. Hence the metonymic-*and*-literal amphiboly in which this type of desubjectified subject is trapped. In the former case, homogeneity is absolutized at the expense of social heterogeneity, with the result that individual and minority rights are nullified. In the latter case, heterogeneity is absolutized to the detriment of political homogeneity, with the result that popular sovereignty dematerializes.

3.4. Let us focus on the metonymic-*and*-literal amphiboly of a dissolving grammar. Within the framework of a demonstrative grammar, the individual stands in for the whole of society, while society stands in for the nonwhole of mankind. Through this chain of metonymic equivalences, every individual is put into relation with mankind at large, but this relation remains purely figurative in nature—*pars pro toto*. Here, no individual represents mankind literally. At all points in the chain, *pars* and *totum* remain at a distance from one another. Individuals remain distinct from society and mankind, just as the whole of society remains distinct from the nonwhole of mankind. America epitomizes this grammatical distribution of places and roles. Although American society is held together by the denial of any axiomatic homogeneity among individuals, all Americans blend into *one* society because they all see social heterogeneity as tracing the boundaries of *one* people. *E pluribus unum*. But suppose now that "there is no such thing as society." Imagine that social heterogeneity is infinitized to the point at which society as such is equated with individuals. If that is the case, the *pars pro toto* relation between individuals and society vanishes into a *pars qua totum* equation, and society starts to dissolve. Social heterogeneity can no longer trace the boundaries of *one* people. But it is also impossible to remove all boundaries, as we continue to live in *one* society. Thus, we are squeezed between a figurative equivalence, *pars pro toto*, and a literal equation, *pars qua totum*. We cannot abandon the former, but we are inclined to literalize it and change it into a delusional equation. Bilogic comes into effect.

3.5. Bilogic does not destroy our societies; rather, it erodes them. The infinitization of social heterogeneity dissolves a given society in a larger and perfectly abstract entity that hyperobjectifies mankind. I call this new entity the human population: the *totum* with which any *pars*—from the individual to the society—can be equated. The individual is the society, in this view, but only on condition that both of them are equated with the human population. If that condition is met, then "everyone" is the society. At the same time, and under the same condition, "everyone" becomes no one. For no one can be literally equated with the human population: no individual, no society. Consequently, one individual is and is not the human population; likewise, one society is and is not the human population. Individuals and society are still there but are mapped onto a surface, the human population, into which they melt. Consider again the idea of fundamental rights. As already emphasized, this notion refers to universal *and* constitutional rights, context-free *and* context-dependent rights, which merge into the same class of rights while having different (national or international) legal status. This double status, or coding, is not without consequences. For one thing, it duplicates constitutional rights and projects them onto the surface of "the human family," which is one of the many names that the human population can take nowadays. In this manner, subjective rights are not revoked. If anything, they are reasserted. Nevertheless, once they are duplicated and recoded, these rights are politically neutralized. Subjective rights now coexist with desubjectified rights, and constitutional rights overlap with universal rights; but the former tend to dissolve into the latter, which are supposed to be more basic and *objective* because they belong to "everyone."

3.6. Bilogic, or the logic of the not-One, dominates here. And this logic, unlike the monologic of the One, can corrupt several forms of political subjectivity. In other words, new fascism, or *soft* fascism, is far more infectious than old fascism, or *hard* fascism. For old fascism to be possible at all, a national metaphor must be in force. A revelatory political grammar revolves around a delusional metaphor that literalizes an axiomatic core metaphor and every peripheral metaphor that is related to it. The phrase "Think with your blood!," for instance, was an ordinary metaphor for Bismarck but became something else for Hitler. This explains why old fascism has never featured as a real possibility in a country like America, where no national metaphor has ever taken root. For a dissolving political grammar to be possible, however, all that is needed is for subjective rights to be in force, no matter whether they are integrated into an axiomatic or a demonstrative grammar. Whatever the case, subjective rights can be duplicated and reshaped into desubjectified rights. No wonder, then, that a schizoid bilogic is more adaptive than a paranoid monologic. The former resembles a virus, the latter a cancer. When the virus goes into action, it never kills the body politic; it simply alters its functioning. At that point, delusional metonymies start inhibiting the axiomatic metaphors or the demonstrative metonymies on which this or that society is grounded, without repealing them. The virus's life relies on the host organism's survival, however compromised the organism's conditions may be. Delusional metonymies do nothing but superimpose a *pars qua totum* equation on all the figures of speech that hint at humanity or mankind. In this light, the only grammar that appears to be immune from bilogic is hard fascism, because in that case subjective rights are not in force and cannot undergo any process of duplication. For this reason, hard fascism is often seen as the most effective response to soft fascism. Recent developments in Europe confirm this trend: either people surrender to soft fascism and neoliberal policies, or they refresh nationalist agendas that are, more often than not, on the brink of ultranationalist radicalization. In some sense, it is true that *there is no alternative* in Europe today. The choice is between two opposite roads to fascism. In America, by contrast, it would be misleading to describe someone like Donald Trump as a genuine fascist (in the European sense of the word). As a matter of fact,

Trump's promise to "make America great again" gives further evidence that new fascism *parasitizes* our democracies and elicits allergic reactions that push "everyone" to look back to the past. Hence the so-called *polarization* between old and new patterns of political propaganda that give expression to a bilogical grammar: in America, the polarization between the old-fashioned champions of American exceptionalism and the heralds of a globalized "human family"; in Europe, the polarization between the old-fashioned champions of European nationalism who sympathize with hard fascism (from Marine Le Pen to Viktor Orbán) and the neoliberal technocrats of the European Union who smile at the rising sun of an "inverted totalitarianism."[10]

4. Bilogic deactivates the people's will and disembodies the people's sovereignty by projecting them onto "another scene," *eine andere Schauplatz*, as Freud would have it. Consider, for example, the scene of European integration. Over the years, legal and political scholars have discussed and disagreed about the process of European integration. In the absence of a European *populus*, how can a European democracy be established? Is anything like that on the horizon? And more generally, what is a *populus*? I will not elaborate on the answers that have been given so far to these questions, for it seems to me that the questions themselves are misplaced when addressing the issue of European integration. Even if a European *demos* does not exist for the moment, a European population is there, and that is enough to move forward with European integration. The result is not democracy, however. The result is a new type of pseudo-democracy.

4.1. As regards the legal foundations of the European Union, no European constitution is in force because the 2005 referendum rejected it (in France and the Netherlands). Nevertheless, there are treaties between European countries, which represent the so-called primary law of the EU. In addition, there exist "regulations," "directives," "recommendations," "decisions," and "opinions" that represent the so-called secondary law created by the European Commission, the European Council, and the European Parliament. By virtue of the "supremacy doctrine," EU law prevails over the Member States' law. The European Court of Justice watches over the application of European law in all countries. After the Lisbon Treaty, passed in 2007, the Charter of Fundamental

Rights of the European Union has become part of EU law. Citizens of the EU hold the "fundamental rights" listed in that charter. If those rights—or those stated in the European Convention on Human Rights of 1950—are violated, citizens of the EU can turn to the European Court of Human Rights or, under particular circumstances, the Court of Justice of the EU.

4.2. As regards European citizenship, article 8 of the Maastricht Treaty says that "every person holding the nationality of a Member State shall be a citizen of the Union." Therefore, all citizens of the Member States are entitled to elect representatives in the European Parliament. Does it follow that they are sovereign over the Union? The answer is not obvious. Again, bilogic comes into play. For example, in matters such as the management of financial crises, the European Parliament has no power to intervene, as it represents the people of twenty-eight (after "Brexit," twenty-seven) countries of which only nineteen to date have adopted the common currency. Fiscal policies, however, are negotiated between the Member States through the intermediary of European institutions (the European Council, the Commission, and the European Central Bank). For this reason, democracy in Europe seems to be relatively safe. Peoples (in the plural) of the Member States continue to exert their sovereignty over the EU through states' representatives—yet problems remain. Recent quarrels over austerity policies have made clear that disagreements between Member States (say, Germany and Greece) can end in the annulment of the people's decisions in this or that country (see the aftermath of the Greek referendum in 2015). Hence the so-called democratic deficit in the EU. But can we really speak of a democratic deficit? Or should we speak, more properly, of a pseudo-democratic drift?

4.3. From a grammatical point of view, the situation in Europe looks particularly interesting. All citizens of the Member States are citizens of the EU. Consequently, they hold constitutional rights at the national level and fundamental rights at the European level. Yet this duplication of rights does not reinforce but rather weakens the people's power, so much so that the concept of democracy is being reconsidered today. The political theorist Catherine Colliot-Thélène, for instance, contends that the notion of popular sovereignty "belongs to the past" and that we should conceive of a "democracy without *demos*."[11] The legal theorist Luigi Ferrajoli, for his part, emphasizes the notion of "democracy through rights" and redefines popular sovereignty as a "summation of fundamental rights."[12] Thus, both Colliot-Thélène and Ferrajoli subscribe to a theory of democracy that downplays, and to a certain extent makes obsolete, the idea of political representation and the assumption that the people's will is sovereign in democracy. For them, power is invisible, and democracy is nothing more than a system of legal protections that defend people against sheer domination. The EU is a practical application of this view of democracy. Although there exists no European *demos*, the European population needs to be protected against all forms of discrimination and abuses of power. As a result, the Court of Justice, not the Parliament, becomes the driving force of democratization. In contrast to the hyperpoliticization of society imposed by hard fascism, a new kind of hyperjuridification of society develops within this framework, one that jeopardizes the people's sovereignty, as though subjective rights alone—whether constitutional or fundamental—might express the essence of democracy.[13]

4.4. The key to understanding such a pseudo-democratic turn is the concept of deactivation. In Freud's *Group Psychology*, the German phrase *Einziehung des Ideals* refers to the deactivation of a regulatory "ideal." According to Freud, every time that deactivation is brought about, people feel freed from all obligations and are overwhelmed by euphoria. Indeed, once the *Ideal* is deactivated, people are no longer encumbered with the gap between what they are and what they ought to be. They are relieved of the burden of failure that otherwise characterizes the life of any subject. But the cost of this feeling of relief is that subjectivity is turned upside down. The ontological subject-supposition is now shaped into a meontological subject-supposition. As Freud explains, people lose their own personality at that moment. This does not mean that they can no longer say *ego* or *nos*, but the first person is negativized. *Ego non sum, nos non sumus.* Think about the current situation in Europe: the national *Ideal* is losing ground, with the result that national communities are dissolving. When Europeans say "we are the people of Europe," the only meaning this sentence has for them is that "we are *not* French, Germans or Italians." The word *Europe* has no value other than that. This is why scholars, politicians, and the general public ask themselves whether Europe might actually acquire a more positive meaning in the future.

4.5. The meontological subject-supposition "we the people of Europe" does not destroy but rather negativizes the political *nos*, thus devitalizing the people's sovereignty. This process hinges on the bilogical coexistence of government and governance. On the one hand, national governments continue to act on behalf of a certain *populus*. On the other hand, European governance watches over national policies and validates them in the last instance. Here, again, we encounter the problem of the so-called democratic deficit. Given that national representatives are closer to people and European institutions are further from them, it seems that the EU suffers from a lack of democratic legitimacy. But is this really so? In the end, it is impossible to tell. In fact, it is true that national governments must comply with European governance, and national representatives must come to terms with European institutions, but it is also true that the latter have been established by national governments on behalf of the people(s). Therefore, we are not allowed to speak of a democratic deficit but only of a pseudo-democratic drift. If national governments must obey European institutions whatever it takes, this is because those governments have been democratically entitled to do so; but the fact remains that the people's sovereignty is thus devitalized.

4.6. Pseudo-democracy is almost invisible from within. With the rise of soft fascism, the people, *populus*, is upstaged by an increasingly passive population, yet democracy keeps up appearances. Even when the people's sovereignty is totally ignored, European institutions can proclaim that they take action for the sake of the European population's rights—for instance, the right to an adequate standard of living that, according to them, would be nullified by "sovereigntist" policies. But rights are exalted while being politically neutralized. Within the European framework, in other words, the people's legal empowerment is conducive to the people's political disempowerment. Law becomes a matter of objective fact that ought to be exempt from political consideration—and the same holds for economy. From the EU's perspective, law and economy should not be subjects of public debate or collective deliberation. Technocracy reigns supreme. New fascism is "techno-fascism," Pasolini had already noted in the 1970s. For him, this was the sign that "neo-capitalism" is spreading all over the world, triggering an "anthropological mutation" of human beings.[14] More soberly, we may speak of a psychopolitical passage. It is not human beings that are changing today but political grammars.

4.7. As Pasolini points out, "antifascism" is one of the emblems of new fascism.[15] Once more, think about current developments in Europe. All kinds of political mobilization against European integration are gathered together under the label of "populism." Unsurprisingly, the political grammar that underpins most protest movements is nationalism, which is regularly inflamed by the nation's decline. As previously emphasized, the more the nation fails and falls to pieces, the louder the appeal to nationalism becomes. As is well known, European integration has heavily destabilized European nations over the past few decades. As a result, we are now witnessing a strong revival of nationalism in Europe. All of this makes perfect sense from a grammatical standpoint. But there is more at stake than just nationalism. In fact, the battle between axiomatic and dissolving political grammars that has broken out on the Continent over the last few years is likely to drive "populist" movements to the edge and prompt the rebirth of hard fascism, which is the only grammar that cannot be parasitized by soft fascism. For this reason, *antifascism* has become one of the watchwords of the European technocratic establishment and, more generally, of neoliberals across the world, who wish to scare their constituencies with dark memories from the past.

4.8. There is another aspect of new fascism that deserves close attention. It is often said that the EU suffers from a democratic deficit because states are no longer the sole depositaries of sovereignty, but only states can be reckoned as true democratic institutions. In reality, as I remarked above, there is no democratic deficit in Europe today, and here is one more piece of evidence: even though the EU designates a set of people and institutions that includes several subsets, each of the subsets turns out to be homeomorphic, and the entire set turns out to be self-similar; this means that every state, *pars*, becomes a fractal subset of a larger *totum*, the EU. Imagine a line. In mathematical terms, a line contains an infinite number of points and every line can be cut into smaller segments, each of which contains an infinite number of points that is exactly the same as before. Thus, the line and the segment, the set and the subset, end up sharing the same cardinality, which is the cardinality of a Cantor set. The size of both the set and the subset is uncountable in a case like this because the line can be cut *ad infinitum*, and the number of possible cuts exceeds the cardinality of natural numbers, that is aleph-o. With regard to this transfinite size, mathematicians therefore speak of aleph-1, the cardinality, or the power, of the continuum. From now on, I will often refer to this notion. Now consider the relationship between the EU and the Member States. As stated in the treaties, decisions made by the EU are considered made by, or in the name of, each of the Member States. Thus, the EU and the states, the set and the subsets, cannot be identified with each other, but they nonetheless equal each other. *Pars qua totum.* The consequences are dire for European democracies. As I have stressed, the people's sovereignty should not be conflated with the state's sovereignty. The latter is a *factum*, the former a *fictio*. The state's sovereignty ought to conform to the people's will as much as possible: this is one of the pillars of modern democracy. But what about the EU? Here the people's sovereignty can be deactivated at any time given that it is possible to establish a *pars qua totum* equation between the state's sovereignty and the EU's authorities. Because each Member State is a fractal subset of the EU, any decision made at the European level equals a decision made at the national level, even when such a decision contravenes the people's "general will." Nevertheless, national governments can implement the EU's decrees without rejecting democracy, for the EU's decrees appear to be issued by none other than national governments and, thereby, on behalf of the *populus*. As a result of this, the power of states (of national governments and bureaucracies) increases dramatically to the detriment of the people's power. As the political scientist Giandomenico Majone observes: "Those who criticize the European Commission for its alleged interference in domestic affairs, for example, do not realize that very little can happen in Brussels without the agreement of the governments and the bureaucracies of the Member States."[16]

5. One of the signs that Europe is facing a new form of fascism, or pseudo-democracy, is the fact that objections to the EU treaties are

forbidden. For the establishment, there is no alternative: take it or leave it—which means: take it. Another sign of fascism is the fact that pseudo-democracy is portrayed as a better or more mature form of democracy. Consider what happened in Europe a few years ago. Sometime around 2013, many had the feeling that democracy was in serious danger. Yet at the peak of the crisis, when thousands of people in Greece were protesting against European institutions, a new debate suddenly broke out. Media, politicians, and opinion-makers started to discuss LGBT rights and gay marriage. Among those against the acknowledgment of LGBT rights and gay marriage, there were some conservatives known for their anti-European sentiment. Among those in favor, there were several pro-European activists. But the interesting thing is that a *tertium non datur* characterized the whole debate. All of a sudden, LGBT rights and European integration became the emblems of the same thing: "democracy through rights"—namely, European democracy. A delusional metonymy was rapidly established, one that equated the *pars*, LGBT rights, with the *totum*, European democracy. Thus, despite the fact that the people's sovereignty was being deactivated, it looked as though Europe and democracy had become synonyms. To crown it all, two weeks before the 2014 European elections, the European population had the opportunity to vote in another election, the 2014 Eurovision Song Contest. As expected, Conchita Wurst, a gay icon from Austria, won the contest. Soon after, Conchita was invited to perform at an antidiscrimination event held at the European Parliament in Brussels. Later, it was the turn of the United Nations in Vienna, where Conchita performed in front of the UN general secretary, Ban Ki-Moon. As a UN official said on that occasion: "Everyone is entitled to enjoy the same basic rights and live a life of worth and dignity without discrimination. This fundamental principle is embedded in the UN Charter and the Universal Declaration of Human Rights. Conchita is a symbol in that sense."[17]

5.1. Let us look more closely at the multiple stages on which Conchita Wurst performed after the Eurovision Song Contest. First, the European stage—Brussels. Then, the global stage, the United Nations in Vienna, which was a national stage as well—Vienna, the Austrian capital. In the end, it might be argued that Conchita performed on all of those stages *simultaneously*. Not because Conchita was bodily present on all of those stages at the same moment but rather because those stages are no longer distinct today. The national stage is indistinguishable from the European stage, just like the European stage is indistinguishable from the global stage. Once more, a delusional metonymy organizes this scenic equation. Austria can be seen as a fractal subset of Europe, just like Europe can be seen as a fractal subset of the entire world. The delusional metonymy has a fractal-like structure. Each time, the *totum* contains the *pars*, but the *pars* can be equated with the *totum*. Conchita is indeed an Austrian singer, but Conchita is at the same time a European singer, as well as a singer of "the human family." Thus, Conchita is "everyone" (male and female) on the stage of the Spectacle, while being no one (neither male nor female). Hence the delusional equation on which soft fascism is based: any individual is (a fractal subset of) the society, and any society is (a fractal subset of) the human population into which the individual dissolves. As Guy Debord put it, "the Spectacle appears at once as society itself, as a part of society, and as a means of unification."[18]

5.2. Interestingly, a dissolving society, like all other fractal-like structures, is closed in on itself and has no outside. There is no room for a *pars* that is not already a *pars qua totum*. There is no place for a "part of no part" (*part des sans-part*), as Jacques Rancière would have it. That is, not everybody can be counted as "everyone." Only those who are already included in a dissolving society are entitled to be "everyone" and find a place in what Debord calls "the society of the Spectacle." All the others, typically migrants, have no right to enter this society because they find themselves outside—which amounts to saying that they find themselves nowhere, for a fractal-like society has no outside. Since these people have never been part of our societies before, they cannot be part of "the human family" into which our societies dissolve. For this reason, they stay in the shadows and live on the margins of our communities. Properly speaking, they do not even have "a life" of their own, because "a life" is now the singular of the collective noun "population."[19] These people are purely and simply unworthy of "a life."

5.3. A dissolving society has no inside either. In the past, social heterogeneity was understood as heterogeneity among individuals. Today, by contrast, heterogeneity is infinitized and tends to dissect the individuals themselves who should constitute the basic elements of society. Thus, the whole of society loses unity and dissolves into individuals; at the same time, individuals lose their own individuality and dissolve into smaller entities: "choices," "behaviors," and "rights." I will address these notions and their interconnection in a moment. For the time being, it is worth emphasizing that the fractal-like structure, which is a mathematical image of the continuum, makes it impossible to suppose that individuals are the ultimate constituents of society. The infinite heterogeneity of society implies the infinite heterogeneity of every individual. The Spectacle glorifies such an infinite blossoming of individuals that appear to be totally unbound from each other. Yet the Spectacle is the realm of non-Truth. The Spectacle does not even lie; rather, it forges our signatures. For individuals are now unbound from themselves.

5.4. The fractal-like structure is crucial to understanding the delusional spacetime of a dissolving society. As regards space, consider again fundamental rights. In Europe, these rights demarcate three different spaces: the national space, the European space, and the global space. First, these rights are stated in national constitutions. Second, they are stated in the Charter of Fundamental Rights of the European Union. Third, they are stated in the Universal Declaration of Human Rights and a number of related documents. These spaces may be visualized as concentric circles that, however, come to coincide. Dissolution and desubjectification are due precisely to the fractal inscription of the inner circle in the outer circles. Through the fractal recoding of rights, a process of depoliticization takes place. The political value of constitutional rights is parasitized and neutralized by the *meta*political value of ever more universal and objective rights. The peoples of Europe are thus projected onto the surface of the European population into which they dissolve.

5.5. As regards time, it splits into two lines: the line of the present and that of the future. The line of the present represents the inner circle, the line of the future the outer circle. When it comes to Europe, the present is the time of European nations; the future is the time of the EU. But present and future do not follow one another. The time of the EU does not come *after* the time of European nations. Rather, present and future coincide. Consider again recent developments in Europe. After the rejection of the European Constitution, European political integration has turned into a new kind of metapolitical integration that paves the way for the political desubjectification of European nations, not the political subjectification of Europe. As a consequence, the present of European nations now dissolves into a future that is about to arrive *and* has already arrived. Here, too, the whole process is framed by the fractal inscription of a smaller circle, the present, in a wider one, the future. Such is the *meta*dimension of a fractal-like society.

5.6. The same sort of perceptual distortion hides behind many current debates about cosmopolitanism. According to David Held, although the goal of a "world government" is unachievable for now, we should nonetheless cherish the dream of a cosmopolitan democracy centered on universal rights.[20] Nations should melt into "the human family," and the present should dissolve into the future, even though cosmopolitan democracy is a distant prospect. In any event, Held argues, we should inscribe the present of national democracies in the future of a worldwide democracy that, contrary to all appearances, does not weaken the role of states. On the contrary, as soon as the sovereign states enter the metadimension of globalization, they acquire an overpowered *meta*sovereignty and a new legal-ethical status. As another proponent of cosmopolitanism put it, "the role of states remains crucial, even if reconfigured in light of legal and ethical norms."[21] For this reason, it seems no exaggeration to say that "the new world order is moral-legal" in nature.[22] For the new world order does nothing but revive an old acquaintance of Europe's, the ethical state, which is the cornerstone of pseudo-democracy.

5.7. Today, like yesterday, the ethical state acts as an inveterate pedagogue. But the new pedagogical credo is far more insidious than the old one because it does not require us to adopt a "newspeak." New fascism simply recodes our traditional language, which becomes progressively neutralized. Let us take an example of such a daily recoding, one that throws light on the critical complicity between the neoliberal state and the big financial institutions that dominate on a global scale. Consider the notion of social justice and the related concepts of economic equality, income redistribution, and the like. These concepts make sense when "we the people" claim social rights and demand justice all together, thus overcoming our individual egoism. But what if "we the people" can no longer speak and act in the first-person plural? When this happens, "we the people" evaporate, and egoism becomes predominant again. That said, we can continue to talk about social justice, provided that we recode our language. For this to be possible, two conditions must be met. First, we must assume that the individual is the society, so that it becomes possible to think of social justice (justice as viewed from the perspective of society as a whole) in terms of individual justice (justice as viewed from the perspective of "everyone"). Second, we must assume that the state's sovereignty no longer identifies with the people's sovereignty, so that it becomes possible to think of the state as a mere exegete of some higher authorities. Under these assumptions, neoliberalism consolidates its dominance. A case in point is the World Bank's Europe and Central Asia Economic Update of November 2016. This document, which provides states with information about how to improve their economic performance, does not give up the quest for social justice. Nevertheless, the quest is recoded here. It becomes a quest for the "economic mobility" of individuals, with no reference to society as a whole and the idea of social equality. In this view, individuals lose attraction to all forms of struggle for economic equality and redistribution of income whenever they "may have expectations of upward mobility that make them prefer less redistribution." In short, "the prospects of becoming richer than average" are likely to persuade everyone, including people in need, to desist from "political polarization" (namely, political mobilization). Yet achieving this result requires a change in "perception," as the World Bank's report emphasizes; and that change is not only theorized but also pursued by this and other similar documents, whose goal is to make people move away from the idea of social justice *qua* economic equality to the idea of social justice *qua* economic mobility:

> For example, people at the lower end of the income distribution may have expectations of upward mobility that make them prefer less redistribution. Societies in which individual effort is believed to be the main source of income formation prefer lower taxes and less redistribution. . . .

Inequality stemming from differences in effort tends to be viewed as more acceptable than the inequality of opportunity (that is, inequality related to circumstances beyond an individual's control, such as place of birth, parents' education, or race). . . .

Life satisfaction, and perhaps political polarization, may be more related to economic mobility, or perceptions of economic mobility, than to GDP growth. The prospects of becoming richer than average may explain why societies with high (or increasing) inequality do not necessarily experience a rise in political polarization or a decline in life satisfaction.[23]

5.7.1. In the World Bank's report, the key word is *perception*. In fact, it is a change in perception that allows us to see the world and delusions as being compatible. Take, for example, the "Je suis Charlie" manifestation that followed the terrorist attacks of January 2015. The main demonstrations took place in Paris and other French towns—the inner circle. Further demonstrations spread across Europe and the rest of the world—the outer circle. In Paris, the French president led the "republican rally" (*marche républicaine*) and launched an appeal for national unity. At the level of the inner circle, the French nation thus came to the fore. The slogan, however, was not "Nous sommes tous français" or "Vive la France" but "Je suis Charlie," and "everyone" began to shout this slogan all around the globe. At the level of the outer circle, the nation thus disappeared. The inscription of the inner circle in the outer circle was the product of a slogan, "Je suis Charlie," which dissolved the French nation in the anonymity of "everyone." But in truth, when did "everyone" join the dead? When did "everyone" become no one? If the true answer is January 7, the day of the Charlie Hebdo attack, then the true answer is false because four days later "everyone" was giving voice to everyone's nonbeing. As Debord says, "in a world that *really* has been turned on its head, truth is a moment of falsehood."[24]

5.7.2. Bilogic promotes a regime of non-Truth that is diametrically opposed to the old fascist monologic of Truth. At the center of a dissolving society stands the meontological supposition *I am nothing*, "Je suis Charlie," which is the contrary of *We are everything*, "Wir sind die Herrenrasse." Importantly, this kind of schizoid negativism does not cancel the subject. Despite appearances, desubjectification still amounts to a particular form of subjectification. Here the subject is derealized, as it were, but not destroyed. By derealization, I do not mean that the real itself disappears; rather, the real—namely, the subject's failure—is experienced as illusion. Hence the subject's sense of relief. As Debord remarks, "Spectacular time is the time of a real transformation experienced as illusion."[25] This explains why the meontological subject-supposition is so hard to detect yet so attractive. When the subject finds its way into nothingness, yelling at the world "Je suis Charlie," it is as though all of its failures are bypassed. A weird feeling of euphoria arises. But who feels this way? If the answer is "everyone," this is because "everyone" is no one. "Everyone" *really* becomes an illusion in "a world that *really* has been turned on its head." Spectacle is the name for such a ubiquitous illusion. The university is the place where this illusion is reinforced on a daily basis.

6. Ever since its foundation, the university has been instrumental in legitimizing and consolidating power, whether at the service of the church, the king, or the state. Today, the role of the university is no less crucial, even though "it is no longer clear what the place of the University is within society nor what the exact nature of that society is," as Bill Readings notes.[26] In the following, I will take up this issue from a grammatical point of view. There is no need to stress that the *technocratic* turn of today's power is largely contingent on the new *technologies* of power developed in the field of contemporary social sciences, from economics to legal studies. But what is the grammar, if any, that underlies academic research focused on such matters?

6.1. In modern times, political parties and the university relate differently to the society in which they operate. Parties represent the latter as a body politic that follows a *subjective* grammar. The university offers a more or less *objective* knowledge of society. But the university is far from immune to political conditioning. Quite the contrary, its role is to bridge the distance between one's knowledge of society and the political nature of one's own society. In this light, the differences between the European university and the American university reflect the differences between European and American societies. In both cases, as Readings makes plain, the university "takes on responsibility for working out the relation between the subject and the state":[27]

Where Fichte's University aspires in its structure to the condition of the state (with plans for funding provided in detail), Humboldt's appears as a productive supplement to the state. . . .

The plan outlined by Humboldt for the University of Berlin synthesized the fundamental reorganization of the discourse on knowledge by which the University took on an indirect or cultural function for the state: that of the simultaneous search for its objective cultural meaning as a historical entity and the subjective moral training of its subjects as potential bearers of that identity. . . . The University is not just a site for contemplation that is then to be transformed into action. The University, that is, is not simply an instrument of state policy; rather, the University must embody thought as action, as striving for an ideal. This is its bond with the state, for state and University are the two sides of a single coin. The University seeks to embody thought as action toward an ideal; the state must seek to realize action as thought, the idea of the nation. The state protects the action of the University; the University safeguards the thought of the state. And each strives to realize the idea of national culture.[28]

This is a very different paradigm from the American university:

The role of the American University is not to bring to light the content of its culture, to realize a national meaning; it is rather to deliver on a national *promise*, a contract. . . . This is because American civil society is structured by the trope of the promise or contract rather than on the basis of a single national ethnicity. Hence where Fichte's university project offers to realize the essence of a *Volk* by revealing its hidden nature in the form of the nation-state, the American University offers to deliver on the promise of a rational civil society. . . .

Thus the *form* of the European idea of culture is preserved in the humanities in the United States, but the cultural form has no inherent content. The content of the canon is grounded upon the moment of social contract rather than the continuity of a historical tradition, and therefore is always open to revision.

This contractual vision of society is what allows Harvard to offer itself "in the service of the nation" or New York University to call itself a "private university in the public service." What such service might mean is not singularly determined by a unitary cultural center. The idea of the nation is always already an abstraction in America.[29]

6.2. Leaving aside some minor discrepancies, Readings's understanding of European and American societies is rather close to mine, and Readings, too, emphasizes that our time is characterized by "the hollowing out of political subjectivity"—namely, depoliticization. Yet, Readings and I do not agree on everything. In particular, he claims that "the hollowing out of political subjectivity" parallels "the hollowing out of the state."[30] As I have stressed, I do not consider this to be the case. Furthermore, Readings seems to believe that depoliticization entails the vanishing of all forms of political order. I would rather say that we live in the age of a "restored order, an order which is an iron one," as Lacan remarked in one of his late seminars.[31] From my point of view, the state and the university are the mainstays, not the hostages, of this new *ordre de fer*.

6.3. One of the distinctive traits of hard fascism is the hyperpoliticization of society. Here the university must comply with a totalitarian Truth sponsored by a totalitarian party. Soft fascism, based on depoliticization, turns the tables. Political parties are marginalized, desubjectification replaces hypersubjectification, and the university is charged with new tasks. Many contend that the university is a *victim* of such a neoliberal reconfiguration of the world. Readings himself takes this view. From my perspective, however, the university is an *agent* of this transformation. The victimizing attitude is due to the fact that those who complain about the metamorphosis of the university come from departments, typically within the humanities, that are indeed victimized. But every time these departments lose ground (and funding), *other* departments gain ground (and funding). Nobody in a department of economics, education, cognitive science, or social and political science feels victimized today. The reason is that these are the departments where a new form of knowledge is growing and coming to prominence. This new form of knowledge follows a new grammar, the grammar of fractal subsets, the same grammar that organizes globalized societies.

6.4. Readings counterposes the new University of Excellence to the old University of Culture and closes his book with a rather pessimistic diagnosis (similar to previous ones).[32] But neither Readings nor anyone else gives us any clues about what kind of knowledge (or "discourse," as Lacan would say) the neoliberal University of Excellence promotes and cultivates. In light of the above, it is possible to make some conjecture concerning the grammatical structure of the neoliberal apparatuses of knowledge. Within the new epistemic framework, the key concepts are right, choice, and behavior. Each of these categories functions as a delusional metonymy in that each of them names a *pars qua totum*— more precisely, a different *pars* of the same *totum*. For this reason, all of these categories are to be understood as *homothetic*: they all refer to the same entity, the human population, which is the ultimate and unique *subjectum* of a dissolving society.

6.5. The university is so important today because it fosters the metapolitical recoding of society. Think about economics. The impact that economic surveys undertaken by eminent academics have on national policies is considerable. The economists who occupy major positions in academia are the same ones who set the agenda in organizations such as the International Monetary Fund or the World Bank, and they have the power to determine the political agenda of many national governments from above, as though they were able to speak a metapolitical language. Let us now turn to the categories of right, choice, and behavior. These are not so much the objects as the *frames of reference* of some significant branches of academic research. Legal and political studies consider the people's rights. Economic and social studies investigate the people's choices. Biological and psychological studies examine the people's behaviors. Needless to say, people cannot be reduced to their own rights, or choices, or behaviors. People are persons—individuals. Nevertheless, from the point of view of the neoliberal university, people are not individuals in the first instance. In some respects, there are no individuals at all, just as there is no such thing as society. Indeed, for neoliberal technocrats and most academic researchers, individuals become relevant only after they have been cut into smaller segments and organized into subsets. Each of these subsets names a *pars*, a part of the individual, and each subset is literally equated with the *totum*: the human population into which every individual dissolves. *Pars qua totum*. Political subjectivity thus disappears into metapolitical objectivity.

6.5.1. In this perspective, individuals *are* insofar as they *are not*, because individuals are trapped in the bilogical and fractal dimension of delusional metonymies. On the one hand, the individual continues to be a discrete entity that enacts rights, choices, and behaviors. On the other hand, rights, choices, and behaviors stop being the attributes of a single and discrete individual, for they are now related to a deeper continuum, to an all-encompassing and perfectly anonymous *subjectum* that is abstracted away from individuals. Consider, again, economics. Today, this science does not take into consideration the individual, the so-called *homo economicus* who tends to maximize profit, but rather choices (technically, "revealed preferences") taken en masse. Economics computes choices and studies their environments (technically, "the markets") without making any additional (and doubtful) assumptions about the rational or irrational nature of the *homo economicus*. Or else, think about the life sciences. Today, molecular biology does not focus on individual organisms but on population behaviors (or "patterns" of behavior) taken en masse. It is a certain behavior, rather than a certain individual, that is encoded in a gene. Genes define individuals and not vice versa. The same holds for psychological research that analyzes human behaviors in relation with cognitive skills and social performances taken en masse. In sum, the same grammar underlies academic research in all of these fields, and this grammar dissolves individuals in the human population, thereby making individuals *be* in the form of *nonbeing*.

6.5.2. But what *is* the human population? As I have said, it is not a collection of individuals; rather, it is a continuum of fractal subsets, typically rights, choices, and behaviors. This means that the human population is a set of a particular kind, a Cantor set, which is self-similar. Briefly put, the human population *is* each of its subsets; it is nothing but rights, choices, and behaviors. From this it follows that all of its subsets are homothetic, because their domains equal the domain of the whole set. Each subset can be equated with another by reason of its transfinite equality with the whole set; thus, all behaviors can be equated with as many choices and rights, all choices can be equated with as many behaviors and rights, and all rights can be equated with as many behaviors and choices. LGBT rights, for example, reflect a certain number of sexual choices and behaviors; but the equation between rights on the one side, and choices and behaviors on the other, remains valid even when we reverse it. In theory, any sexual choice or behavior can be changed into a right. This is why the list of LGBT rights can be extended *ad libitum*. We can talk about LGBTTQIAP rights (Lesbian, Gay, Bisexual, Transgender, Transsexual, Queer, Intersex, Asexual, Pansexual), but we can also expand this catalogue at any moment, adding further choices and behaviors (such as polyamorous, bondage, dominance, masochism, and so forth). There are no a priori limits to the homothetic equation among rights, choices, and behaviors.

6.5.3. From the above, it is clear that the metapolitical recoding of society promotes the hyperjuridification of society (as any choice or behavior can morph into a right) and the infinitization of social heterogeneity. But, in spite of appearances, infinite heterogeneity is no heterogeneity. Again, bilogic takes center stage. The infinitization of social heterogeneity multiplies differences by turning differences between individuals into more detailed and minute differences among behaviors, choices, and rights. Thus, it tends to hybridize people, not to differentiate them, for people are now seen as being composed of elements (behaviors, choices, and rights) taken from the same anonymous continuum, the human population, that nullifies discreteness and distinction among individuals. As a result, the very possibility of claiming one's difference is jeopardized. Not so many years ago, gay people began to fight for their sacrosanct right to inclusion. Today, this fight can be harder than before because of the neutralizing effects produced by the new grammar. Homosexuals and heterosexuals no longer oppose each other. Homosexuality and heterosexuality are part of a wider and infinitely nuanced continuum of sexual behaviors. And the point is that no one *is* these behaviors. No one is in a position to claim one's own *individuality* in front of other people, because the infinitization of social heterogeneity leads to a kind of ironclad uniformity that segregates "everyone" from "everyone." As François Jullien put it, "the *uniform* is the perverted double of that universal which is now being spread by globalization."[33]

6.6. When we speak of the human population in terms of rights (the human family), or choices (the markets), or behaviors (populations in the biological or psychological sense), we always speak about the same uniform and diaphanous continuum, which is not a political but a metapolitical entity. The university is the place where such a ubiquitous entity is brought to life by transforming all proper subsets into fractal subsets of the same Cantor set.

6.6.1. A proper subset is an ordinary subset. For instance, children and adults who live in a certain town are proper subsets of all the people who live in that town. The same holds for males and females. Here the set of all inhabitants is a whole, and different subsets correspond to different parts of that whole. For centuries, human beings have been *counted* this way. But suppose that we classify people according to sexual orientation. This small change of perspective does nothing but introduce two new subsets, heterosexuals and homosexuals, which we differentiate by taking into consideration sexual behavior. In so doing, we are still counting human beings and dividing them into proper subsets. Imagine a village in which ten people live. Five are men; five are women. After dividing them into heterosexuals and homosexuals, we discover that six of them are heterosexuals and four are homosexuals. The total amount of people is always the same, and whether we classify people according to gender or sexual orientation, every subset is a finite part of a finite whole. Now let us introduce a new behavioral definition, say, masochism. One person can be a heterosexual and a masochist, or a homosexual and a masochist, at the same time. As we continue to add further behavioral definitions, things become more and more complicated. In the end, the range of sexual behaviors is infinite, as we know from psychoanalysis. Sexual behaviors are uncountable by definition. So, as soon as we try to grasp and enumerate all of them, they start to multiply like the points on a line, gradually disappearing into a kind of undifferentiated continuum: at that moment, *uncountable* behaviors detach themselves from *countable* human beings. Behaviors start to exist—or *inexist*—on their own. Each person or group of persons (proper subsets of any larger set of human beings) can thus be redefined and recoded in terms of behaviors (fractal subsets of the same uncountable continuum). No one *is* these behaviors, but people can be accounted for in terms of behaviors, for these behaviors turn them into the epiphenomenon of an underlying and uniform *subjectum*,

the human population, which *is* nothing but behaviors. *Pars qua totum.*
Kenneth Burke called this kind of literalized and delusional metonymy
a "real" metonymy:

> "Metonymy" is a device of "poetic realism"—but its partner, "reduc-
> tion," is a device of "scientific realism." Here "poetry" and "behavior-
> ism" meet. For the poet spontaneously knows that "beauty *is* as beauty
> *does*" (that the "state" must be "embodied" in an actualization). He
> knows that human relations require actions, which are *dramatiza-
> tions*, and that the essential medium of drama is the posturing, tonal-
> izing body placed in a material scene. . . .
>
> He also knows, however, that these bodily equivalents are but part
> of the *idiom of expression* involved in the act. They are "figures." They
> are hardly other than "symbolizations." Hence, for all his "archai-
> cizing" usage here, he is not offering his metonymy as a *substantial*
> reduction. For in "poetic realism," states of mind as the motives of
> action are not reducible to materialistic terms. Thus, though there is
> a sense in which both the poetic behaviorist and the scientific behav-
> iorist are exemplifying the strategy of metonymy . . . the first is using
> metonymy as a *terminological* reduction whereas the scientific behav-
> iorist offers his reduction as a "real" reduction.[34]

6.6.2. The human population is the uncountable continuum not
only of behaviors but also of choices. Take, for example, cultures. For
centuries, human communities have been associated with cultures. All
who belonged to the same community were seen as sharing the same
culture. Now things have changed, not only because many different
cultures coexist in our societies but also because people can *choose* their
own culture. People are thought to be free to select from a variety of options, and cultures are ranked among such options. In this perspective,
cultures are what each one of us opts for and not an essential ingredient
of personality traits. This notion is new. Not so long ago, a culture was
considered a background against which the range of possible choices
at one's disposal was fixed. Nowadays, by contrast, cultures are commodified. For this reason, it is not correct to say that ours is a multi-
cultural society. Rather, our societies are becoming a cultural market
in which one's sense of belonging to any culture tends to dissolve, and

people can pick from a fast-growing spectrum of cultures, subcultures, mixed cultures, postcultures, and so on. Cultures are thus redefined in terms of choice, and cultural choices become indistinguishable from choices in general, which are infinite in number. Once more, a finite set of *countable* cultures and peoples is mapped onto a fractal set of options, a continuum of *uncountable* options. The main consequence of this transformation becomes apparent whenever we ask ourselves, Who makes a choice here? Not someone who belongs to a specific culture but rather "everyone," that is, no one. If people can make cultural choices, this is because people do not have any culture on their own, or so "everyone" believes. The human population, namely "everyone," is a neutral and indefinite continuum of choices. As Readings observes, the new university plays a key role in this commodification of cultures. In a dissolving society where the neoliberal faith in the market dominates, "there is no longer any culture to be excluded from," he explains. "The word *culture* no longer names a metadiscursive project with both historical extension and critical contemporaneity from which we might be excluded."[35] If anything, the word *culture* names an object of consumption that the university has the task of providing, after making it accessible and consumable. In this manner, cultures are recoded and deprived of any distant exteriority. A fractal-like society has no outside, as I noted previously, and the university ensures that nothing remains out of reach, that everything becomes available to "everyone." But this entails that the university deprives our society of any interiority. A society with no outside has no inside.

6.6.3. The neoliberal university pursues the hollowing out of society by taking advantage of the homothetic equation among behaviors, choices, and rights. Rights multiply, while being progressively desubjectified and traced back to the meontological continuum of the human population. In this way, they are recoded. The sets of constitutional rights belonging to nationals morph into the fractal set of universal human rights that "everyone" holds. *Entpolitisierung* takes root. As a matter of principle, any behavior or choice can be transformed into a right, and ever new rights can be deduced from the human population's choices and behaviors. The new university is the place where such homothetic transformations are produced, one after the other, thus pursuing the metapolitical recoding of society that ultimately aims at re-placing all subjective, political representations of society with objective, depoliticized knowledge. Seen in this light, depoliticization reveals itself to be an *epistemological* undertaking. This is not to say that depoliticization does not follow a political grammar. *Entpolitisierung*, contrary to Carl Schmitt's belief, does not entail the end of politics or the end of "the political." But the point here is that depoliticization marks the birth of a new alliance between politics and knowledge. The grammar of new fascism, like the grammar of old fascism, is both political and scientific. The difference between the two forms of fascism lies in the fact that hard fascism bet on political hypersubjectification, while soft fascism privileges knowledge, a brand-new form of investigation into human beings, one that fuels and at the same time exploits the people's desubjectification. From legal and political studies to economics, from gender studies to psychology, from cultural studies to education, the same grammar centered on delusional metonymies traces the boundar-ies of today's scientific research. An invisible and binding *ordre de fer* reigns over the university and turns it into the main agent of depoliti-cization. As Readings had realized, no critical inquiry into the present can leave the university out of consideration, and it is clear that a great deal of work is yet to be done as regards the nature and mission of the new university. It is worth repeating that this work should not concern exclusively the way in which the university is being reorganized from a financial, bureaucratic, and institutional point of view. On a broader perspective, what really matters is the way in which academic research is being reorganized—and·the growing harmony that resounds within the university's walls. Is it mere chance that psychoanalysis, the science of subjectivity, is being thrown out of the university's premises?

Conclusion

The Politics of Infinite Sets

What are the causes of the so-called neoliberal revolution? And what is next? As to the first question, there are certainly many causes. The metapolitical recoding of Western societies finds its raison d'être in a number of concomitant factors. It all started with the trauma of Auschwitz and the horrified response to the ultranationalist abomination named Nazism. Then, in a matter of years, further developments started to affect the course of history; economic and technological developments fueled a process of increasing *denationalization*—or, in my own words, of political desubjectification. Against this background, the old political compromises between the people and the state have been progressively altered and undermined. Nowadays, in the age of information technology and unprecedented economic globalization, it seems quite unrealistic to conceive of any return to the past. Moreover, the metapolitical recoding of society is unstoppable because of the parasitic nature of the neoliberal grammar. As already indicated, this grammar is like a virus. It does not destroy but eats the host organism. Thus, on the one hand, it needs the latter to remain alive in one way or another. But, on the other hand, the virus devitalizes the host organism over time. As a result of this double constraint, we witness not so much the death as the most decrepit age of two well-known characters of modern political history: European nationalism and American exceptionalism. Today, no matter how loud their voices may be, there is nothing that can prevent them from becoming exhausted and extinct in the long run. By no means can they get rid of a virus that makes the most of their allergic reactions. But can the virus itself outlive its host organisms? Nobody can predict the future. In the following, after going over some key notions that need further clarification, I will confine myself to some considerations on Europe.

INFINITE

Who are we? How do we count ourselves? It is hard to tell these questions apart. In the classical world, human communities were composed of a finite number of human beings because the cosmos itself and everything in it were deemed to be finite. Then, Christianity came into the world and, with it, infinity. Christians were the children of an infinite God, and they were thought to be infinite in number and in essence, for God had created human beings in His own image, and everybody on Earth could be redeemed by the Savior's blood. With the beginning of the secular age, the star of Christianity started to wane, but the idea of infinity remained in the background. Early modern societies were still Christian in origin, and for them the question was then, How to deal with the infinite heritage of Christianity? Unsurprisingly, the first answers were more or less consonant with the teachings of Christian theology.

Infinitum actu non datur. Infinity does not exist *actually* but only *potentially.* When it comes to human communities, this entails that people are potentially, not actually, infinite in number and in essence. In this perspective, human beings form delimited communities, which nonetheless tend toward infinitization. The connections between nation and humanity on the one side, society and mankind on the other, were so forged as to abide by the principle of potential infinity. After some centuries, however, another possibility—actual infinity—emerged and began to inflame the people's imagination.

The world of potential infinity was the world of early modern democracy, inconclusive by its own nature and infected with "bad infinity."

We may call it a Gaussian world, after the name of the mathematician Carl Friedrich Gauss, who fiercely opposed the idea of actual infinity throughout his life: "I protest against the use of an infinite quantity as an actual entity. This is never allowed in mathematics. The infinite is only a *façon de parler*, in which one properly speaks of limits to which certain ratios can come as near as desired, while others are permitted to increase without bound."[1] The world of actual infinity, by contrast, may be called a Cantorian world, after the name of the mathematician who discovered the "paradise" (David Hilbert's definition) of actual infinite sets. Some consider Georg Cantor's paradise to be the product of his sick imagination. Ludwig Wittgenstein, for instance, labeled Cantor's infinities pure "jokes."[2] Nevertheless, those jokes attest to certain potentialities of human subjectivity, and this is why Lacan and Matte-Blanco paid much attention to Cantor's arguments. For Lacan, in particular, Cantor's infinities were one of the signs that a new frontier in Western civilization had been crossed. Interestingly, Wittgenstein himself was well aware that Cantor's jokes reflected "the sickness of a time"—a sickness that cannot be cured through a philosophical remedy invented by an individual. For a cure to be possible, he said, an alteration in the people's "mode of thought and of life" is required: "The sickness of a time is cured by an alteration in the mode of life of human beings, and it was possible for the sickness of philosophical problems to get cured only through a changed mode of thought and of life, not through a medicine invented by an individual."[3]

Perhaps Wittgenstein is right. Philosophemes are not a cure for problems such as Cantor's infinities. That being said, Wittgenstein's remarks are far from satisfactory for the simple reason that we should not limit ourselves to acknowledging the sickness of a time or of some theoretical puzzles. We should also endeavor to understand how and why we get sick. If we examine Cantor's jokes from this point of view, which is the point of view of psychoanalysis, things look more complex. The question is no longer What is wrong with Cantor's paradise? The question now becomes How do we get into such paradise? And to address this issue, we need to take into account not only philosophy and mathematics but also the people's "mode of thought and of life," as Wittgenstein put it. Nowadays, in fact, we do live in Cantor's paradise, the paradise of the Cantor set, and our own *life* can therefore teach us something about the road that leads to heaven.[4]

MULTITUDO

The Latin word for set is *multitudo*. According to Thomas Aquinas, "multitudo non est aliud quam aggregatio unitatum."[5] If we combine this definition with Thomas Hobbes's famous pronouncements on the *multitudo*, it seems possible to argue that modern politics has been tormented by the problem of infinite sets since the very beginning. In the modern age, the infinitization of human beings brought about by Christianity posed a number of problems, both practical and theoretical. For the Christian gospel, all the people on earth are to be recognized as human beings that can be redeemed by the Savior's blood, whatever their origins and culture may be. Accordingly, every finite set of human beings—*populus* in Hobbes's terminology—is just one among many, and all of these sets are to be seen as the subsets of a potential infinite set of human beings—*multitudo* in Hobbes's terminology. For the father of modern political theory, this amounts to saying that any political community, or "commonwealth," represents a delimited and politically qualified subset of individuals who belong, at the same time, to an unlimited and politically unqualified set of human beings. The notions of *populus* and *multitudo* refer to these distinct yet interconnected sets: the former, the *populus*, is a finite subset of the latter, the *multitudo*, which is a potential infinite set. As Hobbes argues, whoever belongs to the *populus* is part of the *multitudo* as well. For this reason, the two terms are to some extent interchangeable, and Hobbes sometimes uses them without distinction.

The *multitude*, however, is not only the potential infinite set of all human beings. For Hobbes, this concept also refers to the reverse side of the *populus* (or of any "body politic"). In *Leviathan*, for example, when Hobbes explains that the people must count themselves as One "artificial person" in order to establish sovereign power, he makes a point of specifying that sovereign power is "the government of a multitude,"[6] implying thereby that the *multitudo* does not disintegrate the day the sovereign power is "authorized" and the *populus*, or the "political person," is formed and counted as One. On the contrary, the *multitudo* is still there at that moment, although it now appears as the inertial body of the *populus*, on which the sovereign exerts its power.

Therefore, the *populus* and the *multitudo* partially overlap and partially diverge in Hobbes's theorization. The difference between them lies in the fact that the *populus* is always counted as One, whereas the *multitudo* are the Many that cannot be counted. Again, the *populus* is a finite subset of a wider and potentially infinite set, the *multitudo*. When the people are counted, they all equal One, a united and qualified *populus*; when they are not counted, they blend into the Many, an unqualified *multitudo*. The One can be defined as the *political subject* that gives voice to the *summa potestas*; the Many can be defined as the *political object* that is governed by the *summa potestas*. Importantly, the One and the Many are not strangers to each other; they are strictly interrelated.[7]

POPULATION

"Being is said in many ways," Aristotle remarked, and the same holds for the *multitudo*, which is what the two categories of humanity and mankind refer to, each in its own way. As I have argued throughout this book, both categories designate a remainder that challenges and at the same time triggers subjectification. Humanity is the remainder of axiomatic political subjects; mankind is the remainder of demonstrative political subjects. These remainders are ontological in nature because they point to "man" as such, not "the citizen." Consider nationalism. When people become one nation, they acquire power over themselves. Thus, they become sovereign subjects and governed objects, *populus* and *multitudo*, nation and humanity at the same time. As sovereign subjects, they *act*. As governed objects, they simply *are* there. That said, they can *act* collectively and exert power over themselves if and only if each of them *is* there. The object-humanity lies at the heart of the subject-nation, and it is at the level of the object-humanity that the question arises as to which rights are to be ascribed to those who merge into the subject-nation, so as to restrict the arbitrariness of the people's "general will." When it comes to separatism, nothing changes except that axiomatic metaphors give way to demonstrative metonymies and that mankind replaces humanity. Here, too, a political remainder is molded into an object that remains at a distance from the political subject. Because this object and the political *nos* never identify with each other, the process of democratic subjectification and the related process of emancipation can start and go on indefinitely. Modern democracy is contingent on such an unbridgeable gap between *acting* and *being*, between the people's power and the people's resilience.

Things change, though, when the political remainders of nationalism or separatism are thought to be disposable components of democracy. When this happens, delusional metaphors or metonymies come into effect and impact the way in which people perceive themselves and society as a whole. These moments mark the birth of fascism, or pseudo-democracy. Here, the *populus* and the *multitudo* collapse into one another. Within the framework of old fascism, the *multitudo* is absorbed into the *populus*, being into acting. Those who identify with the *populus* bear witness to a new political Truth; those who cannot are doomed to extinction. With new fascism, the situation is reversed. The *populus* dissolves into the *multitudo*, acting into being, with the paradoxical result that being itself becomes indistinguishable from non-being. The human population comes into existence insofar as conflicts are neutralized and political subjects regress into nonexistence.

Given these premises, it is arguable that the human population is the latest manifestation of the *multitudo*, but emphasis must be placed on the fact that the *multitudo* of our time tends to silence the people(s), nourishing a kind of political negativism that puts the life of democracy in danger.

SETS

Humanity and mankind are the potential infinite sets that draw the interior frontiers of axiomatic and demonstrative political subjects, respectively. Both of them are *infinite* sets because both exceed the finite sets of the people that compose a nationalist or separatist society. But both of them are only *potential* infinite sets because they do not possess any actual existence; they just surpass, and delimit, all finite subsets that are included in them. The truth be told, no mathematician would ever use the concept of potential infinite sets with regard to such sets, for no such set is manageable or even conceivable in mathematical terms. We should therefore speak, more properly, of humanity and mankind as the inconceivable infinite sets on which modern democracy is founded. But once we move from the field of mathematics to the field of political history, the key question becomes, What if the infinite sets which lay the foundations for modern democracy were deemed to be conceivable and manageable in political terms? From a mathematical point of view, this would entail leaving the realm of *potential* infinite sets and entering the realm of *actual* infinite sets.

As I have said, these are the sets that Cantor brought into focus: the countable infinite set and the uncountable infinite set. To begin with, consider the set of all even numbers. A one-to-one correspondence can be established between this set (2, 4, 6 . . .) and the set of all natural numbers (1, 2, 3 . . .). It follows that the set of all even numbers can be counted, despite its being infinite. The size of this set equals the size of the set of all natural numbers, and the name of this equinumerosity is aleph-0, the first transfinite number. As Cantor explains, however, not all actual infinite sets can be counted. Consider the set of all real numbers, which includes natural numbers, rational numbers (such as negative integers and fractions), and irrational numbers (such as the square root of 2 and π). On the basis of Cantor's "diagonal argument," it can be proved that this set is larger than the set of all natural numbers and, therefore, uncountable. Still, this set has a size or cardinality. The conclusion that Cantor draws from this argument reads thus: there exists an infinite set that is uncountable and amounts to aleph-1, the second transfinite number.

As I have explained, there seems to be a subterranean pathway that leads from our everyday world, especially the world of fascism, to Cantor's paradise. Within the framework of old fascism, a one-to-one correspondence could be established between, say, the master race and humanity. Although the former was a subset of the latter, the subset (the master race) was equated with the set (humanity). This result was achieved by eradicating all other subsets of humanity (the inferior races). The Nazis' obsession with counting and the notorious accuracy with which they did their calculations are among the signs that aleph-0 is the unconscious cipher of hard fascism and, more generally, the key to delusional metaphors. With new fascism, the uncountable infinite set enters the picture. Take the categories of right, choice, and behavior. Each of them is a *pars qua totum* of the human population. That is to say, each of them is a way of describing and conceiving the human population. But concepts are rather fuzzy here. If the *totum* is a quantity, then the *pars qua totum* is a concept for quantity. Yet this quantity is uncountable, for each *pars* equals the *totum* in this case. As a consequence, the human population is not counted but is nonetheless measured over and over again, amounting as it does to a cipher, aleph-1, which is the invariant unit of measurement for schizophrenic metonymies. On these bases, a plurality of invisible connections (or homothetic transformations) between rights, choices, and behaviors can be envisioned. If rights, choices, and behaviors name different things, this is because they refer not to One thing but to the not-One.

CONTINUUM

The concept of the continuum poses many challenges to common sense. The first thing to note is that it fosters and at the same time forbids measurement. In a sense, the continuum lends itself to infinite measurement precisely because it cannot be measured. The reason for this is that all measurements of the continuum tend to duplicate and reproduce the very unit of measurement, aleph-1. Thus, what is measured and what measures somehow coincide. Take a line. We can divide it into equal segments and use the latter as a unit of measurement for the line as a whole. But then, we can do the same with the segments themselves, cutting them into smaller and smaller fragments. What are we measuring? And what is the unit of measurement? If we repeat this operation *ad infinitum*, the answer is the same for both questions: the continuum. This is why rights, choices, and behaviors, which should measure the human population, end up *being* the human population itself. As should be clear, however, they *are* the human population on condition that they *are not* the human population. Otherwise, how could they measure it?

Another feature of the continuum is no less impressive: whatever it touches turns into the continuum itself. In mathematical terms, if the uncountable set X is a subset of set Y, then Y is uncountable—no matter whether Y is a finite or infinite set. Therefore, if a *pars qua totum*, a part of the continuum, is found to be a subset of a set that is not uncountable in and of itself, the latter nonetheless morphs into an uncountable set. It becomes part of the continuum and acquires the same characteristics, irrespective of what it was a moment before. Therein lies the secret of the metapolitical recoding of our societies. Typically, when some constitutional rights that are ranked among the prerogatives of one countable people are redefined as the universal rights of the human population, then the initial set, one countable people, turns into an uncountable set and dissolves into the faceless continuum of the human population. As a result, the interior frontiers that demarcate one *populus* from the other disappear. Instead, there appears a new pacified *multitudo* in which no one is counted and everyone is measured.

The logical complement of this metapolitical recoding is the meontological supposition: *ego non sum, nos non sumus*. More correctly, we should speak of a bilogical complement here. Indeed, the continuum sucks everything and everyone into nonbeing but only because nonbeing is thus brought into being. Every time that we think of nonbeing, it remains undeniable that we think of it as something that is. Hence the bilogical twist of any meontological supposition. Nonbeing is, or else it becomes unthinkable. Philosophers have often been baffled by this paradox, but psychiatrists and psychoanalysts have also encountered this problem from time to time. Donald Winnicott, for instance, introduced the category of "false self" for the purpose of clarifying the schizoid attitude of people who see themselves as *not being* themselves. Years later, Lacan's notion of "sinthome" (false symptom) pointed more or less in the same direction. Yet the mystery remains. In short, for both philosophers and psychopathologists, the question is How is it possible that nonbeing be understood as being? How to make sense of this patent absurdity? What ties being and nonbeing together? Cantor's theory offers one of the most intriguing explanations: the continuum. From the point of view of set theory, nonbeing appears as an infinite dissolution of being. When this infinite dissolution is taken as *actual*, then nonbeing comes into being. But that does not make nonbeing more real. If anything, the ultimate nature of nonbeing comes to light this way.

LIFE

The ultimate nature of nonbeing is grammatical, and this explains why a false self—singular and plural at the same time, that is to say, "universal"—hides behind such diverse areas of discursive elaboration as those previously analyzed: international law, political representation, European integration, infotainment, and academic research. In all of these cases, the subject is literally nowhere and therefore everywhere. A bilogical grammar dictates that "there is no such thing as society" in a neoliberal world. A monological grammar dictated that "there exists only one society" in the world as viewed from Nazi Germany. It is grammar that renders soft fascism the exact opposite of hard fascism. And grammar helps us to prevent confusion. Take, for example, the much-debated issue of biopolitics. According to Michel Foucault, Nazism pushed the biopolitical drift of late modern societies to extremes.[8] For some, this means that we still need to distance ourselves from Nazism, as we continue to live under the sign of biopolitics.[9] But, beside the fact that Nazism cannot be understood unless we take into account the ultranationalist (not just the biopolitical) roots of Nazi Germany, biopolitics in the neoliberal age and biopolitics in the age of Nazism are not comparable. The two versions of fascism are placed at opposite ends of the biopolitical spectrum.[10] If we look at them from a grammatical point of view, one appears as the inversion of the other.

The grammar of the word *life*, for instance, varies depending on the context. Within the framework of Nazism, *Life* was capitalized, as it was deemed to be the key to the political Truth that the master race embodied. Life was taken as a metaphor of this absolute Truth. But for the revelation of Truth to be possible, this metaphor was to be rendered into literal language. The Truth of Life was to be spelled out through a newspeak capable of resolving the metaphorical surplus value of Life into the literal meaning of biological statements. Hence the *ontological positivism* that characterized Nazism. Science was urged to provide support to politics and thus obliged to meet the party's expectations. Since the Nazi biopolitical subject was thought to be a political-and-natural entity, the Nazis conceived of a political-and-scientific, metaphorical-and-literal Word, which was supposed to disclose the Truth about Life and the glorious fate of the master race.

Nowadays, life has no such metaphorical surplus value. Instead, life has become a continuum into which everything dissolves. Rights, choices, and behaviors are all concepts of the same thing; they all are metonymic embodiments of life, but they do not conceal any glorious truth to be discovered one day, for they are ultimately concepts of the not-One, of "a life," which cannot be appropriated by any subject. In the end, the life of the human family, of the markets, of the human population is the life of no one in particular, as it is the life of every-one. It follows that today's biopolitical desubjectification points in the opposite direction to that of Nazi hypersubjectification. Each *pars qua totum* equation between life and rights, choices, and behaviors does nothing but reinforce the delusional equation between life and the not-One, life and nonbeing. Hence the *ontological negativism* that characterizes our time. Science now attests every day that *ego non sum, nos non sumus.*

DIGNITY

The inverse correlation between the Nazi world and ours becomes evident when we turn our attention to the modern idea of human dignity. This idea and the modern conception of rights are interrelated. The idea of dignity, which is part of the Christian legacy, basically means that human beings are infinite in number and in essence. Humanity and mankind are two different ways of updating the Christian faith in human beings' infinity. Neither of the two categories refers to a finite set of individuals, *populus*. Both of them point to a potential infinite set of human beings, *multitudo*. When a modern *populus* becomes sovereign, a *multitudo*—whether it is shaped into humanity or mankind—is there. This *multitudo* is not only infinite, however. It is also characterized by a number of natural rights that protect the Many against the One, the *populus*. And it is precisely because natural rights are understood as being the endowment of a potentially infinite multitude of human beings that modern people are said to have infinite dignity or "priceless" dignity, as Immanuel Kant put it. Modern people are deemed to be infinite in number and in essence every time that they claim their own rights. That is the secret of their inconceivable dignity.

Nazism posed one of the most serious threats to human dignity. The Nazis dreamt of a perfect identification between *Volk* and humanity, between the conceivable and the inconceivable, between the literal and the metaphorical layers of political language, with the result that the *multitudo* was condemned to extinction—and with it, any remnants of subjective rights and of "priceless" dignity. For the Nazis, human dignity was infinite *and* countable, as they made no distinction between human dignity and the master race's supremacy, which they endeavored to test and quantify with precision. With this end in view, the Nazis divided human beings into two groups: those who epitomized humanity, and those who were said to be alien to humanity. The counting of the former group was to be achieved through the counting, and annihilation, of the latter group. Once all other specimens of humanity had disappeared, the Aryan race could finally appear as the true embodiment of humanity. Hence the obsessive enumeration of those who were unworthy of Life, through which the Nazis sought to establish themselves as the countable infinite set of humanity. In a certain sense, the number tattooed on all victims of the Nazi camps was always the same: aleph-o.

Today, the situation is reversed. Dignity is on everybody's lips. Politicians campaign for it, humanitarian organizations lobby in its name, and the media around the world make grandiose statements about the dignity of all human beings. Yet such an endless apology for human dignity rings hollow. For everyone is endowed with human dignity, but no one can actually lay claim to it. That is to say, everyone is in a position to talk about human dignity *in the third person*, but no one is in a position to claim it *in the first person*. In fact, human dignity has become an attribute of the human population, the latest manifestation of the *multitudo*, into which the *ego* and the *nos* tend to dissolve. Thus, human dignity is preserved as the uncountable benchmark of "a life," but it no longer names the dignity of the people. If anything, it names the dignity of rights, choices, and behaviors that are recoded and abstracted away from the people. Because of this metapolitical recoding, human dignity is desubjectified nowadays, just like subjective rights.

Ours is the infinite dignity of the not-One, aleph-1, which is the cipher of our *nonbeing*.

HOMO EUROPAEUS

What is to be done in this situation? What barricades can be erected against the meontological dissolution of the people? It is difficult to tell, not least because Wittgenstein is right in saying that no medicine invented by an individual can cure the sickness of a time. Yet a healthy dose of skepticism about the role of philosophy or of theory should not push us into assuming that theory cannot tell us anything at all about the future. It is all too obvious that no theoretical interpretation of history can, by itself, transform the world. As Karl Marx famously remarked in his *Theses on Feuerbach*, "the philosophers have only *interpreted* the world, in various ways; the point is to *change* it."[11] Interestingly, however, the most important question goes unanswered here: how to change the world? What does it mean to change the world? In reality, contrary to Marx's belief, any change in the people's mode of thought and of life—or in their subjectivity—reveals itself to be the product of an interpretation from a psychoanalytic point of view. And perhaps Marx should have paid more attention to the very concept of interpretation. For psychoanalysis, an interpretation is, more often than not, an *act*. The psychoanalyst's interpretation of a neurotic symptom is surely not the same as the theoretical interpretation and explanation of neuroses in general. In philosophical terms, the former is a performative speech act, the latter a constative speech act. That said, the psychoanalyst's interpretation of a symptom is necessarily based on a theoretical understanding of a certain situation as a whole, which can be classified as neurosis, for instance, and which is seen as affording some possibilities and not others. With psychoanalysis, in other words, we are in a position to make a distinction and at the same time a connection between abstract, theoretical interpretations and curative, performative interpretations. Can we make a distinction-and-connection of the same type between political theory and political practice? Maybe we can, provided that our *theoretical interpretation* of some past and present situations proves to be compatible with some *political interpretation* of present and future developments, just as an abstract interpretation of neurosis is compatible with a concrete and curative interpretation of this or that symptom.

As regards the theory of political grammars, it amounts to an abstract interpretation of the unconscious foundations of modern democracy. According to this theory, three conditions must be satisfied to give birth to a modern democratic society. First of all, people must rebel collectively against someone or something, thereby starting to speak and act in the first-person plural. Second, people must claim some unalienable rights that have not yet been recognized and ratified at the institutional level. Third, after a period of time, the insurrectional moment must give way to the constitutional moment, and this paramount passage entails that the insurrectional *nos* stabilizes through a political grammar that integrates the *ego*'s demands into the people's collective and sovereign will. If we redefine the entire process of democratization as a process of political emancipation, we may rephrase the above as follows: *Why* do people start a process of political emancipation? Because suffering becomes intolerable. *When* do people start a process of political emancipation? The day they manage to interpret their own suffering as a violation of their own rights. *How* do people start a process of political emancipation? By merging into a political *nos* and claiming their rights collectively. *Against whom or what* do people start a process of political emancipation? Against the state or, more generally, established institutions. Based on these considerations, it does seem possible to conclude that a modern democracy is born every time that the original and unbearable tension between the people and the state finds a way to stabilize without being removed. Indeed, democracy does not mark the end of all suffering. Democracy, especially modern democracy, is only a way to deal with, and thus lessen, the people's suffering. The concept of political grammar refers to this basically unsettled, yet regularized, state of affairs. As I have emphasized in the previous sections, political grammars lay the foundations of modern democracies in that they enable modern societies to cope with their own suffering and dysfunctioning on a secure and solid basis. In this sense, a political grammar is the product of a political interpretation of the unbearable, of the intolerable, which makes it tolerable again and, to a greater or lesser extent, livable.

Over the past century, some political interpretations have been taken to extremes, and the Western world has been pushed into the abyss of fascism. The dream of doing away with all suffering has been taken literally, and that dream has always turned into the nightmare of pseudo-democracy—first with hard fascism, then with soft fascism. The gloomy implications of hard fascism are clear to everybody, those of soft fascism less so. But take, for example, the so-called Islamic menace. Who could seriously argue that the Western world may soon be swamped by hordes of Islamic barbarians? Yet people indulge in such an unpleasant reverie and are mesmerized by the mass media that remind them on a daily basis not that the possibility of falling prey to a terrorist attack is statistically minimal but rather that they find themselves in mortal danger. In all likelihood, one of the reasons for this irrational behavior is that the Islamic beheading of innocent victims becomes a compelling representation of the meontological supposition around which a dissolving society revolves. It is as though people saw themselves in those images of death and remained trapped in them. Thus, people are horrified and become ever more passive. Democratic subjectification is turned upside down. And to stop this process of political petrification, a political—not a theoretical—interpretation is needed. A theoretical interpretation can describe the conditions for a potential improvement or rebirth of democracy. A political interpretation materializes those conditions. From a theoretical (abstract) point of view, modern democracy relies on a chain of either metaphorical or metonymic equivalences that transform the people into *one* people. From a political (concrete) point of view, the perspective changes and the queries become, *Which* metaphors or metonymies can start a process of democratization here and now? *Which* rights are at stake here and now? *Whom or what* are we fighting? None of these questions can be answered easily in the age of the metapolitical recoding of society. All conventional metaphors and metonymies tend to be neutralized by the neoliberal grammar, all rights tend to be desubjectified, and what is more, both the state and the society tend to dissolve into the continuum of a fractal-like world. In our time, globalization is a synonym of denationalization. How can democracy be revived under such circumstances? What is the political counterpart to the theory of political grammars?

To begin with, the survival of democracy cannot be taken for granted. If the neoliberal virus managed to kill all of its host organisms, we would witness the ruin of both democracy and pseudo-democracy. The debate over the compatibility between democracy and globalization has already started in many corners of the Western world. In the end, democracy is a human invention that is subject to decay sooner or later. Having said this, it seems highly unlikely that democracy will disappear in a heartbeat, for at least three reasons. First, we are just at the beginning of the mortal combat between the neoliberal virus and all of its opponents; European nationalism, in particular, is still far from being defeated as a political grammar or ideology. Second, democracy and capitalism are closely intertwined, as many thinkers of the Marxist tradition have clarified, and there is no evidence that capitalism is about to be replaced with a new type of economy. Third, a new political interpretation of the present situation and a renewal of democracy are still possible.

Take Europe. In this case, the survival of democracy is largely contingent on the fate of nationalities and the capability of extending the chain of metaphorical equivalences beyond the borders of national communities. As we have seen, the metapolitical recoding of society leads to the dissolution of all nationalities into the continuum of the human population. A new political interpretation should interrupt this recoding and revive European nationalities within a broader yet delimited context—a *meta*national context, as it were. For this to be possible, two conditions must be satisfied: Europeans must mobilize against someone or something; and new subjective rights must be claimed. As to the first condition, if democracy is to be reframed at a metanational level, then people must mobilize against not only the nation-state but also those institutions that include the nation-state in a supranational space—that is to say, European institutions. As to the second condition, in order to mobilize at a metanational level, Europeans must claim new subjective rights—for instance, the right to hospitality.

Before going on, it is important that we recognize that a political interpretation can achieve a result that a theoretical interpretation cannot achieve: a fracture in the continuum. Think about fundamental rights, which are both context-dependent (constitutional) and context-free (universal) rights. The metapolitical mapping of the former rights onto the latter is possible only on condition that no further rights come into play and decouple the national coding and the international recoding of rights. So, if we start claiming a right that can be granted by the nation-state but cannot be duplicated by international law, we end up in a situation in which the metapolitical recoding is surpassed and interrupted by a new element. The right to hospitality is that sort of element, and it is one that only a political interpretation can bring forth. Imagine that every European has the right to enter other European countries. This right would not necessarily be at variance with the rights already granted by nation-states—the civil, social, and political rights of the citizen—but would be at variance with the current tenets of international law, because it would enshrine the principle that people in Europe are entitled to *enter* a number of foreign countries, and not only to *leave* any country, as the Universal Declaration of Human Rights says.

In my view, if this right were recognized as a metanational right by several countries in Europe, this would greatly help the European population to become a metanational people. I am aware that these considerations may seem paradoxical, as European law already provides for freedom of movement and residence within the territory of the Member States. Article 45 of the Charter of Fundamental Rights of the European Union says, "Every citizen of the Union has the right to move and reside freely within the territory of the Member States." Article 3 of the Treaty on European Union says, "The Union shall offer its citizens an area of freedom, security and justice without internal frontiers, in which the free movement of persons is ensured in conjunction with appropriate measures with respect to external border controls, asylum, immigration and the prevention and combating of crime." Finally, Directive 2004/38/EC of the European Parliament and of the Council says, "Citizenship of the Union confers on every citizen of the Union a primary and individual right to move and reside freely within the territory of the Member States, subject to the limitations and conditions laid down in the Treaty and to the measures adopted to give it effect." So why am I talking about a *new* right to hospitality that should be claimed by Europeans?

The reason is because freedom of movement and residence is likely to be called into question in a matter of years. Originally, Europeans received this right as a gift from above. Everything was decided in high places, with no democratic validation. No antagonistic mobilization, no speech act in the first-person plural, no process of political subjectification paved the way for the aforementioned enactments of European law. But now that Europe is being torn apart by a severe economic, social, and political crisis, Europeans could be deprived of this right at any moment and find themselves obliged to reclaim freedom of movement and residence through political mobilization, thus starting a true process of democratization on a European scale. To clarify this point, let me recapitulate how the present situation in Europe looks from a grammatical point of view. A couple of aspects deserve particular attention.

First of all, the resurgence of nationalism. As a rule, every ontological impasse of the nation is paralleled by an ideological revival of nationalism. With the ascent of neoliberalism, European nations have been seriously challenged by the grammar of soft fascism that maps all national sets onto the fractal sets of rights, choices, and behaviors. Nationalism as we know it cannot stop this process of metapolitical recoding. Nationalism can only be excited by this process. Hence the great instability and the growing tension between nationalism and neoliberalism that has put Europe in jeopardy.

The situation has been aggravated by the attempt to achieve economic integration without political integration. As most economists had warned, the single market and the common currency required that all countries were willing to share their financial resources and assist each other in case of necessity. Yet no sense of belonging to the same *demos* has arisen over the last thirty-five-plus years because European integration has followed the grammar of the meontological supposition and fostered a process of political desubjectification rather than a process of political integration into the same political *nos*.

In view of this, the EU is now heading toward disintegration. The splitting of the eurozone seems to be just a matter of time, with unpredictable consequences for the single market. That does not mean that nationalism is about to win the war against neoliberalism because no current version of nationalism can get rid of the metapolitical recoding of national sets. As things stand now, only ultranationalism might do away with neoliberalism, and European nationalists could actually be driven toward ultranationalism in the years to come. That said, the most interesting thing about the eurozone crisis is that both the birth and the death of the common currency can be traced back to the same grammatical deficit. In the absence of any feeling of proximity and solidarity between people of different nationalities, the Member States were obliged to follow the path of a merely monetary union. But in the absence of those feelings, it turned out to be impossible to back up the euro with the required fiscal transfers from north to south. The euro was thus caught amid the conflict between nationalists and Europeists.

Because of that, not only the euro but also the single market is going to be renegotiated, with the unexpected result that freedom of movement and residence across the Continent might be brought into question at some point. At that moment, however, the right to hospitality might cease to be a right in the third person and become a right in the first person. In general, no significant changes in history are due to the people's awakening to reality; such an illusion is typical of thinkers who feel confident about the political effectiveness of their philosophical interpretation of history. But the fact remains that after more than thirty years of peace without barriers between European countries, people might resist the temptation to rebuild those barriers all of a sudden. It is not unreasonable to imagine that Europeans might even insist that their national societies continue to compose a larger community of nations, a renewed "European Community" instead of the "European Union," and that European institutions continue to perform some particular and limited duties under the control of the European Parliament.

There is no need to go into detail about the legal form that this new arrangement might take. What matters most is that a passage like this would amount to a political interpretation and a democratic re-organization of Europe based on, or largely supported by, the people's demand that freedom of movement and residence all over the Continent be preserved. This interpretation would also allow Europe to survive the demise of the euro. No doubt the collapse of the monetary union would entail the (partial or total) dismantling of the EU's economic governance framework, but it would not imply, automatically, the end of the European project as a whole, as many like to repeat. For instance, European law—and national legislations that now conform to European legislation—could not be undone overnight. All of this took years to accomplish and cannot be annulled all at once. Thus, it is more than plausible that European institutions would continue to exist and be charged with some—residual or new—tasks after the fall of the euro. Only the dream of building a new sovereign entity, the United States of Europe, from the ashes of European nations would vanish at that moment. The good news is that the decline of European nations would be stopped at the same time, and therefore nationalism—which is always inflamed by the nation's decline—would be somewhat sedated. Europe could no longer be thought of as a drastic alternative to nationalities, and the new European Community could not endanger the core metaphor that underpins the existence of each and every European nation. Rather, the former could appear as a new peripheral metaphor of the latter at that point, but one that is common to all European nations this time. Accordingly, nationalism could evolve into a new form of *meta*nationalism, centered on a new transversal and metanational metaphor: the new Europe. Within this context (vaguely reminiscent of what Charles de Gaulle called *Europe des nations*), European citizenship might be characterized not only by the citizen's affiliation to a European nation-state (in accord with De Gaulle's wishes) but also by the possession of a special right, the right to hospitality, the transversal and metanational right vindicated by the peoples of Europe and protected by all nation-states that recognize Europe as a metanational space of freedom. The advantage of this political interpretation of the EU's crisis is there for all to see. A faint ray of democratic subjectification would shine over the Continent, paving the way for the rise of a European people that could be perceived as a common development of European nations, not as a threatening substitute for them. In addition to this, this metanationalist interpretation of the EU's crisis might be followed after a while by a progressive or leftist interpretation aimed at extending the right to hospitality to nationals of third countries—more on that in a moment.

To recapitulate, the upsurge of nationalism is a statement of fact; the conflict between nationalism and neoliberalism is the present, not the future, of Europe, and this conflict can only worsen with the passing of time. As I have observed, in order to make the single market and the common currency really sustainable from a socioeconomic point of view, European nations should communalize their economic policies or else the strong states should pay for the debts of the weaker states. But economic integration in Europe was achieved through the metapolitical recoding of society and under the assumption that people need not undergo a process of subjectification and integration into the same political *nos* for the purpose of living together. Because of this neoliberal framing of political life, no sense of proximity and solidarity has emerged among the peoples of Europe during the past three decades. Worse still, a process of political desubjectification has started all over the Continent, weakening the feelings of proximity and solidarity even among the citizens (*populus*) of each country. Thus, when the economic crisis hit Europe, the only way the worst-off could respond to this situation was to turn away from the meontological supposition of neoliberal Europe and look back to nationalism. That said, neoliberalism is not allergic to nationalism. In fact, the opposite is true: nationalism remains vulnerable to neoliberalism, and neoliberalism in turn needs nationalism. The metapolitical recoding of society requires a preexisting coding, or a grammar, on which the bilogic of soft fascism keeps operating. The virus survives at the expense of a living, not a dead, host organism. Hence the ever harsher polarization between "sovereigntists" and "Europeists" that is the source of trouble in most countries.

Given the high social cost of the euro, hardly sustainable in the long term, nationalists are likely to win the first round against neoliberals.[12] But shortly afterward, the two political fronts might reach a provisional compromise that could lead to a rearrangement of the European political space. Before, during, or after the splitting of the common currency and the renegotiation of the single market, freedom of movement and residence within the territory of European countries might be claimed and reasserted as an unalienable right of all citizens in Europe—the right to hospitality, a right that should not have supremacy over national law but that could be implemented through the national law of most, if not all, European countries. People from both political fronts might find themselves making this claim: people from the neoliberal front, because this claim would second their repugnance against borders;

people from the nationalist front, because this claim would reinforce the nation-state and its prerogatives on the international scale. This convergence would fracture the continuum of the human population. Indeed, the *homo nationalis* would be shaped into a *homo europaeus*, and Europe would change into a metanational metaphor of humanity, one that counterposes the new axiomatic dignity of some (or all) European nationals to the infinite yet ineffective dignity of "everyone." The fact that a fracture in the continuum has been generated would be attested by the unevenness produced by such developments. European nationals would be granted a privilege that differentiates them from all other peoples of the world. The *homo europaeus* would acquire a new right—the right, not just the permission, to move and reside elsewhere in Europe—and a special dignity compared to non-Europeans.

It would be extremely difficult to recode this right and absorb it into the fractal-like structure of neoliberal society, because this right would engender an asymmetry, a curvature in the flat space of soft fascism. However minimal this curvature may seem, it would make an exception and draw a clear line between Europe and the rest of the world. For the first time in history, some (or all) European nations would be aligned along the same political frontier not by virtue of a diktat from above but by virtue of a demand made from below. The goal of awakening a common sense of belonging among the peoples of Europe—a goal that has been pursued in vain for several years now—would be reached not through the dissolution of European nations but thanks to the sense of national belonging that has underpinned the existence of European nation-states for centuries. The *homo europaeus* would be seen as a further achievement of the *homo nationalis* and not as a complete refutation of European history. Thus, it would become easier for Europeans to find common ground and celebrate together the unparalleled historical and cultural dignity of Europe, which must be proudly exalted to keep the European ideal alive.

There is nothing disgraceful about self-absorption. Every process of political subjectification involves taking oneself for someone special. With the sole exception of soft fascism, every time that a new political grammar has been put into practice, the related political subject has claimed to have a particular place in history and a unique role to play.

From a grammatical point of view, nobody is to blame for this senti-ment that provides the subject with a sufficient amount of narcissistic self-esteem. Only when we adopt a normative "view from nowhere," and not a clinical view from within, we feel like being entitled to judge and stigmatize the conceited subjects that confront each other relentlessly. By contrast, when we opt for a grammatical approach to history, we are in a position to realize that these judgments are misplaced and that the "view from nowhere" is far from being politically neutral, because it reflects the process of neoliberal neutralization and of increasing desubjectification that characterizes our time. The normativist's be-lief that democracy can be judged to be good or bad on the basis of moral reasoning, that the political agenda should just implement the most correct or accredited theoretical arguments about the issues at stake, that the people's wishes should be supplanted with more objective decision-making criteria—all of this betrays a radical misconception of democracy. For democracy, in and of itself, is neither good nor bad. Rather, democracy should be understood as a particular context within which our subjective beliefs about what is good and what is bad can find expression and interact with each other, thus giving rise to (more or less) permanent compromises, which I call political grammars, and which ordinarily convey a self-centered view of the world.

As regards the *homo nationalis* and the *homo europaeus*, many may nonetheless feel disturbed by the Eurocentric implications of these metaphors, and the question therefore arises as to what political—not purely theoretical or alleged neutral—interpretation of that feeling could be given in the future. In Europe, the most typical objection to the *homo nationalis* has been socialism over the past two centuries. But what kind of socialist objection to the *homo europaeus* might be made one day? In the long term, if Europe will eventually turn into a metanational metaphor of humanity that fractures the continuum of the human population by bestowing a new right, the right to hos-pitality, on European nationals, a *meta*socialist interpretation of that evolution might do nothing but head toward extending this right to nationals of third countries. Such an extension would necessarily entail strengthening European institutions after the first wave of metanation-alism. In fact, from a metasocialist perspective, European citizenship would become distinct from national citizenship, a new *ius hospitalitatis* would appear beside the *ius soli* and *ius sanguinis* that regulate citizenship within the nation-state, and only European institutions could be charged with the task of issuing European passports for third country nationals. On these premises, moreover, it could also be envisaged that non-European nationals who live and work legally on the Continent be enfranchised without being nationals of a Member State. Even if these people have not obtained citizenship in a European nation-state, they could be seen as members of a potential European constituency that would be larger than the sum of European nationals and would be instrumental in consolidating a less Eurocentric European *demos*—a people of foreigners.

As Hans Kelsen pointed out a century ago, something similar had already been envisioned during one of the most critical times in the history of socialism. In the wake of the Bolshevik Revolution, full political rights were granted to foreigners who lived and worked legally in the newborn Russian Soviet Republic.[13] Kelsen, who had no special affinity with Lenin, defines this innovation as "a step of historic proportions." In the distant future, the same idea may set a European Left against a European Right and nourish the dream of a European parliament elected by a European constituency that is larger than the sum of national constituencies:

> The latest constitutional developments demonstrate that political rights do not necessarily have to be connected to citizenship. Breaking a thousand-year-old barrier, the constitution of Soviet Russia also grants all foreigners, who live in Russia for work-related reasons, full political equality. Given the exceedingly slow progress of the cosmopolitan idea [*Menschheitsgedankens*] in the theory of law, where those foreign to the state were at first considered downright outlaws and only gradually came to be granted civil—but, to this day, typically not political—equality, the Soviet constitution represents a step of historic proportions.[14]

ORGANIC CRISIS

Perhaps the above considerations will remain pure speculation. It is perfectly possible that hard fascism will prevail in some places or that soft fascism will continue to suck blood from the peoples of Europe or that the EU will disintegrate and leave the field open for a narrower confederation of countries guided by the most powerful of all—the reunified Germany. Nobody can make exact predictions about the future. From a theoretical point of view, all we can do is wait and see. There are moments in history when a new beginning is much longed-for, and yet nothing happens. Think about Italy in the first half of the sixteenth century. At that time, Niccolò Machiavelli made a plea for the political integration of the Italian Peninsula, but no "prince" was ready for the appointment with history. Today, the situation in Europe is similar, as no theoretical interpretation of the present can substitute for a political interpretation. Centuries ago, the problem was how to solidify and democratize centralized states. Nowadays, the problem is how to solidify new institutions larger than states while leaving democracy intact. And the future looks grim in this regard.

That said, a glimmer of hope can be found in the theory of political grammars. Indeed, even though the survival of democracy in Europe cannot be taken for granted, there is reason to believe that a new political interpretation will emerge sooner or later and reinvent democracy in one way or another. Ours is the secular age, that is, the age of first-person societies and of modern democracy—at worst, of pseudo-democracy. In our age, a political interpretation is how people render the intolerable tolerable again by reviving an already existing political grammar or, less often, by establishing a new political grammar. The success of political leadership is measured, precisely, by the ability to provide people with an interpretation that enables them to come through an unbearable stalemate. Sometimes people have only one political interpretation at their disposal; at other times, two or more interpretations enter into competition with one another. Whatever the case, it is always a political interpretation that allows people to subjectify a traumatic situation, one that can be so traumatic as to prevent them from being the same as before.

Europe is in agony today because of a crisis that is being interpreted in two opposite ways: neoliberalism and nationalism—with the menace of ultranationalism lurking in the background. But the goal of a political interpretation is to enable most people to subjectify as many critical conditions and unprecedented constraints as possible. The larger the number of the new conditions and constraints that can be accounted for by a political interpretation, the greater the latter's success. And the fact is that neither of the aforementioned interpretations go a long way toward achieving this goal. Neoliberalism does not provide the means to react to the malfunction of the EU—for instance, the malfunction of the common currency in the absence of a communalized fiscal policy—through political mobilization. On the contrary, people are demobilized because of the underlying process of desubjectification and depoliticization that neoliberalism promotes. Owing to this grammatical drawback, an increasing number of people are pushed back into nationalism. But the latter, in turn, falls short of providing the means to subjectify the new conditions and constraints imposed by the growing economic and technological interdependence between countries that make it impossible for any past and isolationist version of nationalism to survive this critical moment in the long run. Furthermore, as I have stated, *nationalism* in the traditional sense of the word has no means with which to stop the metapolitical recoding of society that neoliberalism fuels. Nationalism remains vulnerable to infection by the virus of soft fascism. Hence the impending risk of hard fascism, which is the only grammar immune to contagion.

In view of all this, it is legitimate to conclude that we are at a turning point. As Antonio Gramsci would say, Europe is going through an "organic crisis," which "consists precisely in the fact that the old is dying and the new cannot be born; in this interregnum a great variety of morbid symptoms appear."[15] Back in Gramsci's day, an organic crisis—a crisis that is at once economic, political, social, and ideological and that leads to the rejection of established political parties, economic policies, and value systems—prepared the ground for the rise of hard fascism. Today, it might prepare the ground for a new grammatical arrangement of European society. After a long sequence of shocks, turmoil, and vertiginous vacillations between ineffective alternatives, first metanationalism and then metasocialism might emerge as the most adequate responses to the metapolitical recoding of society. The future will show whether this possibility will become a reality. Better said, the past will show it, as our future is still heavily influenced by the past, and when the past comes back and strikes us with enough energy, it reopens the games and raises the curtain on a new day. *Ego sum, nos sumus*: please close your eyes and try again.

Notes

FOREWORD

1. Jean-Jacques Rousseau, *Discourse on the Sciences and Arts or First Discourse* (1750), in *The Discourses and Other Early Political Writings*, trans. and ed. Victor Gourevitch (Cambridge: Cambridge University Press, 1997), §54, 24.

PREFACE

1. Thomas Hobbes, *Leviathan* (Oxford: Oxford University Press, 1998), 7.

2. Ernest Renan, *Qu'est-ce qu'une nation?* (Paris: Calmann Lévy, 1882), 26.

3. A note for Lacanians: when I speak of "grammar" (in the Lacanian sense), I always mean "phantasy" (in the Lacanian sense). Usually, *grammar* is not considered a key word in Lacan's thought, but Lacan himself is quite clear about the grammatical nature of all phantasies. I will expand on this aspect of his theory throughout the book.

4. Ludwig Wittgenstein, *Philosophical Investigations* (London: Blackwell, 2009), 109.

5. Economic studies based on empirical evidence lead to the same conclusion: trust is contingent on feelings of affinity and a sense of closeness among people. "The effect of heterogeneity on trust is in large partly due to the fact that individuals trust those more similar to themselves. Based upon all these results, can one conclude that if one person is (exogenously) moved from a less to a more homogeneous community he or she will trust others more? This is, of course, a very difficult question, but our results are not inconsistent with an affirmative answer." Alberto Alesina and Eliana La Ferrara, "Who Trusts Others?," *Journal of Public Economics* 85 (2002): 231. The problem here is how to interpret the words *homogeneity* and *heterogeneity*, which economists take for self-evident concepts.

6. See, e.g., David Miller, *Citizenship and National Identity* (Cambridge: Polity, 2000):

That we need such solidarity is something that I intend to take for granted here. I assume that in societies in which economic markets play a central role, there is a strong tendency towards social atomization, where each person looks out for the interests of herself and her immediate social network. As a result it is potentially difficult to mobilize people to provide collective goods, it is difficult to get them to agree to practices of redistribution from which they are not likely personally to benefit, and so forth. These problems can be avoided only where there exists large-scale solidarity, such that people feel themselves to be members of an overarching community, and to have social duties to act for the common good of that community, to help out other members when they are in need, etc.

Nationality is *de facto* the main source of such solidarity. (32)

7. Johann Gottlieb Fichte, *Addresses to the German Nation*, ed. Gregory Moore (Cambridge: Cambridge University Press, 2008), 166.

8. Dieter Grimm, "Does Europe Need a Constitution?," in *The Question of Europe*, ed. Peter Gowan and Perry Anderson (London: Verso, 1997), 252.

9. Jürgen Habermas, *The Inclusion of the Other: Studies in Political Theory*, ed. Ciaran Cronin and Pablo de Greiff (Cambridge, MA: MIT Press, 1998), 155–61.

10. See Dieter Grimm, *Constitutionalism: Past, Present, and Future* (Oxford: Oxford University Press, 2016), 305–11.

11. "Europe in Hard Times. A Conversation with Dieter Grimm and Michael Wilkinson," *Ordines*, no. 1 (2018): 344.

12. Jürgen Habermas, "Entrevista," *El País*, April 25, 2018.

13. Frank Michelman, "Always Under Law?," *Constitutional Commentary* 12, no. 2 (1995): 240–41.

14. Frank Michelman, "Constitutional Authorship by the People," *Notre Dame Law Review* 74, no. 5 (1999): 1624; Bruce Ackermann, "The Storrs Lectures: Discovering the Constitution," *Yale Law Journal* 93, no. 1013 (1984): 1045–49.

15. Jacques Rancière, "Critical Questions on the Theory of Recognition," in Axel Honneth and Jacques Rancière, *Recognition or Disagreement: A Critical Encounter on the Politics of Freedom, Equality, and Identity*, ed. Katia Genel and Jean-Philippe Deranty (New York: Columbia University Press, 2016), 92–93.

16. Axel Honneth and Jacques Rancière, "A Critical Discussion," in Honneth and Rancière, *Recognition or Disagreement*, 123.

17. Honneth and Rancière, 128.

18. Judith Butler, "Can One Lead a Good Life in a Bad Life?," *Radical Philosophy* 176 (2012): 10.

19. In some respects, this book might also be seen as an attempt to explain why Hilary Putnam is right in saying that "we all have to live and judge from within our particular inheritances while remaining open to insights and criticisms from outside." "Must We Choose between Patriotism and Universal Reason?," in *For Love of Country?*, ed. Joshua Cohen (Boston: Beacon, 2002), 97.

20. "My normative aim . . ." Butler, "Can One Lead a Good Life?," 15.

INTRODUCTION: THE CARTESIAN CONNECTION

1. Georg Wilhelm Friedrich Hegel, *Enzyklopädie der philosophischen Wissenschaften im Grundrisse*, vol. 1 (Frankfurt am Main: Suhrkamp, 1970), §64.

2. John Locke, *An Essay Concerning Human Understanding* (London: Penguin, 1997), 312–13.

3. Martin Heidegger, *Being and Time*, trans. John Macquarrie and Edward Robinson (Oxford: Blackwell, 1962), 68.

4. In the field of analytic philosophy, these questions are still at the center of fierce debate, as the two following citations attest:

> On one view the putatively referential use of "I" creates a grammatical illusion. We recall Lichtenberg's critique of Descartes' Cogito: there is thinking going on, but it does not follow that there is something that thinks. The view that there isn't anything at all that thinks I'll call the No-Self view. I do not subscribe to it, for I insist that although *the self is not some thing*, nevertheless *it is not nothing*. (Bas van Fraassen, "Transcendence of the Ego [The Non-Existent Knight]," in *The Self?*, ed. Galen Strawson [Oxford: Blackwell, 2005], 89)

And:

> As is well known, Hume regarded the self as a notion constructed by relating various impressions through resemblance, contiguity, or causation. All we really have is a bundle of perceptions, unified by these relations. Many problems beset this idea. Why should my own impression not equally resemble that of someone else, or be equally contiguous with that of someone else? And similarly, couldn't an impression of mine have a causal relation to that of someone else? In fact, all these things do happen. It is not fair to say that only the impressions that I am aware of count. And, as I have already emphasized, Hume says that we confusedly form the notion of a single, persisting entity because of the close relations between the various impressions. But who is this "we" who do this? (Saul Kripke, "The First Person," in *Philosophical Troubles: Collected Papers*, vol. 1 [Oxford: Oxford University Press, 2011], 306–7)

5. According to Lacan:

"I am thinking, therefore I am" (*cogito ergo sum*) is not simply the formulation in which the link between the transparency of the transcendental subject and his existential affirmation is constituted, at the historical apex of reflection on the conditions of science. Perhaps I am only object and mechanism (and so nothing more than phenomenon), but assuredly, insofar as I think so, I am—absolutely. Philosophers certainly made important corrections here—namely, that in that which is thinking (*cogitans*), I am never doing anything but constituting myself as an object (*cogitatum*). The fact remains that through this extreme purification of the transcendental subject, my existential link to its project seems irrefutable, at least in the form of its actuality, and that *"cogito ergo sum," ubi cogito, ibi sum*, overcomes this objection. (Jacques Lacan, *Écrits: The First Complete Edition in English*, trans. Bruce Fink [New York: Norton, 2005], 429)

6. Lacan, 340.

7. Sigmund Freud, *Group Psychology and the Analysis of the Ego*, in *The Standard Edition of the Complete Psychological Works of Sigmund Freud*, vol. 18 (London: Hogarth, 1955), 69.

8. John Rawls, *The Law of Peoples* (Cambridge, MA: Harvard University Press, 1999), 23.

9. Hans Kelsen, *The Essence and Value of Democracy*, ed. Nadia Urbinati and Carlo Invernizzi Accetti (Lanham, MD: Rowman and Littlefield, 2013), 36.

10. "According to Kelsen, the people in a democracy has no distinct and prior political existence, because its unity is but the unity of a legal order. By denying the prior existence of the people as a political unity, Kelsen, in Schmitt's eyes, collapses constituent into constituted power and politics into law, thereby hypostatizing the legal order into a self-grounding, self-serving, and self-sustaining system of rules." Hans Lindahl, "Constituent Power and Reflexive Identity: Towards an Ontology of Collective Selfhood," in *The Paradox of Constitutionalism: Constituent Power and Constitutional Form*, ed. Martin Loughlin and Neil Walker (Oxford: Oxford University Press, 2007), 9.

11. Kelsen, *The Essence and Value of Democracy*, 36.

12. "There has been a large majority consensus among philosophers of the later twentieth century concerning nationalism, and that consensus has been broadly hostile and dismissive." Neil MacCormick, *Questioning Sovereignty: Law, State, and Nation in the European Commonwealth* (Oxford: Oxford University Press, 2002), 159.

13. For a general survey, see Anthony D. Smith, *Nationalism* (Cambridge: Polity, 2001); and Umut Özkirimli, *Theories of Nationalism* (New York: Palgrave Macmillan, 2010).

14. John Stuart Mill, "Considerations on Representative Government," in *Collected Works*, vol. 19 (Toronto: University of Toronto Press, 1977), 546.

15. Cornelius Castoriadis, *L'institution imaginaire de la société* (Paris: Seuil, 1975); Benedict Anderson, *Imagined Communities: Reflections on the Origin and Spread of Nationalism* (London: Verso, 1983); Bronislaw Baczko, *Les imaginaires sociaux* (Paris: Payot, 1984); Charles Taylor, *Modern Social Imaginaries* (Durham, NC: Duke University Press, 2004).

16. "This is precisely why the unconscious, which tells us the truth about truth, is structured like a language, and why I, in so teaching, tell the truth about Freud who knew how to let the truth—going by the name of the unconscious—speak." Lacan, *Écrits*, 737.

17. G. W. F. Hegel, *Phenomenology of Spirit*, trans. A. V. Miller (Oxford: Oxford University Press, 1977), 110.

18. See Norberto Bobbio, *The Age of Rights*, trans. Allan Cameron (Cambridge: Polity, 1996).

19. Jürgen Habermas has put a strong emphasis on the "co-originality" of private and public autonomy, of human rights and popular sovereignty: "The sought-for internal relation between popular sovereignty and human rights consists in the fact that the system of rights states precisely the conditions under which the forms of communication necessary for the genesis of legitimate law can be legally institutionalized." Jürgen Habermas, *Between Facts and Norms: Contributions to a Discourse Theory of Law and Democracy*, trans. William Rehg (Cambridge, MA: MIT Press, 1996), 104. Habermas's co-originality thesis is closely related to the idea of "constitutional patriotism." As Jan-Werner Müller explains, constitutional patriotism "designates the idea that political attachment ought to center on the norms, the values and, more indirectly, the procedures of a liberal democratic constitution." Jan-Werner Müller, *Constitutional Patriotism* (Princeton, NJ: Princeton University Press, 2007), 1. In the following, I will not discuss the normative value of constitutional patriotism but rather contend that many aspects of modern democracy go unnoticed when we look at them from the point of view of normative political theory.

20. Marcel Mauss, *La nation* (Paris: Presses universitaires de France, 2013), 387.

21. Mauss, 84.

22. Benito Mussolini, "Fascismo," *Enciclopedia Italiana di Scienze, Lettere e Arti*, vol. 14 (Roma: Treccani, 1932). See also the pointed remarks made by Gaetano Salvemini, the Italian historian who was forced into exile by Mussolini: "The Fascists, the Nazis, and the Communists have often labeled the Italian, the German, and the Russian regimes as the *real, true, substantive and most candid* forms of democracy." Gaetano Salvemini, *Sulla democrazia* (Torino: Bollati Boringhieri, 2007), 116–17.

23. By political representation, I mean more specifically "symbolic representation." See Hanna Fenichel Pitkin, *The Concept of Representation* (Berkeley: University of California Press, 1967), 92–111.

24. "As everyone recognizes, fascists had a deep and populist commitment to an 'organic' or 'integral' nation, and this involved an unusually strong sense of its 'enemies,' both abroad and (especially) at home." Michael Mann, *Fascists* (Cambridge: Cambridge University Press, 2004), 13.

25. This point has also been made by Sheldon S. Wolin, *Democracy Incorporated: Managed Democracy and the Specter of Inverted Totalitarianism* (Princeton, NJ: Princeton University Press, 2008).

26. See Alain Touraine, *La fin des sociétés* (Paris: Seuil, 2013).

27. See Wendy Brown, *Undoing the Demos: Neoliberalism's Stealth Revolution* (New York: Zone, 2015).

28. Craig Calhoun, *Nations Matter: Culture, History, and the Cosmopolitan Dream* (London: Routledge, 2007), 80, 84, 114.

29. See, e.g., Étienne Balibar, *Citizen Subject: Foundations for Philosophical Anthropology*, trans. Steven Miller (New York: Fordham University Press, 2016); and Ernesto Laclau, *The Rhetorical Foundations of Society* (London: Verso, 2014).

30. In a similar vein, see also Axel Honneth, *Das Ich im Wir: Studien zur Annerkennungstheorie* (Frankfurt am Main: Suhrkamp, 2010).

31. There are also some similarities between Chantal Mouffe's theory of democracy and mine that are worth noting. See, e.g., Chantal Mouffe, *The Democratic Paradox* (London: Verso, 2000):

> Contrary to those who believe in a necessary harmony between liberalism and democracy, Schmitt makes us see how they conflict, and the dangers the dominance of liberal logic can bring to the exercise of democracy. No doubt there is an opposition between the liberal "grammar" of equality, which postulates universality and reference to "humanity," and the practice of democratic equality, which requires the political moment of discrimination between "us" and "them." However, I think that Schmitt is wrong to present this conflict as a contradiction that is bound to lead liberal democracy to self-destruction. We can accept his insight perfectly well without agreeing with the conclusions he draws. I propose to acknowledge the crucial difference between the liberal and the democratic conceptions of equality, while envisaging their articulation and its consequences in another way. Indeed, such an articulation can be seen as the locus of a *tension* that installs a very important dynamic, which is constitutive of the specificity of liberal democracy as a new political form of society. The democratic logic of constituting the people, and inscribing rights and equality into practices, is necessary to subvert the tendency

towards abstract universalism inherent in liberal discourse. But the articulation with the liberal logic allows us constantly to challenge—through reference to "humanity" and the polemical use of "human rights"—the forms of exclusion that are necessarily inscribed in the political practice of installing those rights and defining "the people" which is going to rule. Notwithstanding the ultimate contradictory nature of the two logics, their articulation therefore has very positive consequences, and there is no reason to share Schmitt's pessimistic verdict concerning liberal democracy. However, we should not be too sanguine about its prospect either. No final resolution or equilibrium between those two conflicting logics is ever possible, and there can be only temporary, pragmatic, unstable and precarious negotiations of the tension between them. Liberal-democratic politics consists, in fact, in the constant process of negotiation and renegotiation—through different hegemonic articulations—of this constitutive paradox. (44-45)

Mouffe contrasts two logics of equality: the liberal logic, based on the principle of "human rights," and the democratic logic, based on the people's mobilization and self-affirmation. According to her, both logics are integral to liberal democracy. I could not agree more. That being said, I do not regard liberalism as a "grammar" and democracy as a "practice." A political grammar, as I understand it, is always already a practice and a compromise between the two logics.

CHAPTER 1: THE CLINICAL APPROACH TO POLITICAL HISTORY

1. Georges Canguilhem, *Writings on Medicine*, trans. Stefanos Geroulanos and Todd Meyers (New York: Fordham University Press, 2012), 45, 48.

2. See Sigmund Freud, *The Dissolution of the Oedipus Complex*, in *The Standard Edition of the Complete Psychological Works of Sigmund Freud*, vol. 19 (London: Hogarth, 1961), 173–79.

3. Jacques Lacan, *Écrits: The First Complete Edition in English*, trans. Bruce Fink (New York: Norton, 2005), 625.

4. Lacan, 11.

5. Lacan, 340.

6. Lacan, 14.

7. See Ludwig Wittgenstein, *Tractatus Logico-Philosophicus* (New York: Routledge, 1974): "Most of the propositions and questions to be found in philosophical works are not false but nonsensical [*unsinnig*]. Consequently we cannot give any answer to questions of this kind, but can only point out that they are nonsensical" (22–23).

8. As Descartes says in his *Meditations on First Philosophy*, the statement *ego sum* is true when I say it or I conceive it in my mind: "Adeo ut, omnibus

satis superque pensitatis, denique statuendum sit hoc pronuntiatum, *Ego sum, ego existo*, quoties a me profertur, vel mente concipitur, necessario esse verum" (Med. 2.25).

9. Jacques Lacan, *Le séminaire, Livre XVI: D'un Autre à l'autre (1968-1969)* (Paris: Seuil, 2006), 30. Unless otherwise noted, all translations of passages from Lacan's seminars are my own.

CHAPTER 2: EMANCIPATIVE GRAMMARS

1. Ernesto Laclau, *On Populist Reason* (London: Verso, 2005), 154.

2. Laclau, 230-31.

3. Sigmund Freud, *Group Psychology and the Analysis of the Ego*, in *The Standard Edition of the Complete Psychological Works of Sigmund Freud*, vol. 18 (London: Hogarth, 1955), 115.

4. Hermann Heller, "Political Democracy and Social Homogeneity," in *Weimar: A Jurisprudence of Crisis*, ed. Arthur J. Jacobson and Bernhard Schlink (Berkeley: University of California Press, 2000), 258.

5. Quoted in Heller, 258.

6. Heller, 258-59.

7. Heller, 260.

8. Heller, 261.

9. Heller, 261.

10. Heller, 261.

11. Heller, 262.

12. Heller, 263.

13. Heller, 262.

14. Heller, 261.

15. Heller, 261.

16. Jacques Rancière, *Disagreement: Politics and Philosophy*, trans. Julie Rose (Minneapolis: University of Minnesota Press, 1999), 35-36.

17. "While doubt has, since Descartes' time, been integrated into the value of judgment, it should certainly be noted that—for the form of assertion studied here—the latter's value depends less upon the doubt which suspends the assertion than on the *anticipated certainty* which first introduced it." Jacques Lacan, *Écrits: The First Complete Edition in English*, trans. Bruce Fink (New York: Norton, 2005), 171.

18. Lacan, *Écrits*, 437.

19. This process is similar, yet not identical, to what is sometimes called "framing" in the field of cognitive research. See, e.g., George Lakoff, *Don't Think of an Elephant! Know Your Values and Frame the Debate* (White River Junction, VT: Chelsea Green, 2004).

20. Charles Tilly, *Contention and Democracy in Europe, 1650-2000* (Cambridge: Cambridge University Press, 2004), 34-35. The same point has been

made by other scholars; see, e.g., Carlo Galli, *Sovranità* (Bologna: Il Mulino, 2019).

21. Laclau's notion of "political discourse" is vaguely reminiscent of Eric Hobsbawn's "public symbolic discourse." See Eric J. Hobsbawm and Terence Ranger, *The Invention of Tradition* (Cambridge: Cambridge University Press, 1983).

22. See George L. Mosse, *The Nationalization of the Masses: Political Symbolism and Mass Movements in Germany from the Napoleonic Wars through the Third Reich* (New York: Howard Ferting, 1974).

CHAPTER 3: HUMAN PROPERTIES

1. Jacques Lacan, *Écrits: The First Complete Edition in English*, trans. Bruce Fink (New York: Norton, 2005), 729.

2. See Lacan, 732–33.

3. Michel Villey, *Le droit et les droits de l'homme* (Paris: Presses universitaires de France, 1983), 78, 115, 129–30. All translations of passages from Villey's books are my own.

4. Michel Villey, *La formation de la pensée juridique moderne* (Paris: Presses universitaires de France, 2006), 593.

5. Villey, 231.

6. Villey, 265.

7. Villey, 267.

8. Thomas Hobbes, *De Cive*, chap. 14, §3.

9. Villey, *Le droit et les droits de l'homme*, 140.

10. Villey, *La formation de la pensée juridique moderne*, 577.

11. Villey, 588.

12. Villey, 579.

13. See, e.g., Brian Tierney, *The Idea of Natural Rights: Studies on Natural Rights, Natural Law, and Church Law, 1150–1625* (Atlanta: Scholars Press for Emory University, 1997).

14. The idea of "proprietates animae naturales" was first introduced by Thomas Aquinas, who saw these properties as an intrinsic feature of man, *potentia*. Aquinas also specified that these properties were neither substance (*substantia*) nor accident (*accidens*). See Alain de Libera, *Archéologie du sujet I: Naissance du sujet* (Paris: Vrin, 2007), 331–37.

15. "Les droits politiques, comme les droits civils, doivent tenir à la qualité de citoyen. Cette propriété légale est la même pour tous." Emmanuel-Joseph Sieyès, *Qu'est-ce que le Tiers État?*, in *Écrits politiques* (Paris: Éditions des archives contemporaines, 1994), 134.

16. Crawford B. Macpherson, *The Political Theory of Possessive Individualism: Hobbes to Locke* (Oxford: Oxford University Press, 2011), 95–96.

17. Macpherson, 97.

18. Macpherson, 153.

19. See Macpherson, 140, 142, 265.

20. Macpherson, 142.

21. See, e.g., Ian Shapiro, *The Evolution of Rights in Liberal Theory* (Cambridge: Cambridge University Press, 1986).

22. See, e.g., Lacan, *Écrits*, 690–91.

23. Jacques Lacan, *The Seminar, Book XIV*, May 10, 1967.

CHAPTER 4: POLITICAL SUBJECTS

1. Jacques Lacan, *Le séminaire, Livre XVI: D'un Autre à l'autre* (Paris: Seuil, 2006), 276.

2. See, e.g., Jacques Lacan, *The Seminar, Book XI: The Four Fundamental Concepts of Psycho-analysis*, trans. Alan Sheridan (New York: Norton, 1981):

> The gap of the unconscious may be said to be *pre-ontological*. I have stressed that all too often forgotten characteristic—forgotten in a way that is not without significance—of the first emergence of the unconscious, namely, that it does not lend itself to ontology. Indeed, what became apparent at first to Freud, to the discoverers, to those who made the first steps, and what still becomes apparent to anyone in analysis who spends time observing what truly belongs to the order of the unconscious, is that it is neither being, nor non-being, but the unrealized. (29–30)

3. Jacques Lacan, *The Seminar, Book XIV*, Jan. 11, 1967.

4. Jacques Lacan, *Écrits: The First Complete Edition in English*, trans. Bruce Fink (New York: Norton, 2005), 691, 731.

5. See Sigmund Freud, *"A Child Is Being Beaten": A Contribution to the Study of the Origin of Sexual Perversions*, in *The Standard Edition of the Complete Psychological Works of Sigmund Freud*, vol. 17 (London: Hogarth, 1955), 175–204.

6. Jacques Lacan, *The Seminar, Book XX: Encore*, trans. Bruce Fink (New York: Norton, 1998), 44.

7. On the "fundamental phantasy," see Jacques Lacan, *Le séminaire, Livre VI: Le désir et son interprétation* (Paris: La Martinière, 2013), 423–42.

8. See Lacan, *The Seminar, Book XIV*, June 21, 1967:

> For phobia, anticipated desire, for hysteria, unsatisfied desire, for obsession, impossible desire. What is the role of the phantasy in this order of neurotic desire? Well then, truth-meaning, I have said. That means the same thing as an axiom: in your interpretation the phantasy has no other role, you have to take it as literally as possible and what you have to do, is to find in each structure a way to define the laws of transformation which assure for this phantasy, in the deduction of the statements of unconscious discourse, *the place of an axiom.*

9. See Lacan, *The Seminar, Book XIV*, June 14, 1967:

[Here is] the aspect that I would call the *demonstration*-aspect, which forms part of this position of the masochist. That he demonstrates—like me on the blackboard, it has the same value—that here alone is the locus of *jouissance*. Demonstrating it forms part of his *jouissance*. And the demonstration is no less valid for all that. All perversion has always this demonstrative dimension. I mean not that it demonstrates for us, but that the pervert himself is a demonstrator. And he is the one who has the intention, not of course the perversion.

10. Jacques Lacan, *Je parle aux murs* (Paris: Seuil, 2011), 19.

11. Lacan, *The Seminar, Book XIV*, May 10, 1967.

12. Lacan, Jan. 18, 1967.

13. Alain Badiou, *Theory of the Subject*, trans. Bruno Bosteels (London: Continuum, 2009); Alain Badiou, *Being and Event*, trans. Oliver Feltham (London: Bloomsbury, 2013).

14. Ludwig Wittgenstein, *Philosophical Investigations* (Oxford: Blackwell, 2009), 123.

15. Jacques Lacan, *The Seminar, Book XII*, Feb. 3, 1965.

16. Ernesto Laclau, *On Populist Reason* (London: Verso, 2005), 116.

17. Ernesto Laclau and Lilian Zac, "Minding the Gap: The Subject of Politics," in *The Making of Political Identities*, ed. Ernesto Laclau (London: Verso, 1994), 11–39.

18. Jacques Lacan, "Of Structure as an Inmixing of an Otherness Prerequisite to Any Subject Whatever," in *The Languages of Criticism and the Sciences of Man: The Structuralist Controversy*, ed. Richard Macksey and Eugenio Donato (Baltimore: Johns Hopkins University Press, 1970), 196–97.

19. The Slovenian theoreticians who draw inspiration from Lacan usually pay greater attention to the ontological implications of notions such as *objet petit a*, phantasy, and drives. That said, they do not seem to grasp the difference between the notion of being and the notion of the real, nor do they place enough emphasis on clinical distinctions among various forms of subjectivity. See, e.g., Mladen Dolar, *A Voice and Nothing More* (Cambridge, MA: MIT Press, 2006); Alenka Zupančič, *What IS Sex?* (Cambridge, MA: MIT Press, 2017); and Slavoj Žižek, *The Parallax View* (Cambridge, MA: MIT Press, 2006).

20. Lacan, "Of Structure as an Inmixing," 189.

21. Sigmund Freud, *Group Psychology and the Analysis of the Ego*, in *The Standard Edition of the Complete Psychological Works of Sigmund Freud*, vol. 18 (London: Hogarth, 1955), 69.

22. For more details, see my introduction to Sigmund Freud, *Psicologia delle masse e analisi dell'Io* (Torino: Einaudi, 2013), vii–li.

23. Freud, *Group Psychology*, 129.

24. Lacan, *Écrits*, 234.

25. Freud, *Group Psychology*, 129.

26. Freud, 93.

27. Lacan, *Écrits*, 234.

28. Jacques Lacan, *Le séminaire, Livre X: L'angoisse* (Paris: Seuil, 2004), 82.

29. Lacan, *The Seminar, Book XIV*, June 21, 1967.

30. Lacan, June 14, 1967.

31. Quoted in Andrew Roberts, *Napoleon: A Life* (New York: Penguin, 2014), xxxvii.

32. Lacan, *The Seminar, Book XIV*, May 10, 1967.

33. Marcel Gauchet, *La Révolution des droits de l'homme* (Paris: Gallimard, 1989), 26.

34. Gauchet, 27.

35. During the nineteenth century, the divide between the existing nation and the true nation took various forms in French public debate. In the early twentieth century, Raymond Carré de Malberg famously interpreted it as a divide between *souveraineté populaire* and *souveraineté nationale*: the former was sovereignty from the point of view of the existing nation (*le peuple*); the latter was sovereignty from the point of view of the true nation (*la nation*). "*Souveraineté du peuple* (popular sovereignty) was in this view a concrete sovereignty, referring to the totality of living individuals, while *souveraineté de la nation* (national sovereignty) was an abstract sovereignty, referring to a collective subject across time made up of present and past generations. The former was realistic, the latter idealized; the former was individualistic and democratic, the latter organic and representative; the former transferred the sovereignty of the monarch to the people, while the second created an entirely new concept of sovereignty." Dieter Grimm, *Sovereignty: The Origin and Future of a Political and Legal Concept*, trans. Belinda Cooper (New York: Columbia University Press, 2015), 43.

36. As John Plamenatz points out, nationalists give voice to a particular *desire*: "the desire to preserve or enhance a people's national or cultural identity when that identity is threatened, or the desire to transform or even create it where it is felt to be inadequate or lacking." John Plamenatz, "Two Types of Nationalism," in *Nationalism: The Nature and Evolution of an Idea*, ed. Eugene Kamenka (Canberra: Australian National University Press, 1973), 23–24. With regard to France, François Hartog has remarked, "Tout au long d'un siècle [the nineteenth century], qui a été si fortement celui des nationalités, l'histoire nationale et l'écriture au nom du futur ont eu en effet partie liée. Dans le cas de la France, il s'agissait d'un futur déjà advenu, mais manqué, dévoyé ou perdu, inachevé en tout cas. 1789 a déjà eu lieu, mais ses promesses sont encore à venir. On est là aussi entre le *déjà* et le *pas encore*." François Hartog, *Régimes d'historicité: Présentisme et expériences du temps* (Paris: Seuil, 2003), 144.

37. Lacan, *The Seminar, Book XIV*, June 14, 1967.

38. Étienne Balibar, *Masses, Classes, Ideas: Studies on Politics and Philosophy before and after Marx*, trans. James Swenson (New York: Routledge, 1994), 212.

39. Étienne Balibar, *Equaliberty: Political Essays*, trans. James Ingram (Durham, NC: Duke University Press, 2014), 307.

40. See Lacan, *The Seminar, Book XIV*, Jan. 18, 1967:

> Nothing can be *said* about what is involved in these structures. Our experience, nevertheless, affirms to us that they dominate. . . . They give their law to the function of desire. But this cannot be *said*, except by *repeating* the grammatical articulations in which they are constituted. Namely, by showing in the sentences that ground them what can be deduced about the different ways the subject may have of dwelling in them. Nothing, I am saying, can be *said* about them, except what we in fact hear, namely, the subject in his *complaint*.

41. Karl Marx, "On the Jewish Question," in *Early Writings*, trans. Rodney Livingstone and Gregor Benton (London: Penguin, 1992), 229.

42. Ernest Renan, *Qu'est-ce qu'une nation?* (Paris: Calmann Lévy, 1882), 26.

43. For more details on this, see Balibar, *Masses, Classes, Ideas*, 61–84; and Ann Laura Stoler, "Interior Frontiers," *Political Concepts* 4, no. 2 (2018): politicalconcepts.org.

44. As Anthony Giddens notes, the birth of a modern nation and the *levée en masse* are usually concomitant, not least because mass conscription is seen as a means of fostering feelings of national loyalty. "The nation-state and the mass army appear together, the twin tokens of citizenship within territorially bordered political communities. . . . In France the *levée en masse* was specifically established in such a way to associate citizenship with active participation in matters urgently affecting the state and as a means of fostering feelings of national loyalty." Anthony Giddens, *The Nation-State and Violence* (Cambridge: Polity, 1987), 233.

45. Balibar, *Equaliberty*, 44.

46. "In discussing the guiding ideas of the eighteenth century, as expressed in the new use of words in the French language, Ferdinand Brunot mentioned *humanité* as the leading new dogma." See Hans Kohn, *The Idea of Nationalism: A Study in Its Origins and Background* (New York: Macmillan, 1946), 227.

47. See Ernest Gellner, *Nations and Nationalism* (Oxford: Blackwell, 1983):

> Chamisso, an *émigré* Frenchman in Germany during the Napoleonic period, wrote a powerful proto-Kafkaesque novel about a man who lost his shadow: though no doubt part of the effectiveness of this novel hinges on

the intended ambiguity of the parable, it is difficult not to suspect that, for the author, the Man without a Shadow was the Man without a Nation. When his followers and acquaintances detect his aberrant shadowlessness they shun the otherwise well-endowed Peter Schlemihl. A man without a nation defies the recognized categories and provokes revulsion. Chamisso's perception—if indeed this is what he intended to convey—was valid enough, but valid only for one kind of human condition, and not for the human condition as such anywhere at any time. A man must have a nationality as he must have a nose and two ears; a deficiency in any of these particulars is not inconceivable and does from time to time occur, but only as a result of some disaster, and it is itself a disaster of a kind. All this seems obvious, though, alas, it is not true. But that it should have come to *seem* so very obviously true is indeed an aspect, or perhaps the very core, of the problem of nationalism. Having a nation is not an inherent attribute of humanity, but it has now come to appear as such. (6)

48. "The signification of the equation Man = Citizen is not so much the definition of a political right as the affirmation of a universal right to politics. Formally, at least—but this is the very type of a form that can become a material weapon—the *Declaration* opens an indefinite sphere for the politicization of rights claims, each of which reiterates in its own way the demand for citizenship or for an institutional, public inscription of freedom and equality." Balibar, *Equaliberty*, 50.

49. See, e.g., Balibar, *Masses, Classes, Ideas*, 191–204; and Étienne Balibar, *Politics and the Other Scene*, trans. Christine Jones, James Swenson, and Chris Turner (London: Verso, 2002).

50. After the publication of Richard Hofstadter's seminal work on the paranoid style in American politics—*The Paranoid Style in American Politics: And Other Essays* (Cambridge, MA: Harvard University Press, 1996)—students of the American Revolution have often stressed, and sometimes overstated, the importance of the paranoid vision of the political world that dominated America in the second half of the eighteenth century; see, e.g., Gordon S. Wood, "Conspiracy and the Paranoid Style: Causality and Deceit in the Eighteenth Century," in *The Idea of America: Reflections on the Birth of the United States* (New York: Penguin, 2011). I will not elaborate on the alleged psychological background of the American Revolution but rather focus on the process of collective subjectification that took place against this background, changing the way the American colonists viewed themselves and the world. "The Revolution was in the minds and hearts of the people; a change in their religious sentiments, of their duties and obligations. . . . *This radical change in the principles, opinions, sentiments, and affections of the people was the real American Revolution*" (John Adams cited in Bernard Bailyn, *The Ideological*

Origins of the American Revolution, enl. ed. [Cambridge, MA: Harvard University Press, 1992], 160).

51. On the ratification process, see Pauline Maier, *Ratification: The People Debate the Constitution, 1787–1788* (New York: Simon and Schuster, 2011).

52. Stanley Cavell, *Disowning Knowledge: In Seven Plays of Shakespeare* (Cambridge: Cambridge University Press, 2003), 115–16.

53. The long controversy over the "General Welfare Clause" of the Constitution confirms the above considerations: the problem was not how to achieve collective happiness but how to make it possible for each individual to pursue happiness without making him too heavy a burden on others. Was Congress entitled to tax and spend? And for what purpose? The questions themselves prove that collective happiness was not understood as being an axiom.

54. Edmund S. Morgan, *Inventing the People: The Rise of Popular Sovereignty in England and America* (New York: Norton, 1989), 262.

55. See Gordon S. Wood, *Empire of Liberty: A History of the Early Republic, 1789–1815* (Oxford: Oxford University Press, 2009):

> Despite the ratification of the Constitution, most Americans knew that they were not yet a nation, at least not in the European sense of the term. At the end of the Declaration of Independence the members of the Continental Congress had been able only to "mutually pledge to each other our Lives, our Fortunes, and our sacred Honor." In 1776 there was nothing else but themselves that they could have dedicated themselves to—no patria, no fatherland, no nation as yet.
>
> Because of extensive immigration, America already had a diverse society, certainly more diverse than most European nations. In addition to seven hundred thousand people of African descent and tens of thousands of native Indians, all the peoples of Europe were present in the country. . . .
>
> Lacking a unique name and ethnicity, the best Americans could do was to locate their national identity and character in something other than the traditional sources of nationhood. . . . (39, 42)

And perhaps most tellingly: "If they were to be a single national people with a national character, Americans would have to invent themselves, and in some sense the whole of American history has been the story of that invention" (41).

56. Lacan, *The Seminar, Book XI*, 185.

57. Lacan, *The Seminar, Book XIV*, May 10, 1967.

58. Lacan, May 31, 1967.

59. See Leonard W. Levy, *Origins of the Bill of Rights* (New Haven, CT: Yale University Press, 2001):

> The Ninth Amendment is the repository for natural rights, including the right to pursue happiness and the right to equality of treatment before the

law. Madison, presenting his proposed amendments, spoke of "the perfect equality of mankind." Other natural rights come within the protection of the amendment as well, among them the right, then important, to hunt and fish, the right to travel, and very likely the right to intimate association or privacy in matters concerning family and sex, at least within the bounds of marriage. Such rights were fundamental to the pursuit of happiness. But no evidence exists to prove that the Framers intended the Ninth Amendment to protect any particular natural rights. The text expressly protects unenumerated rights, but we can only guess what the Framers had in mind. (254)

60. See Mario Del Pero, *Libertà e impero: Gli Stati Uniti e il mondo, 1776–2006* (Roma-Bari: Laterza, 2008), 141–42.

61. As Paul T. McCartney writes: "American national identity has been premised upon the belief that the nation's binding principles are rooted in qualities and capacities shared by all people, everywhere. On the world stage, though, the United States cannot help but act as a single, discrete entity, however universal its pretensions. It is but one state among many. As a result, U.S. foreign policy frequently tries to have it both ways—to assume that America's national interest and the greater good of mankind are one and the same." Paul T. McCartney, "American Nationalism and U.S. Foreign Policy from September 11 to the Iraq War," *Political Science Quarterly* 119, no. 3 (2004): 402.

62. Even those who see America as a "nation" are bound to concede that America is not a nation like all others. "Underneath the nation in the singular, the original nation in the plural remained. In contrast to the European nations, where the primacy of the nation over the individual imposed general uniformity, the unchallenged primacy of the individual allowed—even guaranteed—plurality of tastes, views, attachments, aspirations, and self-definitions, within the shared national framework." Liah Greenfeld, *Nationalism: Five Roads to Modernity* (Cambridge, MA: Harvard University Press, 1993), 482.

63. See Geoff Eley, *Forging Democracy: The History of the Left in Europe, 1850–2000* (Oxford: Oxford University Press, 2002):

If capitalist industrialization transformed the conditions under which democratic ideals had to be pursued, the social meanings of those ideals also changed. As the term "socialism" entered into general currency after 1850, this was the transition it was used to express. "Social" came to signify something more than the common system of institutions and relationships in which people lived and started to imply a desirable contrast to the emergent capitalist form of society. It came to mean "an idea of society as mutual cooperation," as opposed to one based on "individual competition." Indeed, the "*individualist* form of society" associated with the new system of wage labor and private property became rejected as "the enemy of truly *social* forms" in this sense. (21)

64. See John Schwartzmantel, "Nationalism and Socialist Internationalism," in *The Oxford Handbook of the History of Nationalism*, ed. John Breuilly (Oxford: Oxford University Press, 2013):

> Socialist internationalism can be considered as historically the main challenger to nationalism, being its main rival in the field of political ideologies and in terms of movements inspired by those ideologies. One can thus start from a simplistic antithesis between socialist internationalism and nationalism. The former aspired to be a movement aiming to create and develop solidarity between workers (and others) spanning national boundaries. The latter can be viewed as an ideology and movement emphasizing the community and identity of the nation transcending class divisions. "Class" on the one hand, "nation" on the other. (635)

65. When it comes to economic policy, socialists often radicalize— rather than criticize—the nationalist agenda. "On entend par socialisme des idées, des forces, de groupes qui tendent dans une nation moderne à régler l'ensemble de la vie économique. Ce processus s'opère par voie de nationalisation, c'est-à-dire d'instauration de la propriété industrielle et commerciale sous le contrôle de la nation." Marcel Mauss, *La nation* (Paris: Presses universitaires de France, 2013), 254–55.

66. Quoted in Eley, *Forging Democracy*, 126.

67. See Robin Archer, *Why Is There No Labor Party in the United States?* (Princeton, NJ: Princeton University Press, 2008).

CHAPTER 5: THE FREUDIAN PARADIGM OF CRITICAL THEORY

1. Karl Marx and Friedrich Engels, *The German Ideology*, ed. C. J. Arthur (New York: International, 2004), 56–57.

2. See, in particular, Theodor W. Adorno, *Negative Dialectics*, trans. E. B. Ashton (New York: Routledge, 2004); among Derrida's writings, it is difficult to choose one, for the notion of deconstruction is omnipresent across his oeuvre.

3. Friedrich Nietzsche, *Letter to Burkhardt, 6 January* 1889, cited in *The New Nietzsche: Contemporary Styles of Interpretation*, ed. David Allison (New York: Dell, 1977), 36.

4. See, e.g., Sigmund Freud, *Moses and Monotheism: Three Essays*, in *The Standard Edition of the Complete Psychological Works of Sigmund Freud*, vol. 23 (London: Hogarth, 1964), 1–137. For further details on the notion of historical truth, see Bruno Karsenti, *Moïse et l'idée du peuple: La vérité historique*

selon Freud (Paris: Cerf, 2012); and Jocelyn Benoist, "Freud's 'Historical Truth' Revisited," *Research in Psychoanalysis* 23, no. 1 (2017): 37–54.

5. See Jacques Lacan, *The Seminar, Book XX: Encore*, trans. Bruce Fink (New York: Norton, 1998):

> Isn't it thus true that language imposes being upon us and obliges us, as such, to admit that we never have anything by way of being? What we must get used to is substituting the "para-being" (*parêtre*)—the being "*para*," beside—for the being that would take flight. I say the "para-being" (*parêtre*), and not the "appearing" (*paraître*), as the phenomenon has always been called—that beyond which there is supposedly that thing, the noumenon. The latter has, in effect, led us to all sorts of opacifications that can be referred to precisely as obscurantism. (44–45)

On Lacan's paraontology see also Lorenzo Chiesa, *The Not-Two: Logic and God in Lacan* (Cambridge, MA: MIT Press, 2016).

6. The notion of freedom remains rather ambiguous in Foucault's works. It is unclear whether he conceived of human freedom as a historical artifact or a universal endowment of human beings. Sometimes he declares his proximity to a tradition of thought that goes back to Kant, and I myself have insisted on his relation to the Enlightenment in previous contributions; see Davide Tarizzo, *Il pensiero libero: La filosofia francese dopo lo strutturalismo* (Milano: Cortina, 2003); and Davide Tarizzo, *Giochi di potere: Sulla paranoia politica* (Roma-Bari: Laterza, 2007). That said, there are times when he takes a different perspective—for instance, in his analysis of liberalism. Here I will valorize this perspective, which is more consistent with the Freudian twist of Foucault's research.

7. In this paragraph, I will mainly refer to Michel Foucault, *"Society Must Be Defended": Lectures at the Collège de France, 1975–1976*, trans. David Macey (New York: Picador, 2003); Michel Foucault, *Security, Territory, Population: Lectures at the Collège de France, 1977–1978*, trans. Graham Burchell (New York: Picador, 2009); and Michel Foucault, *The Birth of Biopolitics: Lectures at the Collège de France, 1978–1979*, trans. Graham Burchell (New York: Picador, 2010).

CHAPTER 6: THE TWO PATHS TO MODERN DEMOCRACY

1. By the state *qua* institutional fact, I mean "the structure which became dominant in Europe after 1500, the national state," having the following characteristics: "(1) it controlled a well-defined, continuous territory; (2) it was relatively centralized; (3) it was differentiated from other organizations; (4) it reinforced its claims through a tendency to acquire a monopoly over the concentrated means of physical coercion within its territory." Charles Tilly,

"Reflections on the History of European State-Making," in *The Formation of National States in Western Europe*, ed. Charles Tilly (Princeton, NJ: Princeton University Press, 1975), 27.

2. "The idea of the contract brought the people into play and with them the necessity of distinguishing between possessing and exercising sovereignty." Dieter Grimm, *Sovereignty: The Origin and Future of a Political and Legal Concept*, trans. Belinda Cooper (New York: Columbia University Press, 2015), 28.

3. "We could say that metaphor tells us something about one character as considered from the point of view of another character. And to consider A from the point of view of B is, of course, to use B as a *perspective* upon A." Kenneth Burke, *A Grammar of Motives* (Berkeley: University of California Press, 1969), 504.

4. In the following, I will discuss three examples of nationalism, but it is important to keep in mind that the ambiguity between the rights of man and the rights of the citizen is a general and permanent feature of the modern nation as such, which modern constitutions usually bring into focus. For instance, the Italian Constitution of 1948 says, "La Repubblica Italiana riconosce e garantisce i diritti inviolabili dell'uomo" (art. 2); the Spanish Constitution of 1978 says, "La dignidad de la persona, los derechos inviolables que le son inherentes, el libre desarrollo de la personalidad, el respeto a la ley y a los derechos de los demás son fundamento del orden político y de la paz social" (art. 10); the German Grundgesetz of 1949 says, "Das Deutsche Volk bekennt sich darum zu unverletzlichen und unveräußerlichen Menschenrechten als Grundlage jeder menschlichen Gemeinschaft, des Friedens und der Gerechtigkeit in der Welt" (art. 1); and the French Constitution of 1958 restates, "Le peuple français proclame solennellement son attachement aux Droits de l'homme et aux principes de la souveraineté nationale tels qu'ils ont été définis par la Déclaration de 1789" (preamble).

5. See Étienne Balibar, *Equaliberty: Political Essays*, trans. James Ingram (Durham, NC: Duke University Press, 2014).

6. Given that the civic version of the nation has no additional—religious or ethnic—connotation, it is tempting to define it as a "metaphysical" construct, as Benjamin Constant did in the aftermath of the Revolution. Here the nation's "general will" becomes the attribute of an entity that is surrounded by mystery. As Constant notes, this understanding of the nation as a perfectly "abstract being" was likely to facilitate "the usurpation of popular sovereignty by particular individuals or groups claiming to speak for the nation as a whole." Bryan Garsten, "From Popular Sovereignty to Civil Society in Post-Revolutionary France," in *Popular Sovereignty in Historical Perspective*, ed. Richard Bourke and Quentin Skinner (Cambridge: Cambridge University Press, 2016), 256. In other words, Bonapartism was not a fortuitous event,

according to Constant, but a direct consequence of French civic nationalism. From a grammatical point of view, we may perhaps say that, owing to the scarcity of intermediate links (peripheral metaphors of a religious or ethnic nature) between the "nation" (the core metaphor) and the other elements of the political discourse, civic nationalism is less regimented than other types of nationalism; so, leaders are given a freer hand to shape it into their own personality, and there is less reason to deny them the right to speak on behalf of the nation.

7. Jellinek himself makes this point when discussing the Bill of Rights and the theories of natural rights developed by John Locke and William Blackstone:

> When Locke considers property—in which are included life and liberty—as an original right of the individual existing previous to the state, and when he conceives of the state as a society founded to protect his right, which is thus transformed from a natural to a civil right, he by no means ascribes definite fundamental rights to the man living in the state, but rather places such positive restrictions upon the legislative power as follow from the purposes of the state. When closely examined, however, these restrictions are nothing else than the most important stipulations of the Bill of Rights, which was enacted the year before the *Two Treatises on Government* appeared.
>
> Blackstone was the first (1765) to found his doctrine of the absolute rights of persons upon the idea of the personal rights of the individual. Security, liberty, and property are the absolute rights of every Englishman, which from their character are nothing else than the natural liberty that remains to the individual after deducting the legal restraints demanded by the common interest. Laws appear likewise as protectors of these rights—the whole constitution of Parliament, the limitation of the royal prerogative, and along with these the protection of the law courts, the right of petition, and the right to carry arms are treated, exactly in the manner of the Bill of Rights, as rights of Englishmen, and indeed as subordinate rights to assist in guarding the three principal rights. But in spite of his fundamental conception of a natural right, the individual with rights was for Blackstone not man simply, but the English subject. (Georg Jellinek, *The Declaration of the Rights of Man and of Citizens: A Contribution to Modern Constitutional History* [New York: Henry Holt, 1901], 54–56)

8. "[Early modern] English Christians understood contemporary experience and defined their religious identities in relation to biblical Israel, Jewish history and Judaism." Achsah Guibbory, *Christian Identity, Jews, and Israel in Seventeenth-Century England* (Oxford: Oxford University Press, 2010), 1.

9. Linda Colley, *Britons: Forging the Nation,* 1707–1837 (New Haven, CT: Yale University Press, 1992), 33, 54. The history of British nationalism is a highly controversial issue. Colley, who emphasizes the religious inflection of British nationalism, charts the emergence of British national identity with the Act of Union of 1707. From my point of view, the role played by Charles II and the Cavalier Parliament in the making of the Anglican nation should not be underestimated. Indeed, the acts passed after the Restoration laid the foundations for a political *subjectivity* that antedates the affirmation of British *identity.* In a grammatical perspective, the distinction between subjectivity and identity and the fact that subjectivity antedates identity must be clearly highlighted because subjectivity—namely, grammar—is that which prompts the affirmation of identity or the process of national identification. Subjectivity explains why identification starts, why it is bound to follow a predetermined path, and why it never comes to an end, driving people to affirm their national identity with growing exasperation. In this view, the rise of a modern "nation" always implies the birth of a subjectivity or of a certain grammatical background. For further details about religious nationalism, see Hans Kohn, *The Idea of Nationalism: A Study in Its Origins and Background* (New York: Macmillan, 1946); and Anthony W. Marx, *Faith in Nation: Exclusionary Origins of Nationalism* (Oxford: Oxford University Press, 2005).

10. See George L. Mosse, *The Nationalization of the Masses: Political Symbolism and Mass Movements in Germany from the Napoleonic Wars through the Third Reich* (New York: Howard Ferting, 1974).

11. For more on this document, see Ernst Rudolf Huber, *Deutsche Verfassungsgeschichte seit* 1789, Band 2, *Der Kampf um Einheit und Freiheit* 1830 *bis* 1850 (Stuttgart: Kohlhammer, 1988).

12. The *Kulturkampf* and Bismarck's plan to disarm political Catholicism can be interpreted as an unsuccessful attempt to promote a kind of religious—Lutheran—nationalism in the German Empire. "For liberal nationalists, Lutheran Protestantism and German idealism were the sources of Germany's moral and intellectual greatness, while Roman Catholicism was an alien force, hostile to the sovereign state and an impediment to the spiritual unity of the nation." Otto Pflanze, *Bismarck and the Development of Germany,* vol. 2, *The Period of Consolidation,* 1871–1880 (Princeton, NJ: Princeton University Press, 2014), 180. The German Catholics proved too strong for liberal nationalists, however, and their resistance left Germany no choice but ethnonationalism.

13. As Rogers Brubaker notes, French nationalism was "political-ideological, not ethnocultural. But it contributed to the later emergence, during the Napoleonic period, of a German counternationalism in which ethnocultural motifs came to play an important role. Revolutionary expansion, itself driven by political nationalism, thus engendered ethnocultural

nationalism; the 'crusade for liberty' elicited in response the myth, if not the reality, of a 'holy war' of ethnonational resistance." Rogers Brubaker, *Citizenship and Nationhood in France and Germany* (Cambridge, MA: Harvard University Press, 1992), 8.

14. Walker Connor, *Ethnonationalism: The Quest for Understanding* (Princeton, NJ: Princeton University Press, 1994), 93.

15. For more details on this, see Luciano Canfora, *La democrazia: Storia di un'ideologia* (Roma-Bari: Laterza, 2004).

16. "Whether we like it or not, nationalism is the historical force that has provided the political units for democratic governments. 'Nation' is another name for 'We the People.'" Ghia Nodia, "Nationalism and Democracy," in *Nationalism, Ethnic Conflict, and Democracy*, ed. Larry Diamond and Marc F. Plattner (Baltimore: Johns Hopkins University Press, 1994), 7.

17. "Granting sovereignty to the people and recognizing members of the various social strata as political equals are basic tenets of both nationalism and democracy." Yael Tamir, *Why Nationalism* (Princeton, NJ: Princeton University Press, 2019), 35.

18. It follows from the above that a diffuse nationalist sentiment always pervades the whole of national societies, no matter what the people's political opinions are. Michael Billig speaks of this sentiment in terms of "banal nationalism." See Michael Billig, *Banal Nationalism* (London: Sage, 1995).

19. For more details about this, see John Breuilly, *Nationalism and the State* (Manchester: Manchester University Press, 1993).

20. See Quintilian, *Institutio Oratoria*, book 8, chap. 6. These are actually cases of synecdoche, but Quintilian himself stresses that "it is but a short step from synecdoche to metonymy."

21. Some discrepancies between Jakobson's and Lacan's theories have been emphasized in Richard Bradford, *Roman Jakobson: Life, Language, Art* (London: Routledge, 1994), 86–94.

22. See Burke, *A Grammar of Motives*: "We propose to treat *metonymy* and *reduction* as substitutes for each other" (506).

23. Lacan did not take this example from Quintilian, as is often believed, but from the last page of a "childhood grammar book." Jacques Lacan, *Écrits: The First Complete Edition in English*, trans. Bruce Fink (New York: Norton, 2005), 421.

24. "The cause of America is in a great measure the cause of all mankind. . . . O ye that love mankind! Ye that dare oppose, not only the tyranny, but the tyrant, stand forth! Every spot of the old world is over-run with oppression. Freedom hath been hunted round the globe. Asia, and Africa, have long expelled her.—Europe regards her like a stranger, and England hath given her warning to depart. O! receive the fugitive, and prepare in time an asylum for mankind." Thomas Paine, *Common Sense*, in *Rights of Man,*

Common Sense, and Other Political Writings (Oxford: Oxford University Press, 1998), 3, 35.

25. According to the French constitutionalist Raymond Carré de Malberg, "Ce que la Révolution française a fondé en vertu du principe de la souveraineté nationale, c'est le régime représentatif, un regime dans lequel la souveraineté, étant réservée exclusivement à l'être collectif et abstrait nation, ne peut être exercée par qui que ce soit qu'à titre de représentant national. Telle est, en dernière analyse, la signification de la souveraineté nationale." Raymond Carré de Malberg, *Contribution à la Théorie générale de l'État: Tome deuxième* (Paris: CNRS, 1922), 196–97.

26. The metonymic structure of American society explains many ambiguities of the US Constitution. For the framers, "the people" of the Union and "the people" of a US state were equivalent metonyms. Thus, their claims to sovereignty *did* and *did not* contradict each other:

> One of the areas in which the meaning of the constitution is still at issue involves the nature of the sovereignty underlying the federal Constitution. In dealing with that question the [Supreme] Court is divided. Some justices find a national American people in aggregate as the sovereign. This view reflects the understanding most forcefully advanced by Daniel Webster in the 1830s. Other justices consider the people of the states individually as the sovereign who formed the federal Constitution. This alternative view also reflects an understanding articulated in the 1830s in the course of the Nullification crisis. (Christian G. Fritz, *American Sovereigns: The People and America's Constitutional Tradition before the Civil War* [Cambridge: Cambridge University Press, 2008], 296–97)

27. During the New Deal era, when the power of American government expanded as never before, there arose the problem of how to reconcile the new political agenda with America's penchant for individual—rather than collective—happiness. Not only the opponents but also the advocates of the New Deal had to face this problem. Franklin Delano Roosevelt, the US president at the time, put it like this:

> Liberty requires opportunity to make a living. . . . The royalists of the economic order have conceded that political freedom was the business of the government, but they have maintained that economic slavery was nobody's business. They granted that the government could protect the citizen in his right to vote, but they denied that the government could do anything to protect the citizen in his right to work and his right to live. . . . These economic royalists complain that we seek to overthrow the institutions of America. What they really complain of is that we seek to take away their power. Our allegiance to American institutions requires the overthrow of

this kind of power. In vain they seek to hide behind the flag and the Constitution. In their blindness they forget what the flag and the Constitution stand for. (Franklin D. Roosevelt, "A Rendezvous with Destiny," speech before the 1936 Democratic National Convention, June 27, 1936)

28. "The distinctive national culture that Americans have created doesn't underpin, it exists alongside of, American politics. It follows, then, that the people I earlier called Americans simply, Americans and nothing else, have in fact a more complicated existence than those terms suggest. They are American-Americans, one more group of hyphenates." Michael Walzer, "What Does It Mean to Be an American?," *Social Research* 71, no. 3 (2004): 650.

29. Horace Kallen, "Democracy versus the Melting-Pot. A Study of American Nationality," *The Nation*, Feb. 15, 1915.

30. Walzer, "What Does It Mean to Be an American?," 652–53.

31. Martin Luther King Jr., "I Have a Dream," speech delivered at the Lincoln Memorial, Washington, DC, August 28, 1963.

32. Kallen, "Democracy versus the Melting-Pot."

33. Carl Schmitt, *Der Begriff des Politischen* (Berlin: Duncker & Humblot, 1963), 55.

34. Karl Polanyi, *The Great Transformation: The Political and Economic Origins of Our Time* (Boston: Beacon, 2001), 233–34.

CHAPTER 7: FROM DEMOCRACY TO FASCISM

1. See, e.g., Étienne Balibar's channeling of Habermas in Étienne Balibar, *We, the People of Europe? Reflections on Transnational Citizenship*, trans. James Swenson (Princeton, NJ: Princeton University Press, 2004):

> In *Between Facts and Norms*, Habermas presents the construction of citizenship in the work of Rousseau and Kant as representing two successive and only partially satisfactory attempts to combine and reconcile two "principles" that are in an "unacknowledged *competition*," even though both of them "determined the normative self-understanding of constitutional democracies up to the present day." These two principles are the idea of the rights of man considered as the moral (or juridico-moral) foundation of the individual guarantees incorporated into every constitutional order, and the idea of popular sovereignty considered as the political foundation of the existence of a public sphere and its autonomy with respect to particular interests (that is, its generality). (183)

2. On the origins of the American perspective on democracy, see Richard E. Ellis, *The Union at Risk: Jacksonian Democracy, States' Rights, and the Nullification Crisis* (Oxford: Oxford University Press, 1987):

Although the colonial heritage of particularism, the ideology of the Revolution, and the burgeoning of democratic thought all contributed significantly to the creation of a political persuasion that stressed the importance of local autonomy, it was the actual social and economic conditions under which many people lived during the 1780s that sustained the perspective of localism and made it especially meaningful to a large number of Americans. This is because a very substantial portion of the people at this time were small farmers who lived in simple, isolated, and provincial communities. Since at best they had only a tangential connection with the market economy, it was in the interest of these people to want a weak, inactive, and frugal government which would require few taxes and for the most part leave them alone, and for them to believe that whatever government was necessary should be kept as close to home as possible. (2-3)

3. It is debatable whether liberalism has ever been a genuine political option in Europe. The most interesting example of European liberalism is probably the British Liberal Party, which drew inspiration from the American political experiment. America is the country "where both society and the government are most democratic," as the Liberal Party MP John Stuart Mill wrote. John Stuart Mill, *On Liberty* (New Haven, CT: Yale University Press, 2003), 150. Most of the time, however, European "liberals" turned out to be moderate nationalists, and Mill was no exception: "Indeed, many nineteenth-century liberals believed that 'individual liberty and national independence or unity would go together,' and that liberal principles could best be implemented within a homogeneous nation-state. 'Free institutions are next to impossible in a country made up of different nationalities,' argues Mill." Yael Tamir, *Liberal Nationalism* (Princeton, NJ: Princeton University Press, 1993), 140. Leaving aside the question of liberal nationalism, many scholars insist that political moderation has been the most distinctive trait of liberalism in Europe:

Liberal goals were often summed up as the ideals of 1789, revolutionary ideals. But liberals believed that revolutionary means would never attain those revolutionary goals. They rejected 1793, and consistently rejected revolutionary methods. If liberals were sometimes the Party of Change, they were never the Revolutionary Party. Liberal radicalism was moderated by the fact that not even the most daring liberals wanted a revolution to attain their ends. The only acceptable liberal means of changing things was reform; liberals had been convinced by the French Revolution that revolutionary means would lead only to anarchy and despotism. (Alan Kahan, *Liberalism in Nineteenth-Century Europe: The Political Culture of Limited Suffrage* [New York: Palgrave Macmillan, 2003], 1-2)

4. Here I am not considering the case of the "Christian-Democratic" parties born in Germany and Italy soon after World War II, because those developments took place within a historical context that I will examine in the next chapter. In a nutshell, postwar Christian-Democratic parties were basically conservative parties that could no longer adopt a nationalist agenda after the defeat of ultranationalist fascism and the intolerable trauma of Auschwitz. Hence their early engagement in the European project. For more on the role that Christian-Democratic parties played in the making of the European Union, see Wolfram Kaiser, *Christian Democracy and the Origins of European Union* (Cambridge: Cambridge University Press, 2007).

5. The Democratic Socialists of America, which is not a party but a nonprofit organization, is not a faction of the Democratic Party either. This independent organization has at times given critical support to Democratic candidates while remaining very critical of the corporate-funded Democratic Party leadership. Not even Bernie Sanders's New Deal–inspired program in 2016 was judged to be a true socialist program by the DSA, and not without reason.

6. Bruce Ackermann, for example, takes up this issue in his discussion of the American Bicentennial Myth:

> Our public discourse constantly treats the great constitutional achievements of the past as if they contained valuable clues for decoding the meaning of the political present.
>
> This American habit is by no means a universal feature of political society. Public discourse in Russia today does not look back to the nineteenth century in the same respectful way we recall the Civil War amendments; nor do today's Germans allow themselves to recall the 1930's as positively as Americans do when they describe the New Deal's response to the challenges of the Great Depression. For many Europeans, the past two centuries are full of dramatic breaks and false starts. While we have had our share of bitter conflict and profound transformation, modern Americans tell themselves stories that assert the deep continuity of two centuries of constitutional practice, narratives that thoroughly enmesh today's events in a web of constitutional reference stretching back two hundred years to the Founding. While the French have run through five republics since 1789, we have lived in only one. . . .
>
> But must all myths be mystifications? The Greek *mythos* points in a different direction: the narrative we tell ourselves about our Constitution's roots is a deeply significant act of collective self-definition: its continual re-telling plays a critical role in the ongoing construction of national identity. . . .
>
> In part because Americans differ so radically in other respects, our constitutional narrative constitutes us [as] a people. (Bruce Ackermann,

We the People: Foundations [Cambridge, MA: Harvard University Press, 1991], 34, 36)

7. Jacques Lacan, *Écrits: The First Complete Edition in English*, trans. Bruce Fink (New York: Norton, 2005), 423 (translation slightly modified).

8. Jacques Lacan, *The Seminar, Book XIII*, March 23, 1966.

9. The phrases "great experiment of liberty" and "manifest destiny" were famously coined by John L. O'Sullivan in the mid-nineteenth century (*New York Morning News*, Dec. 27, 1845). For more details about this and other aspects of America's self-perception, see Anders Stephanson, *Manifest Destiny: American Expansion and the Empire of Right* (New York: Farrar, Straus and Giroux, 1995). For more on the ceaseless reference to the "infallible" founders, see David Sehat, *The Jefferson Rule: How the Founding Fathers Became Infallible and Our Politics Inflexible* (New York: Simon and Schuster, 2016).

10. See, e.g., Roger Griffin, *The Nature of Fascism* (London: Routledge, 1991); Stanley G. Payne, *A History of Fascism, 1914–1945* (London: Routledge, 1995); and Michael Mann, *Fascists* (Cambridge: Cambridge University Press, 2004).

11. According to Mann, "*fascism is the pursuit of a transcendent and cleansing nation-statism through paramilitarism*. . . . As everyone recognizes, fascists had a deep and populist commitment to an 'organic' or 'integral' nation, and this involved an unusually strong sense of its 'enemies,' both abroad and (especially) at home. Fascists had a very low tolerance of ethnic or cultural diversity, since this would subvert the organic, integral unity of the nation. Aggression against enemies supposedly threatening that organic unity is the original source of fascism's extremism" (Mann, *Fascists*, 13).

12. For more on the Nazis' "use and abuse" of *Life*, see Davide Tarizzo, *Life: A Modern Invention*, trans. Mark William Epstein (Minneapolis: University of Minnesota Press, 2017).

13. Victor Klemperer offers some striking examples of this indistinction between the two regimes of enunciation when he writes about the Nazis' technical metaphors through which human beings were literally objectified, mechanized, and not only compared with machines by way of figurative language:

> A Goebbels sentence such as the following provides more compelling and serious evidence of this intrinsically mechanizing attitude: "In the foreseeable future we will be running at full tilt again (*zu vollen Touren*) in a range of areas." We are thus no longer being compared with machines, we have become machines ourselves. We: that is Goebbels, that is the Nazi government, that is the totality of Hitler's Germany which, in dire distress and critically depleted of energy, is to be spurred on; and this powerful preacher doesn't just compare himself and his faithful followers with

machines, no, he identifies them with them. A more dehumanized way of thinking than the one exposed here would not be conceivable. (Victor Klemperer, *The Language of the Third Reich*, trans. Martin Brady [London: Bloomsbury, 2013], 160)

14. See Jacques Lacan, "On a Question Prior to Any Possible Treatment of Psychosis," in *Écrits*, 445–88.

15. Elias Canetti, *Crowds and Power*, trans. Carol Stewart (New York: Continuum, 1981), 437.

16. Canetti, 183, 188.

17. See, e.g., George L. Mosse, *Nazi Culture: Intellectual, Cultural, and Social Life in the Third Reich* (Madison: University of Wisconsin Press, 2003).

18. Karl Kretschmer, a member of *Einsatzkommando* 4a, writing to his wife in September of 1942; cited in Daniel Jonah Goldhagen, *Hitler's Willing Executioners: Ordinary Germans and the Holocaust* (New York: Knopf, 1996), 404.

19. David Redles, *Hitler's Millennial Reich: Apocalyptic Belief and the Search for Salvation* (New York: New York University Press, 2005), 183.

20. Martin Heidegger, *Die Selbstbehauptung der deutschen Universität* (Breslau: Korn, 1934), 22. As is well known, Heidegger never embraced Nazi biologistic ontology of Being *qua* Life but only because he dreamt of replacing it with a new fundamental ontology of Being *qua* Being. His political involvement is one more piece of evidence that Nazism was widely perceived as an *ontological* revolution.

21. Édouard Calic, *Secret Conversations with Hitler: Two Newly Discovered 1931 Interviews* (New York: John Day, 1971), 68.

22. Elsewhere, I have used Cantor's conceptual tools to examine the Schreber case; see Davide Tarizzo, "The Delusional Metaphor: On Schreber's Anathema," in *Laws of Transition: The Return of Judge Schreber*, ed. Peter Goodrich and Katrin Trüdtedt (Toronto: University of Toronto Press, forthcoming).

23. Claude Lefort, *The Political Forms of Modern Society: Bureaucracy, Democracy, Totalitarianism*, ed. John B. Thompson (Cambridge, MA: MIT Press, 1986), 301–5, 279–80.

24. The notion of totalitarianism has been sharply criticized in Domenico Losurdo, "Towards a Critique of the Category of Totalitarianism," *Historical Materialism* 12, no. 2 (2004): 25–55. For more on this issue see Roberto Esposito, "Totalitarianism or Biopolitics: Concerning the Philosophical Interpretation of the 20th-century," *Critical Inquiry* 39 (2008): 633–45; and Simona Forti, *Il totalitarismo* (Roma-Bari: Laterza, 2001).

25. In Arendt's works, "ideology" means that politics takes on the task of revealing the total, absolute Truth about (more or less) everything. For example, in her *The Origins of Totalitarianism* (New York: Harcourt, 1973), she

writes, "Ideologies are always oriented toward history, even when, as in the case of racism, they seemingly proceed from the premise of nature; here, nature serves merely to explain historical matters and reduce them to matters of nature. The claim to total explanation promises to explain all historical happenings, the total explanation of the past, the total knowledge of the present, and the reliable prediction of the future" (470).

26. As Carl Schmitt explained in 1933:

> The political unity of the current state is a tripartite aggregation of state, movement, *Volk*. This unity differentiates itself from the ground up from the liberal democratic state schema handed down from the nineteenth century, and indeed not only with respect to its ideological assumptions and its common principles but also in all the fundamental lines of construction and organization of the concrete constitution of the state. Every fundamental concept and every meaningful feature is affected by this difference. The new structure of state is distinguished by the fact that the political unity of the *Volk*, and with it the entire ordering of its public life, is presented in three differentiated tiers of order. The three traces of order stand not coordinated, nor next to one another; rather, one of them, namely the movement, carrying both the state and the *Volk*, pervades and leads the other two. (Carl Schmitt, *State, Movement, Volk*, in *The Third Reich Sourcebook*, ed. Anson Rabinbach and Sander L. Gilman [Berkeley: University of California Press, 2013], 58)

One year later, Alfred Rosenberg reiterated the point:

> The revolution of 30 January 1933 is by no means to be confused with a mere extension of the absolute state under a new rubric; rather, it establishes a relationship to the *Volk* and *Volkstum* that differs not only from that established in 1918 but which is also distinct from that of 1871. What has come to pass in this past year and what is yet to come on a much broader scale is not the so-called totality of the state but rather the totality of the National Socialist movement. The state—whether as a mechanized apparatus or as an instrument of domination—is no longer something that should exist independent of the *Volk* and of the movement; it is rather a tool of the prevailing National Socialist worldview. (Alfred Rosenberg, *The Total State?*, in Rabinbach and Gilman, *The Third Reich Sourcebook*, 62–63)

27. See Joseph Stalin, *Political Report of the Central Committee to the Sixteenth Congress of the CPSU*, June 27, 1930:

> It may seem strange that we who stand for the future *merging* of national cultures into one common (both in form and content) culture, with one common language, should at the same time stand for the *flowering* of national cultures at the present moment, in the period of the dictatorship of

the proletariat. But there is nothing strange about it. . . . The flowering of cultures that are national in form and socialist in content under the dictatorship of the proletariat in one country *for the purpose* of merging them into one common socialist (both in form and content) culture, with one common language, when the proletariat is victorious all over the world and when socialism becomes the way of life—it is just this that constitutes the dialectics of the Leninist presentation of the question of national culture.

It may be said that such a presentation of the question is "contradictory." But is there not the same "contradictoriness" in our presentation of the question of the State? We stand for the withering away of the State. At the same time we stand for the strengthening of the dictatorship of the proletariat, which is the mightiest and strongest State power that has ever existed. The highest development of State power with the object of preparing the conditions *for* the withering away of State power—such is the Marxist formula. Is this "contradictory"? Yes, it is "contradictory." But this contradiction is bound up with life, and it fully reflects Marx's dialectics.

28. See David Brandenberger, *National Bolshevism: Stalinist Mass Culture and the Formation of Modern Russian National Identity, 1931–1956* (Cambridge, MA: Harvard University Press, 2002); and David R. Marples, "Stalin: Authoritarian Populist or Great Russian Chauvinist?," *Nationalities Papers* 38, no. 5 (2010): 749–56. The concept of "National Bolshevism" is still debated among historians; see, e.g., Erik van Ree, "The Concept of 'National Bolshevism': An Interpretative Essay," *Journal of Political Ideologies* 6, no. 3 (2001): 289–307.

CHAPTER 8: OLD AND NEW FASCISMS

1. See, e.g., Pier Paolo Pasolini, "Da un fascismo all'altro," in *Saggi sulla politica e sulla società* (Milano: Mondadori, 1999), 1526–31; and Pier Paolo Pasolini, "Intervento al Congresso del Partito Radicale," in *Saggi sulla politica e sulla società*, 706–16.

2. See Ignacio Matte-Blanco, *The Unconscious as Infinite Sets: An Essay on Bi-logic* (London: Karnac, 1975).

3. Alexis de Tocqueville, *Democracy in America*, trans. Henry Reeve (Hazleton: Pennsylvania State University, 2002), 770–71.

4. On schizophrenic disorders see Davide Tarizzo, "La metonimia delirante: Sull'inesistenza di Joyce," *La psicoanalisi* 62 (2018): 132–56.

5. David Harvey, *A Brief History of Neoliberalism* (Oxford: Oxford University Press, 2005), 181.

6. Here I make no distinction between constitutions (and constitutional rights) *sensu stricto* and constitutional documents (and rights) *sensu lato* such as the American Declaration of Independence, the German Reichsgesetz

betreffend die Grundrechte des deutschen Volkes of 1848, or the "unwritten" constitution of the United Kingdom. In all of these cases, natural rights— the "rights of man"—are understood as being context-dependent rights, not context-free rights.

7. Margaret Thatcher, interview for *Woman's Own*, Oct. 31, 1987.

8. See, e.g., Jacques Lacan, *Le séminaire, Livre XIX: . . . Ou pire* (Paris: Seuil, 2011), 193–210.

9. Emilio Gentile, *"In democrazia il popolo è sempre sovrano"* (Roma-Bari: Laterza, 2016). See also Geminello Preterossi, *Ciò che resta della democrazia* (Roma-Bari: Laterza, 2015).

10. Sheldon S. Wolin, *Democracy Incorporated: Managed Democracy and the Specter of Inverted Totalitarianism* (Princeton, NJ: Princeton University Press, 2008).

11. Catherine Colliot-Thélène, *Democracy and Subjective Rights: Democracy without Demos*, trans. Arianne Dorval (London: Rowman and Littlefield, 2018), xxiii.

12. Luigi Ferrajoli, *Principia iuris: Teoria del diritto e della democrazia*, vol. 2 (Roma-Bari: Laterza, 2007), chapter 13. See also Luigi Ferrajoli, *La democrazia attraverso i diritti* (Roma-Bari: Laterza, 2013).

13. In his *Political Constitutionalism: A Republican Defence of the Constitutionality of Democracy* (Cambridge: Cambridge University Press, 2007), Richard Bellamy criticizes this view of democracy, which he calls "*legal* constitutionalism":

> In the first modern constitutions, bills of rights formed a mere preamble or appendix to this procedural constitution. Yet, in recent times the importance of political and legal procedures has been eclipsed by concentration on bills of rights. . . .
>
> Legal constitutionalists acknowledge that no constitution will survive long unless citizens can identify with it. Joseph Raz remarks how a constitution must serve "not only as the lawyers' law, but as the people's law," its main provisions commanding general consent as the "common ideology" that governs public life. In a similar vein, Jürgen Habermas talks of the members of a democratic society being bound together and to their country by means of a "constitutional patriotism." However, once again these theorists locate this moral glue in the "thin" constitution of rights as determined by judicial review, rather than the "thick" constitutional processes of democratic law-making. . . . Citizens are far more likely to identify with laws in which they have had some say. Of course, that say may be very small and be outweighed by what most others say. But the entitlement to have as equal a say as everyone else is the essence of being viewed as a bearer of rights. (6–7)

14. See Pier Paolo Pasolini, "Studio sulla rivoluzione antropologica in Italia," in *Saggi sulla politica e sulla società*, 307–12.

15. See Pier Paolo Pasolini, "Il vero fascismo e quindi il vero antifascismo," in *Saggi sulla politica e sulla società*, 313–18.

16. Giandomenico Majone, *Rethinking the Union of Europe Post-Crisis* (Cambridge: Cambridge University Press, 2014), 261.

17. Quoted in Cynthia Weber, *Queer International Relations: Sovereignty, Sexuality, and the Will to Knowledge* (Oxford: Oxford University Press, 2016), 187.

18. Guy Debord, *The Society of the Spectacle*, trans. Donald Nicholson-Smith (New York: Zone, 1995), 12.

19. See Barbara Duden, *Die Gene in Kopf—der Fötus im Bauch: Historisches zum Frauenkörper* (Hannover: Offizin, 2002), 215–52.

20. See David Held, *Democracy and the Global Order* (Cambridge: Polity, 1995).

21. Richard Falk, *The Declining World Order* (New York: Routledge, 2004), 28.

22. Costas Douzinas, *Human Rights and Empire: The Political Philosophy of Cosmopolitanism* (New York: Routledge, 2007), 148.

23. World Bank, "Polarization and Populism," ECA Economic Update (Washington, DC: World Bank, Nov. 2016), 25, 27, 30.

24. Debord, *Society of the Spectacle*, 14.

25. Debord, 113.

26. Bill Readings, *The University in Ruins* (Cambridge, MA: Harvard University Press, 1996), 2.

27. Readings, 53.

28. Readings, 68–69.

29. Readings, 33–35.

30. Readings, 47–48.

31. Lacan, *The Seminar, Book XXI*, March 19, 1974.

32. See, e.g., Allan Bloom, *The Closing of the American Mind* (New York: Simon and Schuster, 1987).

33. François Jullien, *On the Universal, the Uniform, the Common and Dialogue between Cultures*, trans. Michael Richardson and Krzysztof Fijalowski (Cambridge: Polity, 2014), xi.

34. Kenneth Burke, *A Grammar of Motives* (Berkeley: University of California Press, 1969), 506–7.

35. Readings, *The University in Ruins*, 103.

CONCLUSION: THE POLITICS OF INFINITE SETS

1. Carl Friedrich Gauss to Schumacher, July 21, 1831, cited in Morris Kline, *Mathematical Thought from Ancient to Modern Times*, vol. 3 (Oxford: Oxford University Press, 1990), 993.

2. Ludwig Wittgenstein, *Remarks on the Foundations of Mathematics* (Cambridge, MA: MIT Press, 1983), Part IV, §7.

3. Wittgenstein, Appendix 2, §4.

4. "One of the twentieth century's most significant contributions to philosophy—manifest in the work of the later Wittgenstein and of Heidegger—is a working through of the idea that there can be no viable distinction between the existence of concepts and the lives we live with them. There can be no fundamental divide between thought and life." Jonathan Lear, *Happiness, Death, and the Remainder of Life* (Cambridge, MA: Harvard University Press, 2000), 8.

5. Thomas Aquinas, *Commentary on the Metaphysics Book* 10, lib.10 l.4n12.

6. Thomas Hobbes, *Leviathan* (Oxford: Oxford University Press, 1996), 109–10.

7. For more on Hobbes, see Marco Piasentier and Davide Tarizzo, "'The Government of a Multitude': Hobbes on Political Subjectification," in *The Routledge Handbook of Biopolitics*, ed. Sergei Prozorov and Simona Rentea (New York: Routledge, 2017), 36–49.

8. See Michel Foucault, *The Will to Knowledge* (London: Penguin, 2006).

9. See, e.g., Roberto Esposito, *Terms of the Political: Community, Immunity, Biopolitics*, trans. Rhiannon Noel Welch (New York: Fordham University Press, 2013):

> 1933. –2003. Is it legitimate to turn once again to the question of Nazism seventy years after it took power? The answer, I believe, can only be yes. . . .
>
> . . . The sixty years that separate us from the end of those tragic events form a barrier that nevertheless appears difficult to overcome. It's truly difficult to imagine that it could happen again, at least in the ever-larger space that we still call the West. We wouldn't be theorists of immunization if we thought that the twelve-year Nazi experience failed to produce sufficient antibodies to protect us from its return. Still, such common sense rationalizations aren't able to bring to a close a discourse that, as we've said, remains with us. I'd even add that not only is the problem, or the terrifying laceration, opened by Nazism anything but definitively healed but, in a certain way, it seems to come closer to our condition the more our condition exceeds the confines of modernity. (79, 86)

10. For details, see Davide Tarizzo, *Life: A Modern Invention*, trans. Mark William Epstein (Minneapolis: University of Minnesota Press, 2017).

11. Karl Marx, "Theses on Feuerbach," in *Early Writings*, trans. Rodney Livingstone and Gregor Benton (London: Penguin, 1992), 423.

12. There is a vast literature on the topic. See, e.g., Joseph E. Stiglitz, *The Euro: How a Common Currency Threatens the Future of Europe* (New York:

Norton, 2016); and Alberto Bagnai, *Il tramonto dell'euro* (Reggio Emilia: Imprimatur, 2012).

13. Article 20 of the Soviet Constitution of 1918 says: "In consequence of the solidarity of the toilers of all nations, the Russian Socialist Federated Soviet Republic grants all political rights of Russian citizens to foreigners who live in the territory of the Russian Republic and are engaged in toil and who belong to the toiling class." For more on this constitutional innovation and the future of Europe, see Davide Tarizzo, "Dopo l'euro: L'Europa dell'ospitalità," *Iride* 26, no. 70 (2013): 597–613.

14. Hans Kelsen, *The Essence and Value of Democracy*, ed. Nadia Urbinati and Carlo Invernizzi Accetti (Lanham, MD: Rowman and Littlefield, 2013), 37.

15. Antonio Gramsci, *Quaderni del carcere*, vol. 1 (Torino: Einaudi, 2001), 311.

Index

SQUARE ONE
First Order Questions in the Humanities

Series Editor: **PAUL A. KOTTMAN**